EVERYDAY PRODUCTIONS
OF
BAKED GOODS

EVERYDAY PRODUCTIONS

OF

BAKED GOODS

(2nd Edition)

A. B. BARROWS
F. Inst. B. B.

Senior Lecturer-in-Charge, Bakery School, Tameside College of Technology
Ashton-under-Lyne

CAHNERS BOOKS

A Division of Cahners Publishing Company, Inc.
89 Franklin Street, Boston, Massachusetts 02110

Cahners Books, a Division of Cahners Publishing Company, Inc.
89 Franklin Street, Boston, Massachusetts 02110

First edition 1958
Second edition 1975

ISBN: 0–8436–2062–5

WITH 2 TABLES AND 231 ILLUSTRATIONS

© APPLIED SCIENCE PUBLISHERS LTD 1975

Text set in 11/12 pt Photon Times, printed by photolithography, and bound at The Pitman Press, Bath

CONTENTS

Foreword to the 1st Edition   vii

Foreword to the 2nd Edition   ix

CHAPTER

1. Materials   1

2. Sponge Goods   7

3. Powder-aerated Goods   61

4. Short-paste Goods   81

5. Sweetpaste and Shortbread   96

6. Puff Paste   163

7. Chou Paste   191

8. Ginger Goods   200

9. Cakes and Cake-making   218

10. High Speed Mixing   376

11. Some Conclusions   380

Index   385

FOREWORD TO 1st EDITION

THROUGHOUT the whole of our lives, knowledge in one form or another is offered to us. As we progress and join this most fascinating of all trades, knowledge is passed on by fellow workers, foremen, managers, master bakers, and by the bakery schools and the trade Press. 'Knowledge is Power', and the only knowledge wasted is that not assimilated.

Upon reaching maturity and in our quieter moments, we may reflect that we probably have been unable adequately to express our thanks to our teachers, using the word in its widest possible sense. The only thanks that those teachers would want would be that the knowledge, so willingly given, has been assimilated, the fruits of our own experience added, and the whole passed on to those following. Thus may we assist in our own small way to progress and build a better life.

This book does not in any way pretend to deal with exhibition work, but rather to help the average baker and confectioner to secure the greatest prize of all, that of the thriving, expanding business, with satisfied customers constantly returning. There will always be a niche for the small baker and confectioner who can offer the customer something different, value for money, and a personal service that the plants can never offer.

To the Editor of *Confectionery and Baking Craft,* the photographic department, and the staff who, throughout the many months that this book was originally published in series form, were unfailingly helpful and courteous go my grateful thanks.

The hope that part of my personal debt to the past has been repaid, and that it will assist the reader in securing that greatest prize is the sincere wish of

A. B. BARROWS

Manchester,
1958

FOREWORD TO THE 2nd EDITION

THE first edition of *Everyday Productions of Baked Goods* was published towards the end of rationing and, of necessity, reflected the conditions then prevailing. Having been out of print for some time, it is a cause for satisfaction to any author to know that insistent demand for copies requires another edition.

The opportunity has been taken to bring forward relevant items from the first edition, and to include under the various chapter headings ideas that will be of value in the light of modern trading conditions.

To make the work in such a book live, it is the author's opinion that photographs are vitally necessary, and my sincere thanks must go to former colleague Mr. A. Haselgrove, for his invaluable assistance in this direction. My thanks and appreciation must also go to my former Head of Department and very good friend, Mr. Albert R. Daniel, for his ready and willing permission to use the photographs and captions on Cake Faults in Chapter VIII.

Metric, as well as the familiar Avoirdupois weight is included throughout, and that this formidable task was achieved quickly and in time is due to the tremendous and willing help given by my children, Andrew and Fiona. To both must go my sincere thanks, which must also be extended to my wife for her patience and assistance over the weeks and months that such a work entails.

It is hoped that this edition will assist the Industry as much as did the earlier work, and that it will prove a useful friend and guide to the reader, from student days through to a successful and rewarding business career.

A. B. BARROWS

Manchester,
1973

Chapter 1

MATERIALS

Castor Sugar

It is best to stock two types of castor sugar. For cake-making and general confectionery, such as sponge and meringue work, a sugar of fairly coarse, hard grain is preferred. A fine, floury castor is to be avoided in these instances, for, in use, it will be found that this does not give the same aeration so readily. This is shown particularly in sponge goods, when difficulty may be experienced in whipping up the egg and sugar to a full sponge.

This type of castor sugar can be used confidently in bun doughs and powder-aerated goods where, owing to its quality of being readily dissolved, it does not leave the surface of the goods 'speckled' because of undissolved sugar crystals.

Granulated Sugar

This type of sugar can be obtained in several different degrees of coarseness of grain, the finer grain being almost the equivalent of a fairly coarse castor. Being slightly cheaper it can be used for the production of sponges and other types of goods—cakes by the flour-batter method, for instance—where it can be reasonably certain that the crystals will all be thoroughly dissolved, thus avoiding the 'spotty' appearance on baked goods.

The slightly coarser types are of value in macaroons and for all sugar boiling work, whilst one of extremely coarse character may be found suitable for use in Christmas showpieces, etc., where a 'frosted' effect is desired.

Brown Sugar

Of the several varieties available probably Barbados, or raw sugar as it is sometimes called, will be found the most useful. Ideal in some types of ginger goods, it is invaluable in the production of dundee and dark, heavily-fruited cakes, such as birthday and wedding cakes. Of great assistance in obtaining the correct crumb colour, its use does impart a delicious flavour to the finished article.

Icing Sugar

Obtainable in many grades, two only are essential. The first should be of top quality, good colour, and quite soft, thus rendering sieving unnecessary and obviating any possibility of grease being introduced inadvertently to royal icing, for which this grade will be used exclusively.

A second, cheaper grade, should also be stocked and used solely for dusting and the production of water icing.

Shortening and Compounds

As in all things in life, one gets here what one pays for. This is a very competitive market and the fat should feel smooth and clear when rubbed between finger and thumb. Waxy and flinty fats should be avoided. To be recommended are the golden shortenings, the purest of fats, giving extra quality to the products.

Butter

In many instances a 'must' in order to acquire that delicious flavour. It should contain not more than 12% water, and have a pleasant aroma. It should possess good flavour, free from oiliness or rancidity, with the salt being present only in sufficient quantities to act slightly as a preservative and to bring out the flavour.

Cake Margarine

Of the many brands available, one possessing good creaming qualities should be selected, and, in producing a cake batter, 1 pt (570 g or 0·57 litres) egg should be absorbed to each lb (450 g) margarine without curdling. This, of course, will signify that the product under test is low in water content. When carrying out the test, however, due regard should be given to the temperature of the various ingredients, for cold eggs will naturally tend to curdle the batter.

One other important point to be considered is that of flavour, for one brand I have tried does give a slightly rancid taste to the finished article.

Eggs

Doubtless many readers will find shell eggs quite satisfactory, but where a trade of any size is done, perhaps frozen eggs are the ideal.

These consist of whole eggs, broken, amalgamated, pasteurised, tinned and frozen, usually in 7, 14 and 28 lb (3·25, 6·50 and 13·00 kg) packs. This should be carefully defrosted by allowing the tin to stand under cold running water overnight. As this method is impracticable, it is generally satisfactory to allow the tin to remain unopened in the bakery overnight.

After opening, the contents should be whisked thoroughly to ensure amalgamation. Egg remaining after the day's work is completed should be stored under refrigeration.

Convenient also is dried egg, now perfected in the form of Accelerated Freeze Dried. (AFD).

Egg Whites

Defrosted frozen whites are suitable for many purposes, but I do not include the manufacture of royal icing in this, for often they tend to give the sugar a greenish cast.

To be recommended here is powdered albumen, usually re-constituted at the rate of 3 oz (85 g) albumen to 1 pt (0·57 litres) lukewarm water. For royal icing, quantity may be as low as $1\frac{1}{2}$ oz per pint (75 g per litre) water.

Flour

Probably the raw material that first comes to mind at the word 'bakery', with so many different grades available that confusion can easily be caused.

'Strong' flour is the term used to denote flour suitable for the production of all yeast fermented goods. All wheaten flours contain substances which join together when water is added forming a tough, rubbery material called gluten. In 'strong' flour this is tough, resists extension, is capable of withstanding prolonged periods of fermentation without breaking down and of producing bold fermented goods. Flour of this type is capable of absorbing a high percentage of water.

On occasions, strong flour is used in best quality (i.e. wedding) cakes, where the gluten strength assists in producing a cake with good cutting properties.

A 'weak' flour, i.e. one containing a low percentage of soft gluten, has a low water absorption power. This type of flour is excellent for making short and sweet pastry, some types of biscuit doughs and good quality cakes. Cheaper cakes require flour a little stronger than this. Needless to say, the flour should be of good colour.

It is convenient and less wasteful to empty the bags into a suitable bin, fitted with a lid and kept specially for the purpose.

Baking Powder

This is produced by sieving together two parts of cream powder to one part of bicarbonate of soda four times, keeping the resultant powder in a suitable drum or tin fitted with a lid to exclude air, for any dampness in the atmosphere will cause the powder to react.

Again, care should be taken where the tin is stored, for I know of one bakery where it was kept in the stores close to a newly installed fruit-cleaning machine. Soon after installation and after each time the machine had been used, mixings were spoiled and had the appearance of not containing baking powder. The trouble was finally tracked down to the vibration of the machine separating the powder; the bicarbonate of soda, being heavier than the cream powder, sank to the bottom of the tin.

The making of this is a job usually delegated to the youngest apprentice, but I am strongly in favour of purchasing this ready mixed, the slight extra cost being offset by regularity and time saved, and, if used in the time stated by the manufacturer, will be found to give every satisfaction.

Scone Flour

Called sometimes 'soda flour', 'self raising flour', 'prepared flour', etc.

Produced by sieving together at least four times, 3 oz (85 g) baking powder and 4 lb (1816 g) weak flour, storing as for baking powder.

Its primary use is when baking powder is required in minute quantities, thus obviating mistakes in weighing.

Sultanas

Should be purchased for colour, size and flavour, and cleaned by washing thoroughly in luke-warm water, draining and spreading on boards or tins, previously covered with a cloth, to dry. Unless so treated, the fruit is apt to be gritty to the taste and lack that plump juiciness so necessary. Needless to say, they should be carefully picked over and any stalks, stones or blemished fruit should be removed.

Probably Australian 'Four' or 'Five Crowns' will be found most satisfactory.

Currants

Should be of medium size and good colour and flavour, probably 'Vostizza' being the most acceptable. Cleaning should be carried out as detailed for sultanas.

Glacé Cherries

Medium to fairly large sized cherries for top quality work or, for finishing cakes and gateaux, the smaller variety will prove more economical.

They should be washed in luke warm water to remove the syrup before use, and dried carefully at room temperature.

Glycerine

Here is a commodity which will greatly assist in prolonging the shelf-life of cakes by combating dryness. It is invaluable in cheaper and medium quality mixings, and even in good quality recipes can be used to good advantage.

The amount to use is 1 oz (28 g) glycerine to each lb (450 g) of total fats, and the amount of flour must be increased by 1 oz (28 g) for each ounce of glycerine used. The sugar content should not be interfered with, and the glycerine may be added either at the creaming stage or along with the milk.

Peel

Orange and lemon peels were formerly purchased separately and mixed by the confectioner, but good quality can now be bought ready mixed and give every satisfaction. Some of the cheaper varieties, improperly cured during manufacture, may show, after baking, in the finished cake as white substances and eat rather hard and flinty. This trouble may also arise through prolonged storage. Any remaining in stock should be immersed in a hot sugar syrup and allowed to stand for one week, after which it should be carefully drained and used, when it will be found that this characteristic has disappeared.

Citron

Now on sale as 'caps', cubed, or ready sliced, much time is saved on the old-fashioned method of slicing individually: a very irksome task in busy seasons.

Any caps in stock, however, can be sliced quite satisfactorily and thinly by using a potato peeler.

Colours and Essences

Here, the confectioner is very much on his own and the cheapest colours and essences are not always the most economical. Indeed, many mixings are spoilt by the too liberal use of the essence bottle and, in this respect, probably lemon essence is the most constant offender.

Before regular purchases are made, small sample bottles should be obtained and thorough baking tests carried out.

The amount of colour and essence in any particular mixing should be most carefully measured, and that optimum quantity adhered to rigidly. Indeed, some firms use for this purpose the type of measure to be found in public houses, where a bottle of wine or spirits is inverted over a glass measure. When the tap is turned on, the correct measure only is allowed to run off, the measure refilling automatically. A small measuring glass is kept beside the 'bar' for strict measurement of smaller amounts.

Consideration should be given to the use of natural products, such as fruit pastes, oils, etc., together with liqueurs, to obtain maximum benefit.

Chapter 2

SPONGE GOODS

General Hints

Shell eggs, provided they are fresh, are, of course, ideal for this type of work, but are rather wasteful both in time for cracking and, in addition, rather messy, as it always seems impossible to extract the whites thoroughly.

Ever present, also, is the risk of an 'earthy' or musty egg being inadvertently introduced to the bulk which would, of course, be sufficient to render it entirely useless for our purpose.

The best then remains in frozen egg, which must be carefully defrosted to the correct condition. The best way to do this is, in my opinion, to allow the unopened tin to remain in the warm bakery atmosphere overnight, afterwards open it carefully and pour into a clean hand-bowl of suitable size, whisking to ensure even consistency.

Sugar should be medium castor, free-flowing and of hard grain, the slight coarseness helping to break the grain of the egg and thus bring the sponge to the desired consistency rather more quickly.

Flour should be of weak character possibly high ratio for best results, and all utensils should be thoroughly scalded and cleaned, for the slightest trace of grease can spoil a mixing. In this connection, I have always found it advisable to keep a supply of sugar separate from that generally used, to avoid the possibility of anyone inadvertently putting any greasy sugar into the bulk.

Sponge Drops

1¼ lb or 1 pt (570 g or 0·57 litres) egg   1 lb (450 g) weak flour
1 lb (450 g) sugar

The quantity to be produced at any one mixing will, of course, depend on the facilities available, but as sponge batters deteriorate rapidly, it has been my experience that 1 qt (1·14 litres) of egg is the maximum amount that two people can conveniently handle, one person being employed in working off the sponge, the other baking each sheet as it is completed. Production, however, can be speeded up by employing two machines, starting the second as the first sponge is removed. With careful timing, then, the person employed in working off can be kept supplied with freshly-mixed sponge.

Place the egg and sugar in the machine bowl, fit on the whisk, and commence whisking on second speed. Should the egg be really cold, it will be an advantage to place a gas-ring with a low flame beneath the bowl to bring the sponge to correct condition rather more quickly. When blood-heat has been reached, turn out the gas and change to top speed to complete.

Working off

While this is proceeding, weigh and sieve the flour on to a sheet of clean paper, place on one side, and prepare the bench for working off the sponge.

Using the above quantity, have before you four sheets of greaseproof or silicone paper, cut to size of the sheet tin, one upon the other. Beyond these, with its edge just underneath the four sheets, place a further sheet, upon which is a sieve containing castor sugar. To the right-hand side place four inverted sheet tins, ready to receive the papers after the savoys have been piped out. These are baked on the underside of the sheet tins to keep bottom heat to a minimum. Finally, fit a ⅜-in (8 mm) plain tube into a savoy bag, pushing the end of the bag into the tube to prevent drips, turning down the top of the bag to facilitate holding when filling.

A simple way to discover whether full sponge has been achieved is to stop the machine and count up to six fairly slowly. On reaching 'six' the whisk marks should still be visible.

Remove the bowl from the machine and knock out the whisk. Add the sieved flour to the sponge and clear carefully. To do this, keep the fingers of the right hand open, going right to the bottom of the bowl and gently bringing to the surface, moving the fingers all the time in the manner the conductor of an orchestra brings in the various instruments with his left hand. While this action is proceeding, the left hand should be employed in turning the bowl round slowly. As soon as the flour is incorporated, stop mixing and remove the right hand, for any further manipulation will result in toughness.

Using a cellulose scraper, three-quarters fill the bag and proceed to pipe out bulbs approximately 1½ in (3·8 cm) in diameter. When the first paper has been filled, dredge with castor sugar from the prepared sieve.

Now pick up the paper, using finger and thumb of each hand, at the corners nearest to you, taking the hands upwards and away from you at the same time. This will throw the surplus sugar on to the paper ready to receive it, and then deposit the sheet of drops on to the prepared sheet tins. Bake immediately in a good sound oven of 440°F (225°C) only a few minutes being required, the tops of the drops being a nice delicate golden brown, just firm to the touch. Proceed with piping out in a similar manner until all the sponge has been used.

Finishing

When cool, turn upside down on to a clean cloth or sack, and peel the paper very carefully away from the drops. It will generally be found to come away quite easily, but should any difficulty occur, moisten the paper, using a brush and warm water.

Perhaps the most popular finish for these goods is with fresh, whipped cream. Lay out the required number, flat side uppermost, and pipe in a spot of good quality strawberry, raspberry or apricot jam, or lemon cheese, to give a different, attractive flavour. Then pipe on a liberal whirl of the prepared cream, nicely sweetened and flavoured. I say a liberal whirl advisedly, for I do feel that a cream cake is far too often spoiled by confectioners piping in the cream in a very parsimonious manner and this, to my mind, spoils the article and far too often disappoints the customer.

Place on top of the cream another sponge drop, flat side down. Dredge lightly with icing sugar, and place into a paper case to complete.

Chocolate Halves

For this variety, some buttercream will be necessary. Sandwich the required number of drops together in pairs, using, in this case, a minimum of buttercream, setting the bench out as follows. On the left the drops to be dipped in chocolate, in the centre place the chocolate dipping pan, containing a sufficient amount of chocolate couverture, or properly tempered baker's chocolate, warmed to the correct temperature, and on the right a sheet of clean greaseproof paper ready to receive the finished drops. Take one of the prepared drops in the left hand, pass to the right, and immerse carefully half-way in the chocolate. Remove with an up-and-down motion of the hand, so that the surface tension of the chocolate in the pan will draw from the drop as much surplus as possible. Draw the underside across the edge of the pan to remove the surplus, and place one drop on the greaseproof paper as far away from yourself as possible.

This is necessary, for the attractiveness of the finished article depends upon a clean finish, and pains should be taken to achieve this, so avoid carrying drops from the pan over the other finished goods.

When the chocolate has dried, place in paper cases, when they will be ready for sale. The sheet of greaseproof used to receive the drops can then be scraped, the chocolate being returned to the pan.

Raspberry Sponge Drops

Using the foregoing recipe, after a full sponge has been obtained, add pink colour and raspberry essence, allowing the machine to run until both have been thoroughly incorporated, then proceed as previously indicated.

For finishing either of the above methods can be employed and, in each case, colour the cream a delicate pink and use raspberry flavour.

Chocolate Sponge Drops

$1\frac{1}{4}$ lb or 1 pt (570 g or 0·57 litres) egg	Vanilla essence
1 lb (450 g) castor sugar	Pink colour
14 oz (400 g) weak flour	Chocolate colour and flavour
$2\frac{1}{4}$ oz (64 g) cocoa powder	Bake at 430°F (220°C).

Sieve the cocoa powder and flour together and continue as described previously, adding the colour and flavour last, the pink colour being added to give a more true and richer chocolate colour. Either of the two methods of finishing can be employed, using vanilla-flavoured buttercream for the second.

Savoy Fingers

Many different types of goods have masqueraded in the past as savoy fingers, but the true finger is sold absolutely plain, usually by weight, or tied with a neat ribbon, or sold attractively wrapped in a neat cellulose packet. Whichever variety of presentation is decided upon, it should find a ready market, especially to the busy housewife out shopping with small children.

The recipe is the same as that given for sponge drops. This time, however, the sponge is piped out in rows of neat fingers, care being taken that all are of the same length, approximately $2\frac{1}{2}$–3 in (6·4–7·7 cm). Sugar and bake in the manner already prescribed for sponge drops.

After baking, reverse the paper on to a clean cloth or sack and moisten with warm water. Carefully peel the paper from the fingers and immediately join together in pairs. Owing to the slight moistness from the paper, it will be found that no other medium is necessary for joining together. The fingers are then ready for packing into the type of pack decided upon previously.

Savoy Delights

For this attractive line, pipe out the sponge, as already detailed, into fingers, using for this a $\frac{1}{4}$-in (6 mm) plain tube, piping approximately 2 in (5·2 cm) long. Sugar, bake off, and remove from the papers.

To finish, prepare a mixture of pink and white genoese cuttings, moistened with raspberry jam of good quality, sherry, and a spot of water as necessary. Great care should be exercised when mixing not to crush the genoese too much, the pink and white pieces remaining clearly visible. Pick up one of the fingers and, using a small palette knife, on it spread a liberal amount of filling. Surround with three more biscuits, and place in a small souffle case.

Complete by piping on a liberal whorl of nicely-sweetened and flavoured fresh cream, placing on the top a small piece of cherry, or a spot of red piping jelly and pinch of green almond nibs.

Raspberry Fingers

Using the recipe and method as given for raspberry sponge drops, pipe out fingers, using a $\frac{3}{8}$-in (8 mm) tube, to a length of $2\frac{1}{2}$ in (6·4 cm). Sugar, bake, and remove from the paper as already described. To finish, join two fingers together, using a small quantity of raspberry coloured and flavoured buttercream. Dip carefully diagonally in baker's chocolate or couverture, observing the rules previously mentioned in order to preserve a clean finish.

Chocolate Fingers

These are produced by using the recipe as given for chocolate sponge drops, the finish being similar to that described for raspberry fingers, using, of course, vanilla or chocolate coloured and flavoured buttercream. Instead of dipping diagonally, however, dip each end into the couverture to a depth of $\frac{1}{2}$-in (1·3 cm).

Sponge Bricks or Cakes

Having, by now, acquired the art of gently amalgamating the flour into the sponge, the next task to master is the correct preparation of any tins required, or, as sponge brick tins are generally called, frames.

These are small oblong tins, strapped together in sixes. Great care must be taken to ensure the absolute cleanliness of these, and they should be carefully wiped out every time they have been used, a pointed stick being used to get the corners absolutely clean.

Again, care should be taken in handling the frames, for after constant use they have a tendency to bend, so that the ends of the frames do not 'sit' properly in the oven, resulting in uneven shape and baking of the bricks. To correct this, carefully bend back to the right shape.

When preparing the frames, therefore, first ensure their absolute cleanliness, afterwards greasing thoroughly, paying particular attention to the corners. Pour some finely-sieved castor sugar into the frames, tipping out the surplus, tapping the edges lightly to make sure that this condition has been reached. Sieve a quantity of flour, and repeat the operation, again tapping lightly to ensure that all surplus has been removed. When carrying out this operation, take care that the fingers are kept on the outside of the frames, otherwise trouble may occur when trying to empty after baking.

The following is the recipe:

$1\frac{1}{4}$ lb or 1 pt (570 g or 0·57 litres) egg	$1\frac{1}{4}$ lb (570 g) castor sugar
5 oz (140 g) egg yolk	1 lb 2oz (510 g) weak flour

The method is the same as that given for sponge drops, great care being taken when incorporating the flour to ensure that toughness does not result from overmixing.

Using a savoy bag fitted with a $\frac{3}{4}$-in (1·8 cm) plain tube, two-thirds fill the frames, dredging heavily with castor sugar, afterwards shaking off the surplus.

Most confectioners will find it advisable to bake off the frames at a temperature of 400°F (205°C) on the oven bottom, but as some ovens are rather fierce on bottom heat, the man on the spot will be the best judge as to the necessity or otherwise of a sheet tin.

As soon as the bricks are baked—and care must be exercised during this operation, for over-baking will result in excessive dryness—knock them out from the frames, and allow to cool on a clean cloth or sack. When cold, pack in sixes in attractive cellulose packets, and the bricks are then ready for sale.

Marshmallow Ladies

It would be fatally easy to class the following recipe as 'sponge drops', and utilise those particular bases for this line. To do this would be quite wrong, rob the line of its unique flavour and the variety of that 'something different' to increase and maintain sales.

Prepare:

1 lb (450 g) egg yolk	2 lb (910 g) castor sugar
1 lb (450 g) whole egg	$\frac{1}{8}$-oz (3·5 g) salt

Mix the above together and heat, whilst stirring, over a water bath to 100°F (38°C). Then whisk to a full sponge and add 1 oz (28 g) lemon paste and $\frac{1}{8}$-oz (3·5 g) finely ground aniseed.

Then carefully fold in 2 lb (910 g) weak flour.

Marshmallow ladies

Pipe out in drops, sugar and bake at 450–460°F (230–240°C) as for sponge drops.

To finish, when baked and cold, remove the drops from the paper, and place half those to be finished on the bench flat side uppermost.

Press lightly

Now whisk up sufficient marshmallow, used at the rate of 4 lb (1800 g) stock marshmallow to 1 pt (0·57 litres) of egg whites or albumen. When of piping consistency, stop the machine and fill a savoy bag fitted with $\frac{1}{2}$-in (1·3 cm) plain tube. Pipe a bold bulb on to the drops laid out and, on to this, flat side down, place another drop, just lightly pressing together until the marshmallow shows signs of exuding. Roll the edges in lightly roasted coconut.

Complete by piping on the top a neat, round 'button' of white fondant, into the centre of which place a piece of cherry.

Sponge Sandwiches

This line is, of course, an ever-popular one, but one which, by virtue of that popularity and reasonably easy production given by recipes using stabilisers lends itself quite well for output by the plant baker, who is able to produce in quantity and sell fairly cheaply. The smaller baker can, however, hold his own quite well if he produces a good quality article with a neat, clean finish, for even with the tightness of the family budget, many housewives still prefer to buy for quality, preferring the small baker's product to the general run of the plant product, which has, in all probability, travelled many miles before sale, and is anything up to 24 h old. The watchwords here, then, must be quality, freshness, and clean finish.

Another use for sponge sandwich may also be for gateau bases, the appropriate colour and flavour being added after a full sponge with the egg and sugar has been achieved. Used in this way, the resultant base will be bolder and larger, yet ligher, than the normal sugar batter base, thus enabling the enterprising confectioner to keep his gateau prices within reach of his customers and yet satisfying their desire for best value for money.

The recipe recommended is:

1¼ lb or 1 pt (570 g or 0·57 litres) egg	1 lb (450 g) weak flour
1 lb (450 g) sugar	1 oz (28 g) warm water

Bring the egg and sugar to a full sponge, finally adding the warm water with the machine still running. This is incorporated to give a closer texture to the sponge. Remove the bowl from the machine, knock out the whisk and carefully blend in the flour in the manner already described. Scale into previously greased and floured sandwich tins, the weight usually being 5 oz (140 g) for a 5-in (13 cm) tin, and 6 oz (170·4 g) for a 6-in (15 cm) tin. It is the practice of some confectioners to sugar the tins, also, in the manner described for sponge bricks, and whilst this certainly does give a better-coloured, sweeter-eating crust, it is my opinion that it also gives a certain dryness and is, therefore, better omitted for sandwiches.

Bake the goods carefully at 410°F (210°C) afterwards emptying immediately from the tins and allowing them to cool on a clean sack.

As there are so many ways in which these goods can be finished, and as the baker reflects his personality in that finish, perhaps a few general points on one or two of the more usual finishes may suffice.

Cutting the sandwiches

Many confectioners, I find, quite often spoil an otherwise excellent sandwich by wrong cutting. Their attitude to this simple task appears to indicate that any old knife will do, and they hack away regardless of the consequences. The result is usually torn crumb, the cut resembling a switchback railway, while quite often the point of the knife digs a hole in the bottom of the sandwich.

The correct way is to use a long-bladed saw-knife, placing the left hand firmly straight across the top of the sandwich. Place the knife half-way up the side of the sandwich and employ a sawing motion. Now, using the left hand, commence turning the sandwich round, while still employing a sawing motion with the right. By using this method it will be found that the knife will finish at the starting point, a straight cut will result, and the left hand, being kept on the top of the sandwich, is well out of the way of danger of cuts from the knife. Alternatively, use of a hand genoese cutter is commendable.

Perhaps the most popular mediums to use in finishing sponge sandwiches are jam and fresh cream, nicely flavoured and sweetened, so I propose to give here the three styles I have found to be most popular.

Cream Basket

Scale the sponge at 6½ oz (185 g) into greased and floured 1 lb (450 g) cottage pans, proceeding as already indicated.

When cold, split the sandwich one-third of the way down. Remove the top, cut into two and place on one side. Spread the bottom with a layer of good quality raspberry jam and, using a savoy bag and star tube, pipe a liberal amount of cream along two opposite sides. Now place on the tops over the cream at an angle of 45°, to display the cream to best advantage, and pipe along the joint more cream. Dredge lightly with icing sugar and complete with a piece of cherry in the centre.

Cream Sandwich

Split a 5 in (13 cm) or 6 in (15 cm) sandwich in the centre. Spread the base with apricot or raspberry jam, and, starting in the centre, pipe in a liberal quantity of cream, afterwards replacing the top. Place across the centre a 1½-in (4 cm) strip of wood or cardboard and dredge fairly heavily with icing sugar. Carefully lift the wood straight up, leaving a strip of sandwich untouched by sugar, and the sandwich is then ready for sale.

Strawberry Fool

This, it will be found, is a really good line for those summer days when 'something different' is the demand—and whose mouth does not water at the magical thought of 'strawberries and cream'?

Split in the centre a sandwich baked in 1 lb (450 g) cottage pans. Place the top on one side and, using a plain cutter of appropriate size, remove the centre, leaving a ring of approximate width of ½-in (1·3 cm). Spread the base with a good quality strawberry jam and place the ring back in position.

Using a savoy bag and star tube, half-fill the resultant well with cream, afterwards placing within the cream as liberal a supply of fresh, cleaned and picked strawberries as costings will allow. Pipe on top of these a further layer of cream, afterwards replacing the centre piece, dredging lightly with icing sugar to complete.

Sponge Flans

To the reader it may at first sight seem that these goods come under the heading of 'After-dinner Sweets', but as they are all basically of sponge, I feel that they have a place in this chapter.

The base for these is of the normal sponge sandwich, comprising:

1¼ lb or 1 pt (570 g or 0·57 litres) egg	1 lb (450 g) weak flour
1 lb (450 g) castor sugar	1 oz (28 g) warm water

To finish, split through the centre and layer liberally with cold, well-beaten vanilla custard. Replace the top, mask with quick set jelly and decorate the hollow portion with fruit, neatly arranged, as desired. These may take the form of tinned and well-drained mandarin oranges, cherries, peaches, apricots, pineapple, etc. Brush over with neutral, quick-setting jelly to preserve the glaze of the fruit, and complete by piping whipped and sweetened fresh or synthetic cream around the raised edge, using a large star tube for the purpose.

It is, perhaps, not necessary to mention how popular this line is during the fresh strawberry season, when these luscious fruits are used.

Should large savarin tins not be available, it is, of course, possible to use ordinary sponge sandwiches, removing the centre after splitting with a large plain cutter. The flans are then produced as already detailed, whilst the cut-out centre portions can be used to produce miniature cream sandwiches, for which a ready sale is assured.

Sponge Moulds

No full display of sponge goods can be complete without a selection of sponge moulds, which, if properly made and baked, enhance any shop window, their plain attractiveness lending a certain dignity to the whole. The secret of success is (1) correct preparation of the moulds, (2) correct mixing, and (3) correct baking.

Dealing with the first point, sponge-mould tins can be purchased in a great variety of shapes and sizes, many of them patterned, besides the more normal corrugated type. The preparation of these is identical in each case.

They must, first, be scrupulously cleaned, particular attention being paid to the corners. When it is remembered that these goods are displayed upside down, totally without finish, the necessity for this will be evident. Brush over the mould evenly with well-creamed fat, paying, once again, particular attention to the corners and to the pattern of the mould. Dust out with sieved castor sugar from the supply kept specially for this purpose, knocking the tins carefully to remove the surplus. Finally, dust out the tins with flour, again knocking the tins to remove the surplus. For the patterned moulds, place carefully-selected glacé cherries into the pattern, remembering that the part of the cherry placed into the mould will show in the finished product.

Above I mentioned that one of the secrets is in the baking of these goods, and the moulds should never be allowed to rest directly on the baking sheet. For the smaller moulds, bread tins of various shapes and sizes will be suitable, and for larger ones cake hoops will be ideal. Whatever type of tin is chosen, the mould must be wedged firmly upright, with the bottom of the mould clear of the bottom of the tin in which it is resting. These cradles, as they can be called, are then placed on a sheet tin for baking in the normal manner.

As further protection, bands of brown paper can be tied round the outside of the mould, although the writer has never found this to be necessary.

All these precautions are taken to ensure that the mould does not take on too much colour during baking. This is especially important when using cherries in the patterned moulds, otherwise the cherries are liable to look—and taste—like pieces of coke.

The recipe is:

2 lb 8 oz or 1 qt (1140 g or 1·14 litres) egg	2 lb 12 oz (1250 g) castor sugar
15 oz (430 g) egg yolk	2 lb 10 oz (1190 g) soft flour

The method is identical with that given previously, i.e. whisk eggs, yolks, and sugar to a full sponge, afterwards carefully mixing in the sieved flour and cornflour.

Use Savoy Bag

If dropping the sponge into the mould by hand, there is a danger of air being trapped by dropping in too large a quantity at once, and I would advise the use of a savoy bag fitted with large plain tube, filling the mould round the pattern very carefully, and then continuing to fill the mould not more than two-thirds full. This is important, otherwise, during baking, the sponge may come above and over the sides of the tin, giving a badly misshapen article, thus detracting from the pleasing finish.

It is, of course, difficult to give a hard and fast baking temperature for these goods, as so much will depend on their size, but the oven should be moderately hot, the writer having found a temperature of between 380°F and 410°F (190°C and 210°C) depending on the size of the moulds—to be suitable.

As soon as they are baked and firm to the touch, remove from the tins and allow to cool on a clean, sugared sack, when they are ready for display and sale, after cellulose wrapping to prevent quick drying out.

Madeleines

Using the foregoing recipe, pipe the sponge into tall, greased dariole moulds, approximately two-thirds full, and bake at 400°F (205°C). When baked, remove the cakes from the tins and allow to cool thoroughly. To finish, place firmly on a fork and dip into boiled apricot purée or, using a small palette knife, spread round the sides a thin coating of red jam. Roll in white, medium-desiccated coconut, taking precautions to keep the coconut from the top of the cake, and finish by piping a little white fondant on the top, finally decorating with a small piece of cherry.

SWISS ROLL

This is another line that has been successfully exploited by the plant baker, and any fellow confectioner who has seen this produced on the travelling band will realise how, with low production costs, it is possible for these large firms to produce and market in attractive packs at such a low price. Indeed, in one large plant I visited, I was informed that the particular swiss roll plant was in production for 22 hours out of every 24! To see such a vast amount of swiss roll constantly moving along the band, and to know that this process is continuing for so many hours each day is sufficient for the small baker to ask himself how he can meet—and beat—the plant baker. The answer here is—in quality and variety.

The small confectioner must fight on ground of his own choosing, and variety is one of his biggest weapons.

Plain Roll

1¼ lb or 1 pt (570 g or 0·57 litres) egg   10 oz (280 g) castor sugar
10 oz (280 g) weak flour

Observing all the normal precautions for grease-free utensils, place the eggs and sugar in the machine bowl and commence whisking. Meanwhile, sieve together the flour and cornflour and place on one side.

Using a sheet tin, 30 in × 18 in (76 cm × 46 cm), clean thoroughly, grease and paper, using greaseproof or silicone paper, ensuring that the tin is lined to the exclusion of all wrinkles and air.

When half sponge has been reached, remove from the machine and gently blend in the flour, afterwards transferring the sponge to the prepared sheet tin. Very carefully and, with as few strokes as possible, spread level with a trowel palette knife. There is a certain knack to this, but if the knife is kept parallel to, and approximately ¼-in (6 mm) above, the level of the sheet tin, constantly turning the tin round, the knack will soon be acquired. Bake without delay on biscuit wire or double sheet tin in a sound oven of 440°F (225°C), for 7 min.

On withdrawal from the oven, turn immediately on to a clean sugared sack and remove the paper. It will be found that greaseproof and silicone paper will leave the sponge quite easily. Now, leave the roll to cool thoroughly.

Swiss roll as a week-end 'special', wrapping the roll in a thin layer of almond paste or marzipan, and completing the decoration with either piped or scribbled chocolate and pecan or walnuts.

To test this, lift one corner of the sponge, and slide the hand between the sponge and sack.

Using 1 lb (450 g) of good quality raspberry or apricot jam, or lemon cheese, spread carefully, paying particular attention to the edges. Commence rolling by turning in and pressing well down the first $\frac{1}{2}$-in (1·3 cm) of the sponge, otherwise that bad fault known as tunnels may appear. Now commence rolling up like a carpet. When rolled place a clean sheet of cap or greaseproof alongside the roll, sugar lightly, and roll back within the paper. Leave on one side for $\frac{1}{2}$-h or so to set firmly, unroll from the paper, trim the ends, and cut to required lengths.

Marzipan Roll

Produce a sheet of swiss roll as detailed above, and spread with 1 lb (450 g) white, vanilla-flavoured buttercream. Roll out under the hands a piece of marzipan, nicely coloured pink, approximately $\frac{1}{2}$-in (1·3 cm) thick. Place this along the edge of the roll and commence rolling, afterwards rolling back in paper.

After allowing it a reasonable time to set, remove the roll from the paper and brush over with baker's melted chocolate.

When dry, cut into $\frac{1}{2}$-in (1·3 cm) slices for sale as individual fancies.

Dresden

This method of finish is one introduced by our continental friends and, in my experience, has certainly proved very popular over here.

Produce a sheet of plain roll and, after cooling, with the aid of a piece of wood of correct width, cut the sheet crosswise into 3 in (7·6 cm) strips. Place one of these strips flat side down and, using a savoy bag fitted with a $\frac{1}{4}$-in (6 mm) plain tube, pipe a line of white, vanilla-flavoured buttercream along either side and at the edge. Approximately 1 in (2·6 cm) from either side, pipe two further lines, filling in the hollows formed with raspberry jam.

Place on top a further strip of the sponge and repeat the process with the cream and jam. Place on another strip of sponge, flat side uppermost, and press down lightly.

To finish, brush over or enrobe with baker's chocolate or couverture, melted to the correct temperature, and, while this is still wet, decorate the top with grated chocolate, as shown. Alternatively, after the first coat of chocolate has dried, brush on a further coat and finish by using a comb scraper, finally decorating with a pinch of green almond nibs.

Dresden, with both grated chocolate and combed chocolate finish

Using this latter method of finish, two coats of chocolate are necessary, otherwise the comb will show the sponge beneath.

Coconut Log

Sometimes, through bad spreading, overbaking or incorrect oven temperature, it is obvious that it will be impossible to finish off the roll in the normal manner. To save waste, the following will be found quite practical and will produce an exceedingly attractive and popular line.

Coconut log

When cool, spread the sponge with 1 lb (450 g) delicately-flavoured lemon buttercream. Using a sharp knife, cut ½-in (1·3 cm) from the long side of the sheet and turn in. Now cut along this edge, and turn the cut portion through 90°, standing the cut sides at right angles to the sheet with the edge of the cut pieces running along the edge of the sponge sheet. Cut again and turn in, continuing this process until the sheet of sponge has been used, when the confectioner will be left with a swiss roll square in shape.

Spread the outside thinly with the lemon-flavoured buttercream, roll in pale, roasted coconut, and cut into required lengths for sale, as shown.

Cream Curls

For the confectioner looking for a really attractive, tender-eating sponge line, cream curls should go a long way towards fulfilling the need.

2 lb 8 oz or 1 qt (1140 g or 1·14 litres) egg	2 oz (57 g) hot water
1 lb 2 oz (510 g) castor sugar	vanilla essence
1 lb (450 g) soft flour	egg colour as required
2 oz (57 g) cornflour	

The method used is similar to that previously described for swiss roll—whisk the egg and sugar to a sponge, add the essence and colour as necessary, finally adding the hot water immediately before stopping the machine. Blend the sieved flour and cornflour lightly into the sponge, and divide between two and a half sheet tins, size 30 × 18 in (76 × 46 cm), which have been previously prepared as for swiss roll. Using a trowel palette knife, spread level and bake at 450°F (230°C) only a few mins. being required. It will be found that the sponge on the sheet is, before baking, spread quite thinly. This is quite correct, as there is quite a large amount of oven lift. Any undue bottom heat on the oven should be neutralised by the use of biscuit wires or an upturned sheet tin.

On withdrawal from the oven, reverse the sponge on to a clean cloth or sack to allow to cool, then carefully remove the paper. Using a sharp, plain 3 in (7·6 cm) cutter, cut the sheet sponge into circles, proceeding with care so as to keep waste to the minimum. Place a good spot of strawberry or apricot jam in the centre of each circle, and at opposite ends on the edge of the circle pipe on a liberal shell of nicely whipped and sweetened fresh cream. Now, using the finger and thumb of the right hand, just draw the two plain edges together and pinch lightly, leaving the shells of cream exposed. To complete, dredge lightly with icing sugar and place in paper cases for displays and sale.

To save waste in cutting out the sponge, lightly greased pikelet hoops may be stood on the papered sheet, with the sponge piped in, to the thickness indicated. In this case, use the sheet tin underside up.

Further Varieties of Swiss Roll

The following recipes are all arranged for one sheet of roll, measuring 30 × 18 in (76 × 46 cm). The fruits mentioned can be added to the flour, or dropped into the sponge after the colour and essence have been added, with the machine still running. I would recommend the latter method, for flour adhering to the fruit is apt to show in the finished article. In all cases, the baking temperature is 440°F (230°C) and the baking time 7 min.

Raspberry Roll

Whisk to a full sponge:
  1¼ lb or 1 pt (570 g or 0·57 litres) egg
  10 oz (285 g) castor sugar
Sieve together:
  9 oz (255 g) flour
  1 oz (28 g) cornflour

Add to the full sponge:
  Raspberry flavour
  pink colour
  Filling: 1 lb (450 g) vanilla or raspberry flavoured pink coloured buttercream.

Orange Fruit Roll

Whisk to a full sponge:
  1¼ lb or 1 pt (570 g or 0·57 litres) egg
  10 oz (280 g) castor sugar
Sieve together:
  9 oz (255 g) flour
  1 oz (28 g) cornflour

Add to the full sponge:
  2 oz (57 g) currants
  Orange essence

  Filling: 1 lb (450 g) orange coloured and flavoured buttercream

Pineapple Roll

Whisk to a half sponge:
  1¼ lb or 1 pt (570 g or 0·57 litres) egg
  10 oz (280 g) castor sugar

Sieve together:
  9 oz (255 g) flour
  1 oz (28 g) cornflour

Add to the full sponge:
  2 oz (57 g) crushed, drained pineapple
  lemon-yellow colour

  Filling: 14 oz (400 g) buttercream, coloured lemon-yellow, into which has been beaten 2 oz (57 g) crushed pineapple.

Cherry Almond Roll

Whisk to a half sponge:
  1¼ lb or 1 pt (570 g or 0·57 litres) egg
  10 oz (280 g) castor sugar
Sieve together:
  9 oz (255 g) flour
  1 oz (28 g) cornflour

Add to the full sponge:
  2 oz (57 g) chopped glacé cherries
  almond essence
  pale green colour

  Filling: 1 lb (450 g) white, almond-flavoured buttercream.

A green-coloured swiss roll may, indeed, be controversial, but I feel that any confectioner who tries it will agree with me that it definitely has a place in a scheme for variety in swiss roll. Care must be taken in baking that too much top heat does not affect the colour of the sponge.

Coffee Roll

Whisk to a full sponge:

1¼ lb or 1 pt (570 g or 0·57 litres) egg
10 oz (284 g) castor sugar

Sieve together:

9 oz (255 g) flour
1 oz (28 g) cornflour

Add to the sponge:

coffee colour and essence

Filling: 1 lb (450 g) coffee or vanilla-flavoured buttercream.

Coffee Essences: A word may be said here about coffee essence. This, to me, has appeared to be the most difficult essence of all to obtain from the quality point of view and, in many instances, a large amount has had to be used to obtain a true colour and flavour—so much so that it has had a detrimental effect on the sponge. I have overcome this problem by using one or other of the proprietary 'instant' coffees, mixed to a fairly thick consistency with boiling water and can confidently recommend their use.

Chocolate Roll

Whisk to a full sponge:

1¼ lb or 1 pt (570 g or 0·57 litres) egg
10 oz (280 g) castor sugar

Sieve together:

7 oz (200 g) flour
1 oz (28 g) cornflour
2 oz (57 g) cocoa powder

Add to the full sponge:

vanilla essence
pink colour
chocolate colour

Filling: 1 lb (450 g) vanilla-flavoured buttercream.

A luscious chocolate roll, filled with good quality vanilla buttercream, enrobed with top class baker's chocolate and simply finished with pecans or walnuts is always popular

Chocolate swiss roll produced into chocolate logs, without which Christmas would be incomplete

The rolls are enrobed with chocolate, placed on a log card, with a disc of almond paste placed in position to represent the sawn off branch. Completed with robin, holly piquet and motto, the cards are masked with royal icing, dredged with granulated sugar to give a sparkle. Finally a light dredging of icing sugar, and the logs can be packed into the gay boxes for display and sale.

Ginger Roll

Whisk to a full sponge:

1¼ lb or 1 pt (570 g or 0·57 litres) egg
10 oz (280 g) castor sugar

Sieve together:

9 oz (255 g) flour
1 oz (28 g) cornflour

Add to the full sponge:

2 oz (57 g) crushed ginger
pale caramel colour

Filling: 15 oz (425 g) white buttercream into which has been beaten 1 oz (28 g) ginger syrup.

Hazelnut Roll

Whisk to a full sponge:

1¼ lb or 1 pt (570 g or 0·57 litres) egg
10 oz (280 g) castor sugar

Sieve together:

8 oz (230 g) flour
1 oz (28 g) cornflour
2 oz (57 g) roasted ground hazelnuts

Add to the full sponge:

coffee essence

Filling: 1 lb (450 g) coffee coloured and flavoured buttercream.

BUTTER SPONGES

I do not feel that I can complete this chapter without some reference to butter sponges. Perhaps, through costs and the dearth of good craftsmen, the production of these has declined until—at least to the best of my knowledge—very few bakeries produce them, much preferring to use stabilisers and modern production methods.

No matter how attractively a gateau may be finished, it is a great disappointment to a customer to cut one of these only to find it is 'just the same old cake' inside. No doubt we have all had practical experience of this kind of thing, and so I am continuing this chapter by giving a few recipes and details.

The advantages are, to my mind, great. As against the normal sugar–batter base, the butter sponge has, if properly made, greater bulk, better keeping and better eating qualities, whether modern or traditional is being produced.

Melba Gateau

1¼ lb or 1 pt (570 g or 0·57 litres) egg	13 oz (370 g) weak flour
1¼ lb (570 g) castor sugar	13 oz (370 g) melted butter or margarine
8 oz (230 g) scone flour	vanilla essence

Place the egg and sugar into the machine bowl and commence whisking on second speed. Meanwhile, prepare twelve 1 lb (450 g) cottage pans by greasing thoroughly, then fill with nib almonds, afterwards tipping out all those that do not adhere to the tin. Place the butter or margarine in a suitable tin or basin, and melt to a warm oil. Sieve together the flour, cornflour and scone flour, and finish whisking at top speed until a full sponge is obtained, finally adding the essence. Stop the machine, remove the bowl and whisk, and add the flour in the manner already described. When half cleared, scrape the bowl down, run in the melted butter or margarine and very carefully clear, making certain that the hand does really get to the bottom of the bowl. It will be found that amalgamation is easier if the butter or margarine is only just warm enough to oil.

Divide out equally into the prepared tins, handling as little as possible, and bake at 360°F (180°C). When baked, remove immediately from the tins, placing the gateau on to a clean cloth or sack to cool. Dredge the tops lightly with icing sugar to complete, when they are ready for sale.

These goods are, perhaps, the most difficult of the entire butter-sponge range to produce, owing to the large amount of oil that has to be incorporated into the sponge, but if care is exercised the knack will very soon be acquired.

Gateau Bases

Vanilla

1¼ lb or 1 pt (570 g or 0·57 litres) egg
1 lb 2 oz (510 g) castor sugar
15 oz (430 g) flour
3 oz (85 g) cornflour

8 oz (230 g) melted margarine
egg colour
vanilla essence

Chocolate

1¼ lb or 1 pt (570 g or 0·57 litres) egg
1¼ lb (570 g) castor sugar
1 lb 2 oz (510 g) flour
3 oz (85 g) cocoa powder
6 oz (170 g) melted margarine

1¼ oz (35 g) baking powder
pink colour
chocolate colour
and flavour

The method is as detailed for melba gateau, the colour and flavour being added immediately after full sponge has been obtained, and prior to removing from the machine. The size will, of course, depend upon the individual confectioner's requirements, but the hoops used should not be greased or papered, but merely cleaned thoroughly, the bottoms being drummed with greaseproof paper, and afterwards stood on a sheet tin.

Variations of the base can, of course, be made by using the appropriate colours and flavours. The baking temperature will depend upon the size of base decided on, but generally a temperature of 360–370°F (180–190°C) will be found to be quite satisfactory.

TORTEN

The field here is so wide that I feel that, within the bounds of this book I can only barely touch the fringe—indeed, the possibilities of the subject are almost endless—but I do so in the hope that it will refresh the minds of older readers and fire our younger friends to explore thoroughly the boundless and endless varieties that can be produced to give pleasure and delight both to the producer and to the consumer.

Torten, then, consist of a number of small fancies—14, 16 or 18 in all—depending upon the diameter of the base, each complete (called a torte), and yet when assembled they form a complete gateau. Customers usually purchase torte individually, so the keynote must be variety, both in production and assembly of the different bases, as well as in finish. The caterers will find these invaluable for wedding receptions and parties.

Whilst I intend only to give two recipes, lemon and chocolate, the full range can include orange, raspberry, strawberry, pineapple, banana, and coffee hazelnut, whilst almond, hazelnut and coconut jap circles can be incorporated in the assembly. It will be seen, then, what a wide variety can be produced, especially if sections of different bases are incorporated in the assembly.

Lemon Torten

1 lb (450 g) liquid egg
10½ oz (300 g) castor sugar
5 oz (140 g) weak flour
3¼ oz (100 g) cornflour

4 oz (110 g) melted butter or margarine
zest and juice of 1 lemon, lemon essence or ½ oz (14 g) lemon paste

Chocolate Torten

1 lb (450 g) egg
11 oz (310 g) castor sugar
5 oz (140 g) soft flour
1½ oz (40 g) cornflour

2 oz (57 g) chocolate powder
4 oz (115 g) melted butter or margarine
pink colour
chocolate colour and flavour compound

Method of baking

The method of mixing is identical to that given for gateau bases, the essences, colours and flavours being added after full sponge has been obtained, and immediately prior to removing from the machine. The resultant sponge, in each case, should be divided between two 9–10 in (23–25 cm) hoops, which have been prepared by wiping out thoroughly, and the bottoms being drummed with greaseproof paper.

It will be noted that the hoops are neither greased nor papered, and they should be placed on a sheet tin, care being taken that the sheet selected will not buckle during baking. Bake at 360°F (180°C) on wires or an upturned sheet tin, approximately 35 min being required.

On removal from the oven, remove the paper from the bottom, and insert a long, thin-bladed knife between cake and hoop, running it round carefully to release the sponge, afterwards placing it upside down on a clean cloth or sack to cool. Leave until next day for decorating.

Decorating torten

To decorate, split the torten into three, sandwiching with the appropriate coloured and flavoured buttercream.

If using a contrasting coloured and flavoured portion, place this in the centre, leaving the basic coloured and flavoured sponge top and bottom. Reassemble the sponge and mask the top and sides with the basic coloured

Motifs suitable for piping in chocolate for torte décor

A praline flavoured torte, quickly finished with piped off pieces of chocolate and roasted flaked hazelnuts

A minimal amount of buttercream is used on this chocolate torte, decoration being completed by chocolate dipped roasted almond halves, piped off pieces of chocolate, and roasted almond nibs

Coffee flavoured torte, using buttercream of the same flavour. Whilst the use of buttercream in large quantities is not always acceptable, it does enjoy a certain popularity.

and flavoured buttercream, afterwards masking the sides with roasted coconut, roasted flake almonds, sieved jap or sponge crumbs, chocolate vermicelli or grated chocolate, as appropriate to the flavour of the base. Now place the whole upon a strawboard of suitable size. If available, use a torten divider to mark the base into the required number of segments. Alternatively, mark the centre with a 3 in (7·5 cm) plain cutter, using a long bladed knife to mark in the required number of segments.

Using a small star tube, pipe buttercream of the basic colour and flavour in the form of scrolls, etc., decorating each torte in a similar manner and, finally, decorate with cut chocolate of various shapes and sizes, cherries, angelica, walnuts, hazelnuts, piping jellies, truffle balls, split almonds and coloured almond nibs—although the latter should be used very sparingly, as an excess will cheapen the finish.

Hazelnut Torten

One of the well known and most interesting facets of our industry is how, by a very slight variation, it is possible to produce a line of different taste and flavour. This facet is fully exploited in this line, by a difference in scaling and baking off, i.e. baking quickly as thin discs, as opposed to a torte of $1\frac{1}{2}$–2 in (3·9–5·1 cm) thick.

3 lb (1350 g) egg yolk	1 oz (28 g) cinnamon
3 lb (1350 g) whole egg	1 oz (28 g) salt
3 lb (1350 g) castor sugar	12 oz (340 g) lightly roasted flaked hazelnuts
2 lb 12 oz (1250 g) weak flour	1 lb 6 oz (625 g) melted butter

Sieve together the flour, salt and cinnamon, then mix the roasted flaked hazelnuts well through.

Whisk eggs and sugar to a full sponge, add the sieved flour and partially clear. Finally, add the melted butter and clear very gently.

Divide between shallow, well greased hoops or, if desired, the normal torten hoops. In the first instance bake at 400°F (205°C) but use a temperature of 360°F (180°C) for those of the more usual thickness.

Finish No. 1

Bake three thin discs of 9–10 in (23–25 cm) diameter, sandwiching these together with praline buttercream, masking top and sides with the same medium. Divide the torte into the required number of portions after masking the sides with roasted flaked hazelnuts. Pipe an 'S' scroll on each segment, placing on the outer scroll a de-husked hazelnut, and on the inner a small pinch of mauve decor. Place a 3 in (7·5 cm) cutter in the centre, to ensure that the roasted flaked hazelnuts are neatly kept within bounds.

Finish No. 2

Using the same build up as previously, this time use chocolate buttercream with the segments decorated by piping a 'rope' with a No. 4 piping tube. A chocolate motif is placed lightly in position on each segment, with a chocolate disc lightly placed in position in the centre, surrounded by a shell border.

Hazelnut torte, finish No. 2

Finish No. 3

This is more of a gateau type finish.

Mask the tops and sides with praline buttercream, and the lower part of the sides with chocolate vermicelli. Divide the top into two, covering one half entirely with chocolate vermicelli. On the top of the other half a circle of roasted de-husked hazelnuts are outlined in chocolate with a pinch of green decor in the centre.

Hazelnut torte, finish No. 3

The word 'Praline' is piped first in buttercream, then overpiped in piping chocolate.

Torten Bases/Sponge Sandwiches (All-in method)

Many emulsifiers are based on G.M.S. and/or lecithin, full working instructions being supplied by the Allied Trader producing them under proprietary names.

Having mentioned torten, it will, perhaps, be as well to include here a recipe and method of producing these. Using a proprietary emulsifier, the sponges are very quick to produce, giving wonderfully soft, smooth pleasant eating bases.

6 lb (2720 g) castor sugar	2½ lb (1140 g) emulsifier
6 lb (2720 g) high ratio flour	egg colour
6¼ lb (2840 g) egg	3 oz (85 g) baking powder

Place the egg and emulsifier into a clean machine bowl fitted with whisk, followed by the flour and sugar, previously sieved together. Whisk to maximum volume, which will take about 4 min scraping down bowl and beater as required. Add the baking powder and whisk in over the last half minute. For sponge sandwiches, scale at 6 oz (170 g) into 6 in (15 cm)

Butter sponge torten bases, using the 'all in' method with stabiliser

greased and floured sandwich tins, yield 4½ dozen. Bake at 400°F (205°C) for 20 min.

For butter sponges, add up to 3 lb (1360 g) melted butter, adding whilst on the machine just prior to adding the baking powder. This mixing has the advantages over the traditional butter sponge that no great degree of

Perhaps the most popular finish for fresh cream torte. The butter sponge is split twice filled with appropriately flavoured conserve and whipped cream. The top is thinly masked with whipped cream, and sides masked with whipped cream followed by roasted nib or flaked almonds. Whilst this fruit is grapes, cherries, mandarin oranges and pineapple, all are popular, especially fresh strawberries in early season, which will command a good price

craftsmanship is required, and that, after scaling, the mix can be allowed to stand out of the oven for a considerable length of time before baking at 360–380°F (180–190°C) depending upon the size of the sponge. Colours, flavours, etc. may of course, be added.

Chocolate Sponge Sandwiches

6 lb (2700 g) castor sugar
5¼ lb (2400 g) high ratio flour
12 oz (340 g) cocoa powder
6¼ lb (2800 g) egg

2½ lb (1140 g) emulsifier
chocolate and pink colour
3 oz (85 g) baking powder

Chocolate butter sponge, using stabiliser

6 oz (170 g) chocolate sponge sandwiches with fresh cream and fondant finish. Chocolate fondant on the left, raspberry fondant on the right. A combination gives the Harlequin cream sponge in the centre

Exactly as detailed above including, if desired, the use of melted butter for butter sponge bases.

Dobos Fudge Gateau

Whilst the Dobos Gateau may not be sponge in the true sense, it does perhaps have more affinity here than in any other chapter. Beautifully different to eat, though very simple to produce, it deserves careful handling to ensure the neatness that the cut section shows.

In addition, only a fudge-type icing is really suitable for the finish, for the base does require a soft cutting and eating covering. This is the type of gateau that is something different and more than 'just another finish' in fondant or buttercream!

That point is one that customers will appreciate.

Debos fudge gateau and . . .

. . . as it should be when cut—clean and neat

The recipe is:

1¼ lb or 1 pt (570 g or 0·57 litres) cream
vanilla essence
12 oz (340 g) weak flour

1 lb (450 g) castor sugar
24 fresh, separated eggs

The cream may be either fresh or artificial.

Whisk the egg yolks and sugar quite lightly. Add the cream and vanilla essence, followed by the egg whites which have been previously whisked to a semi-stiff snow. Fold in the flour and gently clear.

It is well worth while having a set of stencils produced from a plastic or other long-lasting material. As a guide, one of 7 in (18 cm) diameter is usually found to be satisfactory.

For stencilling, the sheet tins must be quite heavily greased and just lightly floured. Failure to do this satisfactorily will create waste.

Place the stencil in position on the sheet tin, add sufficient of the mixing spread level, lift the stencil clear and repeat the process until the mixing has been disposed of. Bake at 400°F (205°C), loosen as soon as baked and allow the discs to go cold on the bench or a board.

To finish, layer eight of the discs together with chocolate buttercream, before covering with fudge icing.

Fudge Icing

2 lb (910 g) cube sugar
8 oz (230 g) glucose

15 oz or $\frac{3}{4}$-pt (430 g or 0·43 litres) milk

Boil the above together to 235°F (115°C). Allow to cool to approximately 100°F (38°C).

2 lb (910 g) icing sugar
6 oz (170 g) shortening
2 oz (57 g) egg white
vanilla essence

4 oz (115 g) cocoa
$\frac{1}{4}$-oz (7 g) salt
6 oz (170 g) butter

Cream up the fats quite lightly, add the egg white and essence, followed by the remaining ingredients. Finally add the cooled syrup and beat all well together. Should the fudge be too stiff for use, adjust the consistency with warm milk as required.

As stated, mask the layered discs with the fudge, spattling the top with the tip of the palette knife to provide interest.

Charlotte Russe

Method 1

Two methods can be used to produce this, and the first to be described is that usually used in Britain.

The size to be produced will, of course, depend upon the number for whom the customer is to cater, but a plain, deep, round or oval tin with slightly sloping sides for use as a mould is to be desired.

After ensuring that the tin chosen is scrupulously clean, it should be rinsed out in cold water and well drained. Now prepare a table jelly in the usual manner and pour in sufficient to cover the bottom of the mould to a depth of $\frac{1}{4}$-in (6 mm). Place in a refrigerator to set, then place the chosen fruits—well drained—in position on the jelly to form an attractive pattern, afterwards adding more jelly, now almost at setting-point, just to cover the fruit. Return the mould to the refrigerator to set. If he should be tempted to do this in one operation, the reader will probably find that the fruit will float and will, almost certainly, lose the pattern desired.

Using sponge fingers prepared and baked in the usual way, cut one end square and shape the sides to give a slight taper. When the jelly has set, remove from the refrigerator and place the prepared sponge fingers, upright, with the square end touching the jelly and each finger fitting exactly next to the other.

Now whip 1 pt (0·57 litres) fresh or artificial cream and approximately $1\frac{1}{2}$ oz (40 g) castor sugar to soft piping consistency.

Having previously soaked 1 oz (28 g) leaf gelatine in cold water until flabby—place only the gelatine into a clean saucepan and heat over a very gentle flame until liquid. Add to the whipped cream and amalgamate thoroughly and quickly, for the gelatine will soon commence to set and, unless the operation is carried out quickly, will set in strings, thus spoiling the cream. Pour immediately into the prepared mould, placing gently on top a sponge disc, previously cut from a swiss roll sheet to the size required. Replace in the refrigerator to set.

When required, trim off the tops of the sponge fingers level with the disc, immerse 1 in (2·6 cm) of the base of the mould into a bowl of hot water for a few seconds only, remove, wipe off the moisture, place a suitable dish or tray on the top and reverse both together, afterwards lifting the mould clear. If desired, a narrow ribbon may be tied round the sponge fingers to complete the decoration.

In the foregoing, it will be noted that no mention has been made of flavours, though these are of great importance to give the charlotte russe good eating quality.

Combinations will come readily to mind, but a great favourite is orange jelly, with well-drained mandarin oranges inset, with the cream coloured a pale orange and flavoured with the liqueur, orange curaçao. So far as possible I would prefer a liqueur flavour with some of the fruit mixed in with the cream.

Method 2

This, continental in origin, is rather quicker to produce than the variety previously described, but, nevertheless, delightful to eat. Indeed, with the jellied cream in this instance being of rather softer chracter than the former, it may hold more attraction for many palates.

The mould is here dispensed with, and a hoop, size again depending upon the number to be catered for, approximately $1\frac{1}{2}$ in (4 cm) high, used.

From a sheet of swiss roll, cut a disc to fit inside the hoop and spread with apricot jam, afterwards placing the disc upon a strawboard, rather larger in size than the hoop, to permit ease of handling. Now place the hoop in position round the disc of sponge.

Prepare sufficient savoy fingers by cutting to a height of approximately $2\frac{1}{2}$ in (6·5 cm), trimming the sides and standing upright inside the hoop.

To prepare the jellied cream, place 1 oz (28 g) leaf gelatine in cold water and soak until flabby.

Place 8 oz (230 g) whole egg and 8 oz (230 g) castor sugar into a suitable machine bowl and commence whisking to a full sponge, meanwhile bringing to the boil 1 pt (0·568 litres) fresh milk, afterwards adding the gelatine and stirring well to dissolve. Allow to go cold before adding to the sponged egg and sugar, whisking by hand to amalgamate, with a spot of egg colour and sufficient rum to give a good flavour.

Add 1 lb 14 oz (850 g) by weight of fresh cream, previously whipped and sweetened, stirring well. Pour the mixture into the prepared hoops to within $\frac{1}{2}$-in (1·3 cm) of the tops of the sponge fingers, and place in the refrigerator to set.

When this has been achieved, remove from the refrigerator and lift the hoop clear. Mask the base, where sponge fingers and disc join, with whipped and sweetened fresh cream, followed by roasted flake almonds.

To finish the top, pipe a basket-work pattern in whipped and sweetened fresh cream.

Using a small star tube, pipe the first line down the centre. Turn the charlotte russe at right angles to the body and pipe a loop over the first line at the far right-hand end. Leave a space sufficient for another loop, then pipe a further loop, and so on, until the other end of the line is reached. Turn the charlotte russe round to its original position, and pipe a second line from one end to the other, parallel to the first, and close enough just to hide the joint where the loops join the jellied cream.

Commence again with the loops, after once more turning the charlotte russe round, this time starting in the space between the original loops, continuing in this manner until one half is completed. Now turn the charlotte russe round, and complete the other half in a similar manner.

It should be mentioned that this operation is far easier and quicker to do than to describe!

To complete, place a pinch of green nib almonds in the centre.

Charlotte Royale

Cut a disc of greaseproof paper slightly larger than the hoop to be used, place on a strawboard, with hoop in position, as described for the second charlotte russe.

Starting in the centre of the hoop, place thin slices of swiss roll to cover the base completely. Around the sides place savoy fingers as previously described or, alternatively, a strip of sponge approximately $2\frac{1}{2}$ in (6·5 cm) high cut from a sheet of swiss roll. Using the jellied cream as previously described, pour in to within $\frac{1}{2}$-in (1·3 cm) of the top, afterwards placing in position a disc of sponge cut from a sheet of swiss roll.

Allow to set in the refrigerator and, when required, cut the sponge fingers level with the disc. Reverse on to another strawboard, remove the greaseproof paper and hoop, and brush over the surface of the now exposed swiss roll with boiled apricot purée.

Complete by piping round the edge with whipped and sweetened fresh cream and affixing a gay ribbon round the sides.

OTHELLOS AND PETITS FOURS GLACE

It is, perhaps, unfortunate that these goods are not more widely produced, for they offer a fine opportunity for the individual craftsman to shine by providing a variety of differently flavoured fillings, and thus a further outlet for him to express his personality and at the same time to produce the 'different' type of goods so necessary to keep and expand his trade.

A fine set of Othellos or, more properly, petits fours glace. From the left, Desdemonas, white fondant with caramelised walnut finish, pineapple, with marzipan collar and crushed pineapple centre, coffee, completed with chocolate/coffee bean. The mandarin segment beneath the fondant is indicative of orange curacao flavoured filling whilst, far right, the true Othello, is enrobed in chocolate fondant

The bases for othellos are dry in character and insipid to the taste, thus providing the ideal vehicle for a wide variety of fillings and finishes.

Recipe for Othello Base

42 fresh eggs	1 lb 10 oz (740 g) soft flour
1 lb 9 oz (710 g) castor sugar	1 lb (450 g) cornflour

The usual strict grease-free precautions must be taken before commencing mixing.

The eggs, by number instead of the more usual weight, refer to standard size, and adjustment will have to be made should these be of the small or large variety.

Separate the eggs, place the whites into a suitable machine bowl along with 1 lb 2 oz (510 g) of the sugar, and commence whisking to full peak on top speed.

Meanwhile, commence whisking the yolks and the remaining sugar in a hand bowl sufficiently to break these down and to dissolve the sugar. It is not necessary to whisk them to a sponge.

When the meringue has reached full peak, put the machine on bottom speed, add the yolks and sugar, allow to amalgamate and then remove from the machine. Knock out the whisk, blending in the previously sieved flour and cornflour gently by hand. When all is thoroughly blended, pipe out in round bulbs, of approximately 1 in (2·6 cm) diameter, and oval bulbs of a size in keeping. Dust lightly with flour, and bake at 360°F (180°C) with damper or oven door open to ensure a thorough, steam-free drying out.

When baked, allow to become cold before preparing for finishing. This consists of pairing each bulb, cutting the rounded top of one to produce a flat base on which to stand without rolling, and making a hollow in the flat base of each to enclose the filling. When filled, the halves of the othello should fit flush, and none of the filling should be apparent to the customer.

The ideal medium for the filling is well-beaten, cold vanilla custard with flavourings added, using true liqueurs where applicable. This, after being enclosed for a short time will soften the biscuit and, if flavoured correctly, will give an article second to none in palate appeal.

An alternative recipe for Othellos is:

15 oz or $\frac{3}{4}$-pt (430 g or 0·43 litres) egg white	8 oz (230 g) weak flour
10 oz (280 g) castor sugar	4 oz (115 g) cornflour
$7\frac{1}{2}$ oz (215 g) egg yolk	

Whisk the egg whites and half the sugar to half peak. Meanwhile, whisk yolks and the remainder of the sugar by hand to a partial sponge. Blend the meringue into the sponge, add the sieved flour and cornflour, clear, work off as detailed, baking and drying out at 375–400°F (190–205°C).

Vanilla Cream Othellos (Desdemonas)

Use equal quantities of vanilla custard and whipped and sweetened fresh cream. Fill the biscuits and when complete brush the tops with boiled apricot purée.

Dip in white fondant, brought to normal dipping temperature and consistency, to cover completely the joint between the two biscuits, and complete with a whirl of white piping fondant and a caramelised walnut.

Kirsch

Flavour sufficient of the custard with kirsch and fill as already indicated. Brush the tops with the boiled apricot purée, mask with pale pink fondant, and complete with a whirl of the same coloured fondant and a small piece of cherry.

Coffee

Rum-flavoured vanilla custard is used as the filling, with the othello masked in coffee-coloured and flavoured fondant.

Complete with a whirl of the same medium and a roasted hazelnut.

Chocolate

Soften sufficient praline paste to a smooth cream and add the required amount of vanilla custard, a little at a time, to produce a smooth filling for the bases. Mask with apricot purée, dip in chocolate-coloured and flavoured fondant, completing with a whirl surmounted by a silver dragée.

Pineapple

For this variety, flavour the vanilla custard with glacé pineapple syrup and small pieces of chopped fresh or tinned pineapple. Fill the othellos, brush the tops with apricot purée and dip in pineapple-coloured fondant, reduced by adding pineapple syrup in place of water or stock syrup.

Complete with a whirl of the same coloured fondant and a small piece of well-drained glacé pineapple.

Apples

For these flavour the custard with a spot of pistachio essence, fill the biscuits, and mask with apricot purée.

Roll out sufficient natural-coloured marzipan and cut with a 2 in (5 cm) cutter. Wrap the othellos neatly, bringing the edges of the marzipan to hide the joint, and place them in rows along the bench. Using a suitable brush dipped in apple green colour and stamped on a sheet of paper until amost dry, brush along one side of the row of othellos. Wash and dry the brush, then using pink colour, repeat the process along the other side. Complete by pressing a small currant in the top centre to represent the core of the apple.

Peaches

Using plain vanilla custard as the filling, proceed as for apples, using in this case the pink colour on both sides to represent the 'blush' of the peach. Mark in the 'crack' with a modelling tool or the back of a knife, completing with artificial leaf.

Potatoes

Oval biscuits are used for this variety, with the praline-vanilla custard filling. Proceed as for the peaches, using natural-coloured marzipan rolled out thinly. When all are covered, moisten with a slightly water-dampened brush, and dust lightly with a mixture comprising two-thirds cocoa powder and one-third icing sugar. Brush off the surplus dust and make one or two cuts in each to represent the eyes.

Preparation for sale

With all the above lines, of course, the othellos are placed in paper cases before being offered for sale.

It should, perhaps, be made clear that the shelf life of these goods is strictly limited. Again, they should be finished as soon as possible after being filled, for, if left any length of time, it will be found that the vanilla has softened the biscuit to the extent of making enrobing very difficult.

In any continental variety of petits fours glacés, othellos similar to these described are extremely popular and, for cocktail parties, if produced approximately two-thirds the normal size, they enjoy great popularity.

Tutti-Frutti

This exceedingly sweet line is not one that commends itself to all tastes, yet is sufficiently popular to be deserving of a place in any variety of fancies.

Using bold othello bases place the required number on the bench, flat side down, and on the top of each place a small amount of mixture comprising chopped fruits, such as cherries, glacé pineapple and crystallised pear, just bound together with white, vanilla-flavoured buttercream, dredging lightly with icing sugar to act as a 'key'.

Allow a short period in the refrigerator to harden, then enrobe with white fondant, using this thinly enough to allow the fruit to be discernible. Another reason for thin fondant is, of course, to keep the degree of sweetness down to a minimum.

A word of warning: an acquaintance did on one occasion use savoys as a base in place of othellos on the grounds of being 'too busy to bother with othellos'. The whole point of using an othello is that it does assist in some measure to counteract the sweetness and preserve a balance.

The moral is, if time or other circumstance does not permit a line to be properly produced, it is better to play safe and forget it. To follow our friend's example is to invite trouble.

Russe Slice

This fancy is rather unusual, yet, if sufficient suitable refrigeration space is available, may be made well in advance for finishing as required.

Roll out sufficient, well-rested puff-paste cuttings to approximately $\frac{1}{16}$-in (1·53 mm) thick, dock well, cut into 3 in (7·6 cm) strips and give another good rest before baking at 380°F (195°C). Allow to go cold, then spread with almond-flavoured buttercream, dotting this latter with maraschino cherries.

To produce the russe cream, whisk together:

5 oz (140 g) castor sugar   10 oz or $\frac{1}{2}$-pt (280 g or 0·28 litres) egg yolk

To produce a firm sponge, add any liqueur desired, plus:

1$\frac{1}{2}$ oz (43 g) lemon paste   2$\frac{1}{4}$ oz (64 g) leaf gelatine, previously soaked
                                                                    until flabby and warmed to a liquid

Finally add and amalgamate 2 lb 8 oz or 1 qt (1140 g or 1·14 litres) whipped and unsweetened cream.

Cover the prepared slice with the russe cream, shape into a semi-circle and cover with a thin layer of sheet sponge, placing into a refrigerator to set. The spreading must, of course, be accomplished quickly. Alternatively, use a

Russe slice

semi-circular 'trough'-shaped tin, setting sponge in position before filling with the russe cream.

To finish, spread the sponge with raspberry-coloured and -flavoured, cold, quick-set jelly and, when set, dredge heavily with icing sugar before cutting into slices. A greaseproof 'finger paper' should be placed under each slice for ease of handling.

Pineapple Chocolate Roll

This is another of those lines of restricted shelf-life, yet delicious to eat. Invaluable to the catering confectioner, it can also be useful to the reader possessing a deep freeze. The quantities given are sufficient for one sheet for a tin measuring 30 × 18 in (76 × 46·6 cm).

8 oz (230 g) castor sugar	6 oz (170 g) weak flour
1¼ lb (570 g) egg	chocolate colour and flavour
2 oz (57 g) cocoa	

Produce in the normal way for swiss roll, transfer to a papered sheet tin, spread level and bake at 440°F (225°C) for approximately 7 min.

Allow to cool, reverse on to a sugared cloth or sack, remove the paper and divide down the centre, thus now having two strips of sponge 30 × 9 in

(76 × 23 cm). Spread with whipped and sweetened fresh cream to a depth of ½-in (1·3 cm), dotting with drained and chopped tinned or fresh pineapple. Roll lengthwise and refrigerate to become firm before spreading the exterior with pineapple jam and rolling in fine roasted nib almonds.

Pineapple chocolate roll

Cut into 1 in (2·6 cm) slices and decorate each with a segment of crystallised pineapple.

Hazelnut Dainties

A traditional buttersponge base into which roasted ground hazelnuts are incorporated is the basis for this line, which is unusual, well flavoured and well worthy of a place in the production schedule.

For these you need:

1¾ lb (800 g) castor sugar
1 lb (450 g) whole egg
1 lb (450 g) egg yolk
1 lb 2 oz (510 g) weak flour

14 oz (400 g) cornflour
12 oz (340 g) roasted ground hazelnuts
1¼ lb (570 g) melted butter
vanilla essence

A flavour to enjoy. Hazelnut dainties No. 1 and . . .

Produced by the normal butter sponge process, pipe into greased, small bun tins for the first type of finish. For the second finish, the greased tins should be 'nutted' before piping in the mixing. Bake at 350°F (180°C), and empty from the tins as soon as baked.

. . . No. 2

No. 1 Finish

Mask the sides with praline buttercream, followed by roasted flaked hazelnuts. Pipe a good whirl of similar buttercream on the top and, at an angle of 45°, place a disc of chocolate, previously piped on to wax or greaseproof paper, and in the centre of which was placed a roasted hazelnut.

No. 2 Finish

Cut the 'nutted' buns horizontally into two through the centre and pipe on to the bottom half a good layer of cream, fresh, whipped and sweetened, or buttercream, and replace the top half. Dredge with icing sugar to complete.

Mocha Slice

The amount given below is suitable for one sheet tin measuring 30 × 18 in (76 × 46 cm) prepared and lined as for swiss roll:

1 lb (450 g) castor sugar
1¼ lb or 1 pt (570 g or 0.57 litres) egg
14 oz (400 g) flour

2 oz (57 g) cornflour
3 oz (85 g) melted butter or margarine
vanilla essence

Using the usual grease-free precautions, whisk up the eggs and sugar to full sponge, adding the essence immediately prior to removing from the machine. Add the sieved flour and cornflour, and when half incorporated add the melted butter or margarine and complete the mixing, using great care not to toughen or overmix.

Transfer gently to the prepared sheet tin and spread level, afterwards baking on wires or upturned sheet tins at 420–430°F (215–220°C). When baked remove from the oven and reverse on to a sugared cloth or sack to go cold.

To finish, strip off the paper, moistening with warm water if necessary, and if only one sheet is being produced divide into two. Upon one half mask that side previously in contact with the paper with boiled apricot pureé, followed by coffee-coloured and -flavoured fondant. When set cut into fingers measuring $2\frac{1}{2} \times 1$ in ($6 \cdot 4 \times 2 \cdot 6$ cm).

Now mask the top of the remaining half with a reasonable layer of coffee-coloured and -flavoured buttercream, and, placing the cut slices in position, cut into the size indicated, wiping the knife constantly to prevent buttercream smears appearing on the fondant.

Complete by piping on the name 'Mocha' with cool chocolate fondant.

Chocolate Coconut Slices

Goods produced basically from coconut are always popular and prove to be ready sellers. These varieties make use of this material to help 'ring the changes'.

Produce as for a buttersponge, by whisking together sugar, salt, eggs and vanilla, then add the flour, partially clear, add the melted fats and chocolate together. Finally, add the coconut and clear well. Although the method is as for buttersponge, this latter is so tight as to make the possibility of a collapse utterly remote.

$2\frac{1}{4}$ lb (1250 g) castor sugar	10 oz (280 g) high-ratio fat
$\frac{3}{4}$-oz (21 g) salt	8 oz (230 g) butter or margarine
1 lb 5 oz (600 g) egg	1 lb (450 g) liquid chocolate
$\frac{1}{4}$-oz (7 g) vanilla essence	2 lb (910 g) fine coconut
1 lb (450 g) flour	

Deposit on a well-greased sheet tin, measuring 18×22 in (46×56 cm) fitted with a stick to prevent flowing. Spread level and bake at 360–370°F (180–190°C). When baked, the slice should remain chewy.

Type No. 1

Cut into $2\frac{1}{2}$ in ($6 \cdot 4$ cm) strips and mask the top and sides with chocolate buttercream, followed by very pale roasted coconut. Cut into 1 in ($2 \cdot 6$ cm) fingers, segments or triangles as desired.

Type No. 2

This is perhaps the simplest finish of all. Cut into $2\frac{1}{2}$ in (6·4 cm) strips, sprinkle with white cake coating and cut into the desired shapes.

Type No. 3

Enrobe the $2\frac{1}{2}$ in (6·4 cm) strips with milk couverture or baker's chocolate and allow to set. Re-enrobe, comb, add a sprinkle of green nib almonds down the centre, and cut as desired.

Hazelnut Gateau

Something different if properly made, it is deliciously tender to eat. It is certainly not cheap to make but, please, think hard before using any substitutes.

First, line a sheet tin measuring 28 × 18 in (71 × 46 cm) with greaseproof paper in the normal way, placing a stick at the end to prevent flowing.

Ingredients needed are:

3 lb 7 oz or $2\frac{3}{4}$ pt (1560 g or 1·56 litres) egg $1\frac{1}{2}$ lb (680 g) castor sugar

Whisk the above together to full sponge.

4 oz (110 g) cornflour   12 oz (340 g) roasted ground hazelnuts
8 oz (230 g) weak flour $1\frac{1}{4}$ lb (570 g) roasted ground almonds

Sieve together, add and half clear.

Hazelnut gateau and . . .

. . . fancies from the same base

Finally, add, and very carefully clear, 12 oz (340 g) melted butter or margarine.

Transfer carefully to the prepared sheet tin, spread level and bake at 370–380°F (190–195°C).

When cold, reverse on to the bench, strip off the paper and, for the gateau, sandwich two thicknesses together using coffee or praline buttercream. Cut into oblongs of the desired size after first masking the tops with a similar buttercream, then place in a refrigerator for a short time to allow the cream to set.

Remove from the refrigerator, remask the top and comb with a comb scraper. Mask the sides, first with a similar cream then with roasted, flaked hazelnuts and complete with three whirls of the buttercream and a roasted whole hazelnut on each.

For the fancy, a single thickness of genoese is used, masked all over, then rolled in roasted, flaked hazelnuts. Dredge lightly with icing sugar and complete with a whirl of buttercream and a whole roasted hazelnut.

Plain Fingers

These are a cross between a sponge or savoy finger and othello, yet they combine the sweetness of the savoy flavour, of the jap finger. It is possible to produce these bases in advance and store them in the drying cupboard for use as required.

The fingers are, apart from sweetness, quite neutral in taste and are therefore suitable for finishing using a wide variety of flavourings.

Whisk to half meringue:

1¼ lb or 1 pt (570 g or 0·57 litres) egg white   1 lb (450 g) castor sugar

Whisk to full sponge and amalgamate to the above:

1¼ lb or 1 pt (570 g or 0·57 litres) egg yolk   1 lb (450 g) castor sugar

Blend and clear carefully:

2 lb (910 g) weak flour

Pipe out, using savoy bag with ⅜-in (9 mm) or ½-in (1·3 cm) plain savoy tube, into 2½ in (6·4 cm) fingers on greased and floured sheet tins. Bake on wires at 340°F (170°C) and when baked it should be possible to lift the fingers from the sheet. As previously mentioned, store in the drying cupboard for use as required.

Plain fingers, sprinkled with almond nibs before baking, joined into pairs with lemon butter-cream, completed with a pinch of green almond decor

No. 1

In the first of these, nib almonds are scattered over the piped fingers and baked as indicated. Join two together with buttercream, flavoured and coloured by the addition of lemon cheese, and complete with a small pinch of green nib almonds.

To show variety, the cream can be piped in with a $\frac{3}{16}$-in (5 mm) plain savoy tube as in the illustrations, but if the reader preferred, a star tube could be used.

Half dipped in chocolate before joining together with ganasche, a pinch of green decor completes

Strawberry buttercream is the medium for joining these plain fingers together, with half dipping in chocolate and a walnut to complete

The plain fingers are 'tip dipped' in chocolate before joining together with praline buttercream, completed with neat diagonal sprinkling of chocolate

No. 2

Lengthwise, dip one half of the fingers in chocolate—either baker's or couverture. When set, join in pairs with praline buttercream and place a pinch of mauve almond nibs in the centre of each.

No. 3

Join the fingers in pairs with coffee buttercream, dip half-way into chocolate and complete with a half walnut at the joint.

No. 4

Dip the tips of each finger into chocolate and, when set, join into pairs with well-beaten, rum-flavoured buttercream.

Coconut Honey Balls

1 lb (450 g) egg	1 lb (450 g) honey
1½ lb (680 g) castor sugar	2¾ lb (1250 g) fine coconut
¼-oz (7 g) salt	8 oz (230 g) castor sugar
¼-oz (7 g) cream of tartar	

Whisk eggs, the first quantity of sugar, salt and cream of tartar to a full sponge, add the honey and mix in. Remove the bowl from the machine, add the coconut and second quantity of sugar previously sieved together, and clear well by hand. Qualities of honey differ and vary in consistency, so if the mixing is too soft to mould then a little more coconut may be added.

Scale into $1\frac{1}{4}$–$1\frac{1}{2}$ oz (35–43 g) pieces, mould round and place upon sheet tins, well greased and floured or, if preferred, covered with wafer paper. Bake at 350°F (180°C).

When cold, immerse the bases in chocolate and leave standing on greaseproof paper until set, when they are ready to be placed in paper cases for sale.

Hazelmalt Fingers

Though, for convenience, these are called fingers, they can, as the photograph shows, just as easily be produced as drops.

Group 1:

1 lb 14 oz or $1\frac{1}{2}$ pt (850 g or 0·85 litres) egg white or albumen	$1\frac{1}{2}$ lb (680 g) castor sugar pinch of salt

Group 2:

10 yolks ($\frac{1}{2}$-pt) (280 g)	8 oz (230 g) sugar

Group 3:

12 oz (340 g) flour	12 oz (340 g) roasted ground hazelnuts

Whisk the ingredients of group 1 to a meringue and at the same time those of group 2 to a sponge. Amalgamate them afterwards, folding in and carefully clearing the previously sieved group 3.

Strong Flavour

Pipe out in $2\frac{1}{2}$ in (6·4 cm) fingers with a savoy bag fitted with $\frac{3}{8}$-in (9 mm) plain tube on to well-greased and lightly floured sheet tins, baking at 320°F (160°C) until they may be moved along the sheet. If not wanted for immediate finishing, they should be stored in a drying cupboard.

To finish, sandwich in pairs with a mixture comprising equal quantities of buttercream and royal icing, flavoured quite strongly with malt. Enrobe with chocolate and finish with a single silver dragée.

An alternative flavour to malt would be lemon, using lemon paste, and rum, using liqueur, not essence.

Lemon and rum may be used to flavour these fingers and drops in place of malt

Fluted Fingers

From a sheet of plain swiss roll cut slices $2\frac{1}{2}$ in (6·4 cm) wide. Place on to papered sheet tins and spread with strawberry jam. Prepare the following mixing by the sugar-batter method:

1 lb (450 g) butter	2 lb (910 g) flour
1 lb (450 g) castor sugar	egg colour
10 oz or $\frac{1}{2}$-pt (280 g or 0·28 litres) egg	vanilla essence

Using a star tube and savoy bag, pipe parallel lines lengthwise along the prepared strips, each touching the next. Bake on wires at 350°F (180°C) and, immediately on withdrawal from the oven, glaze with boiling apricot jam, followed immediately with thin water icing or fondant, and sprinkle with roasted almonds prior to cutting to fingers of the desired size.

Raisin Slice

This is another tasty line using raisins, and may be produced either in the 'trough'-shaped frangipane tins, or, alternatively, on an ordinary sheet tin. In either case, line the chosen tin thinly with a good sweet-paste, masking this with apricot jam.

1 lb 6 oz (620 g) castor sugar $\frac{1}{2}$-oz (14 g) baking powder
2 oz (57 g) honey $1\frac{1}{2}$ lb (680 g) chopped raisins
$1\frac{1}{2}$ lb (680 g) egg   6 oz (170 g) roasted nib almonds
1 lb 2 oz (510 g) flour $\frac{1}{2}$-oz (14 g) salt

Produce a full sponge in the normal way with the castor sugar, honey and eggs. Remove from the machine, add the sieved flour, salt and baking powder, partially clear, add the fruit and nuts and clear. Divide into the 'trough' tins or, if using an ordinary sheet tin, spread over an area measuring 18 × 24 in (46 × 61 cm) fitted with a stick to prevent flowing. Bake at 380–390°F (195–200°C).

Raisin slice using sheets

After baking, and when cold, a simple finish should suffice. For the troughs, mask with boiled apricot purée, followed by white fondant, completing with a half walnut to each 1 in (2·6 cm) slice.

For the sheets, cut into $2\frac{1}{2}$ in (6·4 cm) slices, masking top and sides with lemon buttercream, followed by roasted, flaked almonds. Place a genoese stick along the centre, dredge with icing sugar, remove the stick and cut into 1 in (2·6 cm) fingers.

Raisin slice 'trough' variety

Walfruit Slices

Some lines are sufficiently rich in both appearance and eating quality that no adornment after baking is required, this particular line fitting quite neatly into that category. Preferably produced in trough-shaped tins, it may also be made on a sheet tin and cut into slices.

Line up the trough-shaped tins with sweetpaste, making the base with pineapple jam. Prepare the filling from:

3 lb (1360 g) weak flour $\frac{1}{2}$-oz (14 g) salt
1¾ oz (50 g) baking powder

Sieve together, then add half to the fruit and nuts:

2¼ lb (1020 g) chopped dates 3 lb (1360 g) broken walnuts
2 lb 10 oz (1190 g) cherries

Mix together, with half of the above:

4½ lb (2040 g) egg egg colour
6 lb (2720 g) sugar vanilla essence

Whisk together the eggs and sugar to full sponge, adding colour and essence just prior to taking off the machine. Remove, knock out the whisk, partially blend in the flour, add the fruit/flour mix and clear well.

Divide into the trough tins or, if baking on a sheet, scale at 8 lb (3700 g) to a 30 × 18 in (76 × 46 cm) sweetpaste-lined tin. Bake at 350–360°F (175–180°C) for approximately 25–30 min.

Walfruit slices

If baked on sheet tins, cut whilst still warm, but if trough tins are used tip on to a clean cloth or sack to cool.

Russian Slice

Another popular name for this is 'wine slice' but should only be used if wine, or, to be more precise, sherry is used in the manufacture.

This is another outlet for scrap, but only pieces of differently coloured cake should be used, the crumbs being used in different ways. Too much crumb will produce an indistinguished looking mass.

For each complete sheet to be produced, two sheets of sponge will be required.

Prepare a sheet tin by papering with greaseproof paper after thorough cleaning, and upon this place one of the sheets of sponge, top uppermost.

Now, produce the filling by mixing the pieces of cake together, and make a bay, pouring into this sufficient apricot purée, boiling, to moisten. Mix gently together, first with a spatula, then with the hands to ensure that every piece is moistened, turning as gently as possible so as not to break down the pieces. A small amount of hot water is permissible to ensure that the filling is not too sticky, yet moist. If desired, and costs permit, add sherry. Now, transfer the whole to the prepared sheet and spread level, paying particular attention to corners and sides.

On to the top of this place the second sheet of sponge, top down, cover with greaseproof paper and a clean, reversed, sheet tin. Place in a corner of the bakery out of the way and weight the sheet tin, bags of flour being admirable for the purpose, and leave overnight or until required.

To finish, remove the weights, lift off the top sheet tin, strip off the paper and ice with water icing, marbling in a contrasting colour. The slice may then be cut individually into fancies or, alternatively, sold as a large unit.

Drescan

This is an adaptation of the very popular Dresden, and comprises sheet sponge (such as swiss roll) produced slightly thicker than usual, with a few chopped or broken pecans added to the sponge.

Drescan

After spreading, baking and cooling, cut the sponge into three inch strips. Place the first strip, top uppermost, and, using a savoy bag fitted with a $\frac{1}{4}$-in (6 mm) plain tube, pipe a line of white, vanilla flavoured buttercream along either side, at the edge. About 1 in (2·6 cm) from either side pipe two further lines, filling in the spaces formed with pineapple conserve. Place another 3 in (7·6 cm) strip of the sponge on the top, this time, top down, pressing lightly to adhere. Enrobe with baker's chocolate, allow to set, enrobe again, this time combing with comb scraper and decorating with whole pecan nuts.

TRIFLES

These are an ever popular sweet and, from our viewpoint, provide an excellent and profitable means of disposal of dry and broken sponges. This, however, does not mean that these are a receptacle for anything that happens to be lying around. Indeed, so easy is it for the customer to produce her own, that it is incumbent upon us to produce an absolutely first rate article. The size, of course, depends upon many and variable factors, but clear, plastic dishes of all sizes are available, so that the production of trifles can become an integral part of a 'Hostess Service', as well as normal shop sale.

The whole character should be of a soft-eating article, so the inclusion of nuts of various types is, to me, strictly not to be considered. The base should be of jammed sponge, to be soaked with a syrup of pronounced sherry flavour. This latter is cheap enough, in the context of price obtainable for a first class article, and the flavour should be sufficient to percolate through the vanilla custard and cream topping. The sugar syrup can be a normal stock syrup, or fruit juice can be utilised, as can dessert fruit if desired, but I feel that fruit is better not included. On to the sponge can be added ratafia biscuits if desired. A layer of vanilla custard should now be poured over the sponge whilst still hot, and should be produced rather softer than one would make it for any other purpose. Remember that the confection must be soft eating, which does not include rubbery custard!

Topping should not be with anything other than fresh cream, whipped to piping consistency, and piped on using savoy bag and star tube. Far too often is one served with fresh cream that has been passed through the air whip, so that the remaining smudge might just as well not exist for any pleasure given to the consumer. Final decoration is generally with small pieces of cherry, etc., but chocolate vermicelli should *never* be sprinkled on the tops of trifles, as is often seen.

Chapter 3

POWDER-AERATED GOODS

The production of goods generally under this heading appears to have steadily declined over the past years. How much this is a result of a more affluent society, or how much a result of indifference on the part of the industry is hard to say, but the main goods in this category seem to be the ring of scones and a few tea scones.

Whilst the latter appear to be of generally fair quality and workmanship, the former quite often resemble some overgrown rock cake with a rough appearance. More milk than egg appears to be used in the final 'wash', giving a stale appearance at the outset and, quite often, a sodary after-taste completes the downfall of the ring, and can account for dwindling sales and popularity.

First, what of the materials to be used? Flour should be of medium strength, and the sugar a fine castor. For scones, a good shortening should be employed, although, for a really high-class trade where a good price may be obtained, a proportion of this may be exchanged for butter.

Similarly, a proportion of the liquids may take the form of egg or egg whites in place of milk—if reconstituted the quantities should be 2 oz (57 g) milk powder to 1 pt (0·57 litres) water.

Baking powder should be of the normal 2 and 1 variety, using two parts of cream powder to one part of bicarbonate of soda. Cream powder is preferred to cream of tartar, for goods containing the latter begin to work quickly, as this is more soluble in cold water, hence the necessity for quick working off and immediate baking. Goods made with powder comprising cream powder may be left for a short period—usually 20 min or so—to rest after working off. This will ease any toughness occasioned by mixing and working off.

Methods of Mixing

(1) Creaming method

Place the fat and sugar into a suitably sized bowl—or machine bowl fitted with beater if the amount warrants it—and cream until light and the sugar is dissolved, slightly warming if necessary. Add the sieved flour and baking powder, and rub in. Now add the liquid and clear, finally adding any fruit required and dispersing evenly.

(2) Rub-in method

Sieve together the flour and baking powder on to the bench and, if the fats are hard, rub down to a smooth consistency, afterwards adding to the flour and rubbing in finely. Make a bay, place the sugar in the centre, add the liquids and dissolve the sugar. Commence drawing in the flour from the inside of the bay, finally drawing in all the flour and working down really well to produce a smooth, clear dough, afterwards dispersing any fruit required evenly throughout the dough. Once again, should the amount warrant it, this method may be adopted by using a machine, but this time using a dough hook in place of a beater.

(3) Batter method

Sieve together the flour and baking powder and place on one side. Place the sugar and fat into a suitably sized bowl and cream until light, afterwards adding the liquid in several stages. Finally, add the sieved flour and baking powder, clear, and disperse any fruit required throughout the dough.

(4) All-in method

This method was used in an establishment prewar solely for producing small tea scones, which, in those days, were sold at a $\frac{1}{2}$d each. The trade in these was terrific, and this method was adopted to save much valuable time in the mornings. All the dry ingredients—including fruit—were weighed the previous day, rubbed in, and the whole bagged in clean sacks. The following morning $4\frac{1}{2}$ lb (2040 g) of the dry ingredients were weighed out and mixed, by hand, with $1\frac{1}{2}$ pt (0·85 litres) milk, to produce a clear dough.

This, in turn, was pinned out and cut with a 2 in (5·1 cm) cutter to produce $4\frac{1}{2}$ dozen tea scones, and woe betide the operative who failed to get the correct yield! The resultant tea scone was of a slightly rough appearance due to undissolved sugar, but general appearance and eating quality were quite good, as a large trade testified.

Commercial Scone Rings

5 lb (2270 g) flour
4 oz (114 g) baking powder
10 oz (280 g) sugar

10 oz (280 g) shortening
3 lb 2 oz or $2\frac{1}{2}$ pt (1420 g or 1·42 litres) milk
10 oz (280 g) sultanas

Enriched Scone Rings

5 lb (2270 g) flour
4 oz (114 g) baking powder
10 oz (280 g) castor sugar
4 oz (114 g) butter

6 oz (170 g) shortening
15 oz or $\frac{1}{4}$-pt (430 g or 0·43 litre) egg
2 lb 3 oz or $1\frac{3}{4}$ pt (1000 g or 1 litre) milk
10 oz (280 g) sultanas

Bold, with clean cuts, sultana scone rings (left) and the little seen ginger scone rings, popular where introduced

As will be noticed, the above recipes are for sultana scones, but if plain rings are required the fruit will be deleted. Whilst there may be some divergence of opinion as to the quantity of fruit required, the amounts given will be found to be quite satisfactory.

Mix by any of the first three methods detailed, paying particular attention to the final clearance—the stage, I find, where many confectioners make the mistake of being so concerned to 'mix lightly' that they fail to clear properly, hence the 'rocky' appearance.

In discussing this point on one occasion with a few fellow confectioners, one of the number present opined that to mix thoroughly was to produce the 'exhibition' type of scone. Surely, whatever type of goods we are producing, our aim should be to produce the 'exhibition' type in everything, taking the word exhibition at its full literal sense, meaning that which is best?

Also, continued our speaker, he was sure that that type would not sell in his business. Further enquiry elicited the information that his scone trade was very poor, amounting to a few rings of the 'home-made' type daily. That, I feel, is the answer to his argument. Only an article that looks professional and is free of after-taste will find favour.

The traditional scaling weight of rings of scones is 10 oz (280 g), but probably due to the price factor this has been reduced somewhat and, for present-day needs, a weight of perhaps 8 oz (230 g) will prove most suitable.

Scale, mould round, and pin round to a disc of approximately $\frac{3}{4}$ in (1·9 cm) thick. Transfer carefully to a clean, lightly-greased sheet tin, and divide into four, using a scotch scraper for the purpose.

Egg-wash carefully, using a wash comprising whole eggs to which one or two yolks have been added, the whole having been well beaten to provide a smooth wash. Using a brush of soft bristle, take particular care that the egg does not run into the cracks, making strokes away from the cuts, and from the corners outwards.

During this operation, any sultanas protruding from the rings should be removed, for during baking they burn and resemble pieces of coke.

Allow to stand in the rack for a short period to recover and, if time and costs permit, apply a second egg-wash, afterwards baking at 450°F (230°C). If the oven displays undue bottom heat, bake on a biscuit wire or upturned sheet tin to prevent a thick, dark undercrust.

Currant Tea Scones

As will be noticed from the following recipes, all are variations from scone rings, slight adjustments being made here and there, with variations in the type of finish.

The following recipe will be found very similar to that given for rings of scones, but is sure to find favour if correctly made, and one or two simple rules are observed.

Whilst a period of rest after the goods have been worked off is essential, they should be worked off immediately after mixing. To allow the mixed scone dough to stand whilst another job is completed is fatal. An oven temperature of 470–480°F (245–250°C) is desirable, as are wires or upturned sheet tins to prevent bottom heat.

Finally, I have preference for a dry heat, having found by experience that a much nicer article is produced if the work can be so arranged that the tea scones are the sole occupants of the oven during baking.

6 lb (2720 g) flour
4½ oz (130 g) baking powder
12 oz (340 g) sugar
12 oz (340 g) shortening

3¾ lb or 3 pt (1700 g or 1·7 litres) milk
12 oz (340 g) currants
spot of egg colour (if desired)

Perfection in afternoon tea scones, with well glazed tops, straight white sides, good fruit distribution and even size

Mix the dough by one of the methods already detailed, divide into two, and commence rolling out the first portion, using a minimum of dusting flour, and constantly turning the dough round to prevent it sticking to the bench and to obtain an even thickness. Pin down to ⅛-in (4·5 mm) and cut with a 2 in (5·1 cm) plain cutter, carefully, keeping the scrap down to a minimum.

Place the cut portions on to a clean, lightly-greased sheet tin, taking care to keep the shapes quite round and quite close together.

Press the cuttings lightly together, and place in the centre of the second piece of dough, enclosing by turning over the edges. Turn the dough over, to expose the smooth surface, and again repeat the pinning and cutting out process, afterwards transferring the cut shapes to the sheet tins.

The scrap may now be drawn together and rolled again, but usually I find that if this is done the tail end of the mixing does show some signs of toughness, and I prefer to work off the scrap into quarter scones, which obviates the toughness and gives yet another variety.

To do this, scale off the dough at 5 oz (140 g) and mould round, afterwards pinning to a diameter of 5 in (13 cm). Cut evenly into four, and place the cut portions on to a separate, clean, lightly-greased sheet tin. Egg-wash all the scones produced, taking care that none runs down the sides, and allow to stand in the rack for 20 min. After this period has elapsed, egg-wash again, and bake the tea scones as already detailed.

The quarter scones should be baked at 420–430°F (215–220°C) and, when set, but before they have commenced to take on colour, draw to the mouth of the oven, and turn carefully, using a palette knife for the purpose.

Care must be taken to turn at exactly the right moment, for if turned too soon the bottom will bulge, and if turned too late, instead of a flat, shiny surfaced top, the result will be a small coloured disc, thereby detracting from the finished appearance.

The recipe, as given, should produce approximately twelve-dozen scones.

Tea Scones, Using Yeast and Powder Aeration

An enriched type of tea scone may be produced using yeast and powder aeration.

In this case, the texture is slightly more open but, externally, a bolder, lighter article, with shorter eating properties may be produced. To offset the increased cost, the dough may be rolled slightly thinner, and this gives a greater yield.

6 lb (2730 g) flour	$1\frac{1}{4}$ lb or 1 pt (570 g or 0·57 litres) egg
4 oz (110 g) baking powder	$2\frac{1}{4}$ lb or 1 qt (1140 g or 1·14 litres) milk
12 oz (340 g) sugar	3 oz (85 g) yeast
12 oz (340 g) shortening	12 oz (340 g) currants

A little egg colour may be used, but every care should be taken to avoid a vivid yellow.

Break down the yeast in the cold milk and mix by any of the first three methods detailed, adding the egg to the milk and whisking well just prior to adding to the remainder of the ingredients. Clear really well and, finally, add the cleaned fruit, dispersing evenly through the dough. Work off as already detailed for tea scones but, in this case, a slightly longer rest is advisable and I find about 45 min to be ideal. Egg-wash again, and bake as already detailed.

Cherry Scones

Variety, with good effect, may be introduced into what we can call the stock lines of scones, and I find that where introduced cherry scones have proved to be immensely popular.

5 lb (2270 g) flour	12 oz (340 g) shortening
4 oz (110 g) baking powder	3 lb 2 oz (1420 g) milk
10 oz (280 g) castor sugar	12 oz (340 g) cherries

Popular afternoon cherry tea scones, with sugar glazed tops

Mix as already detailed; the cherries, having been washed and dried, should be lightly chopped and dispersed throughout the dough.

Two types of finish are now possible. The first is to continue as for tea scones, using the method as detailed above, but, as this is an entirely different line, another finish is recommended.

For this, and using the minimum of dusting flour, pin out the dough to a rectangle, keeping the edges straight and corners as square as possible until the dough is approximately $\frac{1}{2}$-in (1·3 cm) thick. Brush over the surface with a mixture comprising half egg whites and half water, afterwards dredging lightly with castor sugar. Now, using a sharp knife, cut into strips 3 in (7·6 cm) wide and divide, afterwards, each strip into individual pieces 1$\frac{1}{2}$ in (3·8 cm) wide. Alternatively, cut out with an oval cutter of the desired size. Transfer carefully to a clean, lightly-greased sheet tin, and bake at 430°F (220°C).

Ginger Scones

5 lb (2270 g) flour	3 lb 2 oz or 2$\frac{1}{4}$ pt (1420 g or 1·42 litres) milk
4 oz (110 g) baking powder	1$\frac{1}{4}$ oz (35 g) ginger *or*
10 oz (280 g) castor sugar	12 oz (340 g) ginger crush
10 oz (280 g) shortening	egg colour

Produce the scone dough by any of the first three methods detailed, adding the ginger crush, if used, along with the milk. Scale off at 10 oz (280 g). Mould round, and pin to a thickness of approximately $\frac{3}{4}$-in (1·9 cm). Place on lightly greased sheet tin, and cut across three times with a scotch scraper. Egg-wash, allow the usual period for rest, egg-wash again, and bake at 460°F (240°C).

Chocolate Scones

These items present a novel and interesting line, and are generally welcomed at children's birthday parties, especially if made quite small and dainty. Contrary to what might be expected, the chocolate nibs do retain their shape in the oven, and should be grated from a block of couverture, afterwards being put through a coarse sieve to remove any dust.

4 lb (1820 g) flour	10 oz (280 g) shortening
3 oz (85 g) baking powder	2$\frac{1}{4}$ lb or 1 qt (1140 g or 1·14 litres) milk
10 oz (280 g) sugar	14 oz (400 g) chocolate nibs

Make into a clear dough by one of the methods enumerated, afterwards dividing the dough into halves. Pin down the first half to approximately $\frac{1}{4}$-in (6 mm) thick, and cut with a 1$\frac{1}{2}$ in (3·8 cm) or 2 in (5·1 cm) plain cutter, spacing the cutter carefully to avoid undue scrap. Place the cut scones on to a clean, lightly greased sheet tin, and gather up the scraps, keeping as free from dusting flour as possible, afterwards pressing lightly together and placing in the centre of the second portion. Work off as already detailed, afterwards gathering together the small amount of scrap and working off with the minimum of handling.

Egg-wash carefully with a strong wash, allow the usual period of rest, egg-wash again, and bake on wires or an upturned sheet tin at 460°F (240°C).

Coconut Scones

Here, again, is another interesting line, and one that has proved very popular.

3½ lb (1590 g) flour
8 oz (230 g) coconut flour
3 oz (85 g) baking powder

10 oz (280 g) shortening
12 oz (340 g) castor sugar
2½ lb or 1 qt (1140 g or 1·14 litres) milk

In addition, a spot of lemon oil or, preferably, the juice and zest of one lemon, or lemon paste will most certainly assist in bringing out the flavour of the coconut, whilst coconut flour is preferred to desiccated coconut.

Coconut scone rings

Sieve the flour and baking powder together, afterwards mixing with the coconut flour and passing through a coarse sieve. Mix with the remaining ingredients to produce a smooth, clear dough.

Scale at 8 oz (230 g) and mould round, afterwards pinning out to approximately ⅜-in (4·5 mm) thick. Wash with a weak egg-wash, and reverse the rings on to a heap of medium desiccated coconut, afterwards placing the rings on to a clean, lightly greased sheet tin, paying particular attention to the shape.

Cut through each ring three times with a scotch scraper and, after the usual period of rest, bake at 450°F (230°C).

Wheatmeal Scones

2 lb (910 g) white flour	$\frac{1}{2}$-oz (14 g) salt
2 lb (910 g) wheatmeal	4 oz (110 g) castor sugar
3 oz (85 g) baking powder	2$\frac{1}{2}$ lb or 1 qt (1140 g or 1·14 litres) milk
12 oz (340 g) shortening	

Sieve together the white flour and baking powder, afterwards adding the wheatmeal, and proceed to make into the usual scone dough. Using wheatmeal for dusting, scale off at 8 oz (230 g) mould round, and transfer to the prepared sheet tin, afterwards dividing into four with a scotch scraper.

As these scones have a traditionally rough appearance, it is not usual to egg-wash, but to bake immediately in a good, sound oven of 470°F (245°C).

Wholemeal Scones

2 lb (910 g) wholemeal	6 oz (170 g) butter or margarine
2 lb (910 g) white flour	12 oz (340 g) castor sugar
3 oz (85 g) baking powder	2$\frac{1}{2}$ lb or 1 qt (1140 g or 1·14 litres) milk
1 oz (28 g) salt	1 oz (28 g) black jack
6 oz (170 g) shortening	

Although richer than its close relative, the wheatmeal scone, this line should attract those customers—even though a vociferous minority—who see such harm in white flour and who prefer wholemeal in any form of bread and confectionery.

Make up as already detailed for wheatmeal scones, and, if desired fruited, 8 oz (230 g) cleaned and picked sultanas may be added to the quantity given, baking at once at 450°F (230°C).

Whilst it is only a personal opinion, I do feel that wholemeal and wheatmeal scones tend to eat dry, especially in hot summer weather, and to obviate this, have found that 2 oz (57 g) glycerine, added to the given quantities, proves most beneficial.

Treacle Scones

4 lb (1820 g) flour	12 oz (340 g) black treacle or syrup
3 oz (85 g) baking powder	$\frac{1}{4}$-oz (7 g) mixed spice
8 oz (230 g) shortening	1 lb 14 oz or 1$\frac{1}{2}$ pt (850 g or 0·85 litres) milk

Sieve the dry ingredients together, rub in the fat, make a bay, add the treacle or syrup to the milk, thoroughly amalgamating before making the whole into a smooth, clear dough.

Scale off at 10 oz (280 g) mould round, and, using a scotch scraper, divide into six equal portions. Transfer carefully to a clean, lightly greased sheet tin, egg-wash, allow to recover, and bake at 460°F (240°C), reversing carefully to complete baking after the scones are set, but before too much colour has been taken on. A palette-knife will, of course, be found most useful for this purpose.

The use of black treacle entirely does give quite a distinctive flavour, but many people do find a rather bitter after-taste. With this in mind, then, the advisability of using proportions of treacle and syrup—say, half and half—should be studied when putting these into production.

General Remarks

Besides the varieties already given, the changes may still be rung by using a basic dough and adding 8 oz (230 g) chopped dates to each 4 lb (1820 g) flour used, or, using a plain scone dough, cutting to the required shape, egg-washing and dipping in sugar nibs.

The shapes, also, should offer as much variety as possible, and in this connection it is quite a good plan to scale the dough and cut in a divider, leaving the pieces exactly as they come out of the pan. Made up in this way, variety of shape is present, whilst the weight of each individual scone is exactly correct, with no scrap left for working off.

Doughnuts

In this country we are used to seeing doughnuts mainly sugared with castor sugar and, perhaps, occasionally glazed, but that is generally the limit. Our American colleagues quite often use the doughnut as a base, giving a variety of finishes, and it is from that angle that we shall consider them.

A typical American doughnut recipe is:

4 lb (1820 g) flour	10 oz or ½-pt (280 g or 0·28 litres) egg
1¾ oz (50 g) baking powder	2¼ lb or 1 qt (1140 g or 1·14 litres) milk
½-oz (14 g) salt	vanilla essence
4 oz (110 g) shortening	pinch mace or cinnamon
1 lb 2 oz (510 g) sugar	

Comparison of this and the following recipe will show the significant differences. The second recipe is, of course, softer and requires quick handling with a little dusting flour. Both may be made by the rubbing-in method, clearing very well at the end.

To work off, take a portion of the dough and pin out to slightly less than ½-in (1·3 cm) thick. Cut with a double cutter if one is available or, alternatively,

American ring doughnuts with water icing finish . . .

cut with a $2\frac{1}{2}$ in (6·4 cm) plain cutter, removing centres with a 1 in (2·6 cm) plain cutter. Fry in oil at a temperature of 360°F (180°C), and allow to cool before finishing. This can be accomplished by:

   (a) Immersing completely in thin water icing or fondant.
   (b) As above, afterwards rolling in coconut.
   (c) Enrobing in coffee fondant or water icing.

. . . and masking in coconut

Enrobed with coffee fondant

(d) Half dipping in baker's chocolate.

(e) Complete enrobing in baker's chocolate, then masking with roasted flaked almonds.

Half dipped in baker's chocolate or . . .

. . . wholly dipped and masked with roasted flaked almonds

Fried Scone Dough Rings

As a change from the fermented type of doughnut, these may find favour, inasmuch as valuable time is saved by cutting out the period of fermentation, whilst from the customer's point of view, they are of good eating quality.

4 lb (1820 g) flour
3 oz (85 g) baking powder
6 oz (170 g) shortening

6 oz (170 g) castor sugar
2½ lb or 1 qt (1140 g or 1·14 litres) milk

Mixed as for ordinary scone dough, they are then worked off in the manner of the fermented doughnut, taking care to keep the pieces to be fried fairly thin to ensure that they are thoroughly cooked.

Rock Buns

In many confectioners' shops where these goods are displayed it would appear that the confectioner responsible has gone all out to justify the name.

Having succeeded in breaking the bun, the customer often finds that the remains are a mass of crumbs, which, when tasted, have such a strong 'bite' that the customer eventually gives up the unequal struggle and, from our point of view, that is another sale lost and a black mark against the trade in general. How many master bakers and executives, I wonder, regularly sample their own goods in this category?

The first recipe is excellent of its kind if properly made and handled.

No. 1

4 lb (1820 g) flour
3 oz (85 g) baking powder
$\frac{1}{2}$-oz (14 g) salt
8 oz (230 g) shortening
10 oz (280 g) butter or margarine
1$\frac{1}{4}$ lb (570 g) castor sugar
1 lb (450 g) egg

15 oz or $\frac{3}{4}$-pt (430 g or 0·43 litres) milk
12 oz (340 g) currants
6 oz (170 g) sultanas
6 oz (170 g) peel
egg colour
lemon paste or oil of lemon

No. 2—Cheaper Recipe

A slightly cheaper recipe is:

3 lb (1360 g) flour
2$\frac{1}{4}$ oz (64 g) baking powder
8 oz (230 g) shortening
4 oz (110 g) margarine
$\frac{3}{4}$-oz (21 g) salt
12 oz (340 g) castor sugar
5 oz or $\frac{1}{4}$-pt (140 g or 0·14 litres) egg

1$\frac{1}{4}$ lb (570 g) milk
10 oz (280 g) currants
4 oz (110 g) sultanas
2 oz (57 g) peel
egg colour
lemon paste or oil of lemon

A well made selection of the old favourites of rock, rice and raspberry buns

Sieve together the flour and baking powder, make a fairly large bay, and in this cream together the fats and sugars. When light, add the eggs in three portions, together with the colour and essence, finally breaking in the milk. Take in the remaining ingredients to produce a clear, short dough, finally dispersing the fruit evenly.

Drop out in $1\frac{3}{4}$ oz (50 g) pieces on to a cleaned, lightly-greased sheet tin. Egg wash, if desired, by employing a 'dabbing' motion, so as not to disturb the 'rocky' contours, and complete by placing a pinch of castor sugar or sugar nibs on the centre of each. Bake at 450°F (230°C) using a wire or upturned sheet tin, if necessary, to obtain a rich, golden brown.

It is possible to cheapen these goods by replacing butter and eggs with shortening and milk, and increasing the amount of baking powder, but that, of course, brings us back to the opening remarks of this chapter. So, if a good quality article cannot be made and sold to show a reasonable return, in all seriousness I would say do not produce the article. Make something else, for, interested as we all are in our trade, we must not lose sight of the fact that we are also in it to make a living!

Rice Buns

No. 1

3 lb (1360 g) flour
2 oz (57 g) baking powder
$\frac{1}{2}$-oz (14 g) salt
8 oz (230 g) butter or margarine
4 oz (110 g) shortening

10 oz (280 g) castor sugar
14 oz (400 g) egg
$1\frac{1}{4}$ lb or 1 pt (570 g or 0·57 litres) milk
4 oz (110 g) ground rice
vanilla essence

No. 2

3 lb (1360 g) flour
$2\frac{1}{4}$ oz (63 g) baking powder
$\frac{3}{4}$-oz (21 g) salt
12 oz (340 g) shortening
12 oz (340 g) castor sugar

5 oz or $\frac{1}{4}$-pt (140 g or 0·14 litres) egg
1 lb 14 oz or $1\frac{1}{2}$ pt (850 g or 0·8 litres) milk
8 oz (230 g) ground rice
egg colour
vanilla essence

Sieve together the ground rice, flour and baking powder, afterwards rubbing in the fat. Make a bay, placing in this the sugar and salt, thoroughly dissolving with the egg, afterwards adding the milk and essence, and making up the whole into a smooth dough.

Scale at $3\frac{1}{2}$ oz (100 g) divide each into two and mould round, and here speed will be an asset, for the dough will be found to be of a rather sticky nature.

Place in rotation on the bench and wash carefully with milk or egg and milk wash, completing by dipping in granulated or castor sugar and placing on greased sheet tins, allowing each of the buns sufficient room for expansion during baking at 440°F (225°C).

Raspberry Buns

No. 1

4 lb (1820 g) flour
3 oz (85 g) baking powder
½-oz (14 g) salt
10 oz (280 g) butter or margarine

6 oz (170 g) shortening
1 lb (450 g) castor sugar
1 lb (450 g) egg
1¼ lb or 1 pt (570 g or 0·57 litres) milk
vanilla essence

No. 2

3 lb (1360 g) flour
2½ oz (71 g) baking powder
12 oz (340 g) shortening
12 oz (340 g) castor sugar
10 oz or ½-pt (280 g or 0·28 litres) egg

¾-oz (21 g) salt
1¼ lb or 1 pt (570 g or 0·57 litres) milk
egg colour
vanilla essence

Produce a smooth clear dough as for rice buns. Scale off at 3½ oz (100 g), divide into two, mould round and place in rotation on the bench. Wash the buns with milk, dip into castor sugar and place in position on to a lightly greased tin.

Make a depression in the centre, afterwards piping in a little good quality raspberry jam, taking care not to be too generous with the jam, otherwise there is every likelihood of it boiling over and producing a messy-looking article. Bake off to an attractive golden brown at 440°F (225°C).

Alternatively, of course, the jam may be piped inside the bun prior to moulding, but this method is no longer commercial.

No matter how regular and well made are goods in this category, the time comes sooner or later when the customer tires of the 'stock' lines and something different is required.

The following varieties are given to fill this need so that the proportion of comparatively unfinished baked goods is kept to the same level, therefore not incurring more labour in the day's production.

Almond Buns

These are actually a slight variation on the raspberry buns, using either of the doughs previously given for these goods, with the addition of a spot of almond essence.

Work off as already detailed, piping into the depression a reasonable amount of almond filling, prepared by mixing together the following:

1½ oz (43 g) ground rice
4 oz (110 g) egg white (approx.)
6 oz (170 g) ground almonds

6 oz (170 g) sieved sponge crumbs
6 oz (170 g) castor sugar

Bake at 430–440°F (220–230°C).

Cherry Buns

4 lb (1820 g) flour
3 oz (85 g) baking powder
12 oz (340 g) shortening
8 oz (230 g) margarine
1 lb (450 g) castor sugar

1¼ lb or 1 pt (570 g or 0·57 litres) egg
1¼ lb or 1 pt (570 g or 0·57 litres) milk
12 oz (340 g) chopped cherries
egg colour

Make into a dough by one or other of the methods already given, finally adding the cherries and dispersing evenly throughout the dough. Scale at 3½ oz (100 g) for two, mould round, and place in rotation on the bench. Wash with milk or milk and egg wash, dip into castor sugar and place on to a greased sheet tin, leaving room for expansion during baking.

Finish by placing a half cherry in the centre of each, depressing firmly, as the cherry will, of course, rise during baking.

An alternative to the sugar finish would, of course, be to egg wash, leaving the final decoration to the cherry. Bake at 430–440°F (220–230°C), double traying, if necessary, to guard against undue bottom heat.

Coconut Buns

4 lb (1820 g) flour
3 oz (85 g) baking powder
8 oz (230 g) coconut flour
8 oz (230 g) shortening
8 oz (230 g) margarine

1 lb (450 g) castor sugar
10 oz or ½-pt (280 g or 0·28 litres) egg
1 lb 14 oz or 1½ pt (850 g or 0·85 litres) milk
egg colour
juice and zest of two lemons or lemon paste

Having produced a smooth, clear dough, scale at 3½ oz (100 g), divide into two and mould round, placing the buns in rotation on the bench.

Wash with milk or milk and egg, dip into fine or medium desiccated coconut, afterwards placing in position on the prepared sheet tin. Flatten slightly with the flat of the hand and, using a cellulose scraper or suitable knife, make four shallow cuts across the bun to enable the dough to open attractively during baking at 440°F (225°C).

Coffee Buns

4 lb (1820 g) flour
3 oz (85 g) baking powder
1 lb (450 g) shortening
1 lb (450 g) margarine
1 lb (450 g) Barbados sugar

1 lb (450 g) castor sugar
3 oz (85 g) coffee essence
10 oz or ½-pt (280 g or 0·28 litres) egg
1½ lb (680 g) currants

Almost a shortbread in character, the coffee bun does enjoy a certain popularity.

Make up into a smooth, clear short dough and scale at $3\frac{1}{2}$ oz (100 g) for two. Mould round, then slightly oval, placing on greased sheet tins, allowing sufficient room for flowing during baking at 380–390°F (190–200°C). Flatten slightly with the hand, egg-wash and fork lightly.

If costs permit, the addition of a small amount of chopped walnuts to the mixing and a top decoration of a half walnut add immensely to the attractiveness of this line.

Paris Buns

4 lb (1820 g) flour
3 oz (85 g) baking powder
$1\frac{1}{2}$ lb (680 g) castor sugar
8 oz (230 g) shortening
4 oz (110 g) margarine

$1\frac{1}{4}$ lb or 1 pt (570 g or 0·57 litres) egg
$2\frac{1}{2}$ lb or 1 qt (1140 g or 1·14 litres) milk
1 lb (450 g) sultanas
egg colour

Using the above recipe, produce a well-toughened, fairly slack dough and drop by hand on to well-greased sheet tins in rocky heaps, leaving sufficient room for expansion during baking. Egg-wash by employing a 'dabbing' motion so as not to disturb the rocky contours unduly, and finish by adding a pinch of castor or granulated sugar or a pinch of sugar nibs. Afterwards bake carefully at 420°F (215°C).

Vanilla Fingers

4 lb (1820 g) flour
3 oz (85 g) baking powder
8 oz (230 g) shortening
4 oz (110 g) margarine

12 oz (340 g) sugar
$2\frac{1}{2}$ lb or 1 qt (1140 g or 1·14 litres) milk
vanilla essence

Produce a clear dough by one of the methods enumerated and scale at $3\frac{1}{2}$ oz (100 g) for two. Mould round and then into finger shapes, afterwards placing in position on a lightly greased sheet tin. Egg-wash and bake carefully at 420°F (215°C).

When the fingers are baked and cold, finish carefully by icing with white, vanilla-flavoured fondant.

Using this mixing, variety can be introduced by colouring and appropriately flavouring the dough and fondant with raspberry, strawberry, orange, chocolate, etc.

In the case of chocolate, substitute 8 oz (230 g) cocoa powder for a similar weight of flour; chocolate colour and flavour also being used, together with a few spots of pink colour to give a truer chocolate colour.

Lemon Buns

4 lb (1820 g) flour
3 oz (85 g) baking powder
8 oz (230 g) shortening
8 oz (230 g) margarine
1 lb (450 g) castor sugar

1 lb 14 oz or 1½ pt (850 g or 0·85 litres) milk
¼-oz (14 g) salt
10 oz or ½-pt (280 g or 0·28 litres) egg
egg colour
lemon essence, oil or paste

This dough is very similar in character to that for paris buns and should be mixed and dropped on to greased sheet tins in a similar manner.

Bake at 410–420°F (210–215°C) in lemon coloured and flavoured fondant, warmed to the correct consistency. Great care should, of course, be taken to keep the finish neat and clean, for goods of this kind can so easily look messy.

Coffee Fingers

3½ lb (1530 g) flour
2½ oz (70 g) baking powder
8 oz (230 g) shortening
6 oz (170 g) margarine
7 oz (200 g) Barbados sugar

7 oz (200 g) castor sugar
2½ oz (70 g) coffee essence
10 oz or ½-pt (280 g or 0·28 litres) egg
1¼ lb or 1 pt (570 g or 0·57 litres) milk

Work off as already detailed for vanilla fingers, in this case, of course, using coffee coloured and flavoured fondant.

Chapter 4

SHORT-PASTE GOODS

Many good reputations have been built on the production of a range of pastry goods and, conversely, these goods have proved a stumbling block to other confectioners, although a little care should produce excellent goods, build business and enhance the confectioner's reputation. Whilst the recipe does, of course, have a great bearing on the matter, correct handling, I feel, matters equally, if not more.

Some time ago an acquaintance asked my opinion of his baked custards. The appearance they presented was really poor, with the paste having blistered and shrunk, and, on asking for the recipe used, I was surprised to learn that it was top quality, though the appearance and taste would suggest that pie paste cuttings of inferior quality had been used.

As the reader will have guessed, the answer lay in wrong handling, for quite often a cheaper recipe, with correct handling, can prove superior to a top quality recipe carelessly or inexpertly handled.

Before the more widespread use of mixers and blocking machines, the paste was made by hand on the bench, with the various types of tins laboriously lined by hand. It is still generally necessary to line some of the tins by hand—large plate tarts and large custards, for instance, but for the smaller items the blocking machine, with a size to suit every type of establishment, has now so gained a hold that it is doubtful whether any but the extremely small bakeries manage without today. With the advent of the blocker, new methods of mixing were devised and have now become normal practice.

Having now gone through the general preamble let us get down to what I consider suitable recipes. These are numerous, of course, but those chosen will give wide appeal wherever used.

First Quality

No. 1

4 lb (1820 g) flour	10 oz or $\frac{1}{2}$-pt (280 g or 0·28 litres) water
8 oz (230 g) margarine	1 oz (28 g) salt
1$\frac{1}{2}$ lb (680 g) shortening	$\frac{3}{4}$-oz (21 g) baking powder (2 : 1)
6 oz (170 g) castor sugar	egg colour

No. 2

5 lb (2280 g) flour	15 oz (430 g) castor sugar
2$\frac{1}{4}$ lb (1140 g) shortening	15 oz (430 g) water
1 oz (28 g) salt	egg colour

Both recipes are produced by the 'rubbing in' method, and are suitable for either hand working or machine blocking.

Hand mixing

Sieve together the flour and baking powder, rub down the fats if hard and rub into the flour until a consistency of fine bread crumbs is obtained, afterwards making a bay. Dissolve the sugar and salt in the egg colour and water, place in the bay and draw in the rubbed-in flour and fat, mixing all as lightly as possible. Over-mixing should be avoided, although the small amount of baking powder added will, during the various resting periods during working off, ease out any slight toughness.

The sugar is added for sweetening and colour for, during baking, the sugar will caramelise and the baked goods will take on that rich golden brown so attractive to this class of goods.

Machine mixing

Sieve the flour and baking powder into a machine bowl fitted with the dough hook, add the fats, which should be rubbed down if hard and 'flinty', and start the machine on slow speed. When the resultant mixture has the appearance of fine bread crumbs, add the water into which the sugar and salt have been dissolved, and allow the machine to mix the paste thoroughly, when it will be ready for use.

Second Quality

Whilst the methods given above represent the more orthodox way, the following recipe and method are extremely satisfactory either for hand or machine use.

Group 1:

3 lb (1360 g) flour   3 lb (1360 g) shortening

Group 2:

1½ oz (43 g) salt   1¼ lb (800 g) water
12 oz (340 g) sugar   egg colour

Group 3:

5 lb (2270 g) flour   1½ oz (43 g) baking powder

Place the materials in Group 1 in a machine bowl fitted with the cake beater, and start the machine on slow speed until a paste-like consistency is obtained, afterwards changing to fast speed to cream quite lightly, warming slightly if the fats are at all hard.

Meanwhile, dissolve the ingredients in Group 2, and sieve together the flour and baking powder, constituting Group 3. Scrape down the bowl and beater as necessary, and when the mixture has attained the indicated lightness add Group 3, now running the machine at slow speed until the mix has attained the consistency of fine bread crumbs. Pour in the liquor, commence mixing on slow speed. Finally, change to second speed, clearing until the paste leaves the side of the bowl quite cleanly.

The disposal of scrap and cuttings can prove quite a headache unless carefully watched, but using this method of paste-making the problem is solved, for reasonable amounts of scrap can be added during the creaming process. Thus fresh paste may be constantly used if carefully watched, and so obviate any danger of shrinkage and 'blowing'.

The usual pitfall when using this method is failure to cream Group 1 sufficiently light.

One other tip received some time ago in connection with paste was, if the crumb situation was getting out of hand, to soak a certain amount of sieved cake crumbs in water and add to the paste.

I have tried this, and used 2 lb (910 g) sieved cake crumbs in 1 pt (0·57 litres) cold water, adding to the paste, with no alteration in recipe, along with the sugar and water, otherwise mixing as already indicated. The result was quite satisfactory in every way, and I pass it on with the only comment that any paste so produced should be used the same day to prevent sourness developing.

As previously mentioned, scrap should be kept to a minimum, yet it is surprising how many operatives still use guesswork when 'pasting up', preparatory to blocking. This is quite wrong, for the paste should be weighed and cut on the divider. It is a simple enough matter to block one or two tins, previously weighed empty, then weigh after blocking, and so calculate the exact amount of paste required to be cut on a 30- or 36-piece divider, allowing, of course, a fraction over for correct blocking.

By instituting and adhering to this method strictly the most inexperienced worker should be able to be left safely to 'paste up' without much valuable time being spent on supervision.

Mince Pies

The mince pie will, if correctly made, be very popular, but care will have to be exercised in producing them. Hard, misshapen articles will not do, neither will some haphazard filling comprising 50% apple, 20% fruit, 5% sugar, and the remainder water, so let us, for a moment, turn our attention to the filling.

Many excellent mincemeats are now on the market, and opinion varies considerably as to whether the mincemeat should be bought or 'home produced'. The answer to this lies with the individual, and should only be arrived at if a careful survey has been made regarding costs. Time is an important factor, remember, so sufficient samples should be obtained, inspected, baked and tasted. There are certainly some excellent products on the market, and samples should be well tested and then bought as per sample.

It should also be remembered that all the reputable conserve manufacturers only arrive at and market their produce after much patient and careful research. No confectioner should be so foolish as to destroy the flavour by indiscriminately adding apples and dried fruit. The only addition permissible, I feel, is that of a spot of water if the mincemeat, after being well stirred, is found to be too stiff, and this should be added very carefully. The aim should be to produce a filling on the juicy side, but certainly not 'wet'.

Mincemeat

To the confectioner desiring to produce his own, here is a recipe which has been well tried and proved satisfactory.

12 lb (5450 g) currants	1½ oz (42 g) salt
4½ lb (2050 g) seedless raisins	4 oz (110 g) mixed spice
5 lb (2270 g) sultanas	10 oz or ½-pt (280 g or 0·28 litres) rum
11 lb (5000 g) apples	10 oz or ½-pt (280 g or 0·28 litres) brandy
2½ lb (1140 g) mixed peel	5 oz (140 g) black treacle
5½ lb (2500 g) Barbados sugar	zest and juice of 10 oranges, and 10 lemons
5½ lb (2500 g) suet	or 5 oz (140 g) lemon paste, 5 oz (140 g)
1½ lb (680 g) glycerine	orange paste

It is necessary to take all possible precautions to prevent fermentation, and to that end all benches, bowls and utensils should be absolutely free of flour before work commences. Apples should be of the hard, sour variety, carefully inspected for bruises and flaws, well wiped, and afterwards cut into quarters with the cores removed.

Suet as obtained from the butcher should be of good quality, cut into convenient size pieces with all skin, etc., removed. Prepacked suet, usually dusted with flour, is not generally considered to be suitable.

Set up the mincing attachment on the machine, fitted with a medium-sized cutter, and start passing the apple, raisins and suet consecutively through until all have been minced. Mix thoroughly with the remainder of the ingredients, the dried fruit having, of course, been previously washed, picked and dried; stir well to amalgamate thoroughly.

The finished mincemeat should then be allowed to stand for at least a week, being occasionally stirred whilst in bulk, before being packed in clean jars or other suitable containers. This will allow the fruit to swell and the flavour to permeate through the bulk. If possible, allow a further four or five weeks to elapse before using, then adding, as necessary, a spot of water to obtain the consistency required.

Small Mince Pies

For the small patty-shaped mince pies, wipe sufficient tins and divide the requisite amount of paste on the dough divider. Paste up the tins and block, filling afterwards with the mincemeat, the quantity having been pre-determined by careful costing, ensuring, of course, that each pie contains a similar amount.

Pin out sufficient short paste very thinly, using a minimum of dusting flour, and cut with a plain or fluted cutter of a size to fit comfortably the inner circle of the top.

Using a clean piece of cloth folded carefully to fit a cottage pan, pour sufficient cold water into the tin so that the cloth will act as a damp pad. Now touch the underside of the lid on to the pad to moisten it, and place in position on the filled pie. Using the top of a cutter slightly smaller than the lid, press gently to ensure that the lid adheres to the bottom and complete by piercing a small hole in the top with a metal skewer or tip of a french knife to permit the steam to escape.

Bake carefully at 430–440°F (220–225°C), and then, as they are beginning to take on a rich colour, draw to the mouth of the oven and dredge with castor sugar, afterwards returning to the oven for a few minutes to enable the sugar to set.

It is quite a practice to dredge these fairly heavily with icing sugar after baking, but this, I feel, is incorrect, for all too often the sugar smears and looks anything but attractive when the customer gets the pies home.

Large Mince Pies

These prove quite popular in winter-time, and often the housewife will purchase one to use as an after-dinner sweet.

Before the advent of the cardboard plate, it was customary to bake these on metal plates, and what a stir was caused when a customer was waiting for one, and it had to be removed from the plate whilst hot, straight from the oven! The cardboard plate, and now those produced from aluminium foil, have eliminated all this, and with the hygienic and labour-saving aspect in mind, not to mention the saving in breakages, the small extra cost incurred is, I feel, well worth the small outlay.

The correct amount of paste, pre-determined by costing, should be weighed, carefully moulded round and pinned out slightly larger than the plate, using the minimum of dusting flour. Now reverse the disc and line the plate carefully, ensuring that no air is trapped between the plate and paste by smoothing carefully by passing the fingers from the centre to the outside edge of the plate. Place in this a reasonable amount of mincemeat and pin out, quite thinly, sufficient paste for the lid, afterwards marking in a pattern with the pastry wheel. Moisten the edges with pastry brush and cold water, and place the lid carefully over the plate. Thumb the edges carefully to secure adhesion, and trim with a suitable knife.

Care should be exercised over this latter operation, and the knife should be held at an angle of 45° away from the plate with the hand underneath the plate. To cut off level with the plate means that, when baked and shrinkage occurs, the pie will be found to have shrunk slightly smaller than the plate, thus spoiling the appearance.

Now thumb up the cut edge and, using a small knife held like a pencil, hand notch. This is quite a simple operation, so often spoiled, yet extremely easy. Hold the paste edge with thumb and forefinger of the left hand and cut the paste alongside the thumb, drawing the knife towards you whilst, at the same time, gently easing the thumb back, continuing round the pie until complete.

Place the finished pies on a sheet tin and bake at 420°F (215°C) sugaring as for the small pies, after which they are ready for display and sale.

Small Jam Tarts

If fiction is to be believed, these are the favourite confection of all schoolboys: we in the trade find them to be in steady demand.

For the machine-blocked variety, clean and paste up the tins or foils as for mince pies, afterwards blocking in the usual manner.

For hand-lining, pin the paste to the required thickness using a minimum of dusting flour and constantly turning the paste. Cut with a fluted cutter of the appropriate size, reverse each disc and thumb up carefully and evenly in the cleaned patty tins, afterwards placing the lined tins in position on a sheet tin.

Small jam and lemon cheese tarts

The method of filling requires a few moments' thought, for quite often jam tarts are filled by taking a handful of jam and sliding what should be the correct amount into the case, or, by using a spoon. In either case the result is all too often messy, with jam trickling between the fingers or from underneath the spoon, dropping on the edges of the tarts, or on to the sheet tin. If direct loss through tarts sticking to the tins does not occur, the result is a messy-looking tart and a wastage of jam, which should be avoided.

The best method to fill the tarts is by use of a savoy bag and a $\frac{1}{2}$-in (1·3 cm) plain tube. Filled this way, the finished job can be accomplished quite cleanly. The type of jam used should also be considered for, to give added variety, two or three kinds should be used. Indeed, one big firm have, I noticed, tackled this problem of variety and presentation in the ideal way, and now pack six tarts in a cardboard box with transparent film 'window'. The contents consist of two raspberry, two apricot, and two lemon cheese tarts. The result must be a very great increase in sales appeal. As both material and labour costs in production of this line are quire low, this is commendable.

Bake the tarts carefully at 430–440°F (220–225°C), and here a true indication of correct baking is that the jam should boil. When cold, it will be found that jam baked thus has set quite well. If required, a finish of a small star of whipped and sweetened fresh or synthetic cream may be piped in the centre.

Large Jam Tarts

Pin out the paste to a reasonable thickness, reverse and carefully line fluted or plain tins—personally, I prefer fluted for this line.

Varieties of jam and lemon cheese tarts using foil plates

If using the latter, trim the edges by using the flat of the hand with an outward and downward 'brushing' motion. Use sufficient jam to give the bottom of the paste a reasonable cover, but do not over-fill, or the jam may boil over and wastage occur.

Level the jam, then roll out some paste quite thinly, cut into narrow strips and decorate with lattice work.

Alternatively, and decidedly quicker if any quantity is to be produced, reduce sufficient paste with water to piping consistency and pipe on the lattice work using a fairly large plain tube fitted in a savoy tube in a savoy bag. Bake at 420–440°F (215–225°C), depending on size and, when cold, empty by carefully turning upside down, removing the tin, then carefully reversing the pastry.

Fruit Tarts

Here, again, is the basis of a large range using a variety of fillings. Apple, apple and raspberry, apple and blackcurrant, rhubarb, damson, gooseberry, red currant and raspberry, bilberry, strawberry, and plum are to name but a few, and yet it is surprising how the public remain faithful to the apple tart. However, a choice of three or four varieties should, I feel, always be offered for sale, and the treatment of the fruit does merit some little consideration.

Many confectioners advocate stewing the fruit with sufficient sugar, allowing it to go cold, and then filling out the prepared cases. Personally, I do not care for this method, for all too often, when eaten, the filling is merely a pulpy mess, often resembling jam. My preference is to use the fruit raw, washed and cleaned or peeled if fresh, otherwise straight from the bottle or tin, using sufficient sugar to sweeten.

The argument against this method is that the sugar may tend to form into a lump and the fruit remain uncooked. The answer to the latter objection is thorough baking, and if the oven is of the correct temperature and the tarts properly baked, which includes bringing the fruit to the boil, the first trouble will be non-existent. The second objection also concerns apple tarts, and the answer is to chop the fruit reasonably small.

Also to be considered are the prepared fruit pie fillings or alternatively, the use of a pre-gelatinised starch with tinned or bottled fruit. I must confess to some original suspicion of these fillings, but public comments, unsolicited, overheard during the organisation and running of working bakeries at numerous exhibitions by the author were convincing. Cherry pie fillings, well laden with luscious whole cherries, closely followed by blackcurrant, were undoubtedly the most popular.

Small Fruit Tarts

Carefully wipe out the tins to be used, placing a white greaseproof paper case in each. The use of foils obviates the need for cases. Having calculated the amount of paste required for each, weigh the correct amount and cut on the dough divider, afterwards placing a piece of paste in each tin or foil, operating the block in the usual manner.

To prevent shrinkage, it is generally advocated that the blocked tarts should be allowed to stand but by using paste made from the recipes given earlier, and with careful handling, the rest should not be necessary.

Two-thirds fill the tarts with the fruit, add sugar and, in the case of apple or other fresh fruits, a spot of water. If using bottled fruit, the water should be omitted and the fruit juice used. In the case of fruit pie fillings, no additions of any sort are required.

Roll out some short paste very thinly, cut out small circles with a plain or fluted cutter just slightly smaller than the top of the tart, mark the centre with the point of a knife and place carefully in position. Bake at 440°F (225°C) and be certain to allow the fruit to come to the boil.

If desired, a decoration of castor or icing sugar may be added after baking.

Charlottes

A very close relative of the fruit tart, but nevertheless extremely popular, especially when made using apples, or strawberry filling.

Fruit charlottes, employing fresh, whipped cream in a whorl and a ring. For sale as fruit tarts, a lid would be added before baking

Produce as already indicated for small fruit tarts, but in this case the lid is omitted. When cold, remove from the tins and pipe on a whorl of whipped and sweetened fresh cream, and complete with a sprinkle of green nibs.

Large Fruit Tarts

These are produced in a similar manner to large mince pies.

The fruit should be used as already indicated for the smaller tarts, with lid and finish as for the large mince pies.

Just one word of warning, however. Some fruits, damsons and blackcurrants for instance, have, when baked, an almost identically coloured juice and appearance, and it is often difficult for the confectioner to decide which is which simply by eye: the difficulty experienced by shop assistants is correspondingly greater. To overcome the possibility of disappointment and perhaps more serious trouble, it is a good plan to have a well-known system of designs marked in the pastry top, so that a quick glance is all that is required for the sales staff to give the potential customer the correct answer.

Large fruit tarts, using a proprietary filling. Note the clean cut obtained

Small Custards

Block as for small fruit tarts and, if possible, allow the lined tins to stand for an hour or so to acquire a skin. Whilst this is not strictly necessary, it is desirable to prevent any seeping of the filling into the paste.

To produce a really good filling the only ingredients should be fresh shell eggs, castor sugar, and fresh milk. Whilst many confectioners do make quite a good custard using frozen egg and reconstituted milk, the finished product always lacks the wonderful flavour of the true egg custard, whilst frozen eggs can vary in quality from tin to tin to an extent that occasionally trouble is experienced in getting them to set.

The best filling then, is

3 lb (1360 g) fresh, liquid egg   10 lb or 4 qt (4550 g or 4·55 litres) fresh milk
1¼ lb (570 g) castor sugar

A second quality filling, that is quite successful, although not of such outstanding flavour, can be made, using

2½ lb (1140 g) liquid egg   4 oz (110 g) cornflour
1¼ lb (570 g) castor sugar   10 lb or 4 qt (4550 g or 4·55 litres) milk

Measure the eggs carefully, discarding any that may be doubtful in freshness, and place in a round-bottomed handbowl of suitable size. Sieve on to this the castor sugar and cornflour if using the second recipe, and whisk to dissolve the sugar and break the grain of the eggs. When all is thoroughly amalgamated, add the milk, stirring constantly the whole time, but not whisking too energetically, for if a froth is formed and transferred to the custards, it will burn and become mottled during baking.

Small custards, using foils to save wastage by breaking. Note the clean cut of a perfect 'set'

Using a conveniently sized jug of good pouring habits, and stirring the custard thoroughly prior to each filling, fill the pastry-lined tins to within approximately $\frac{1}{4}$-in (6 mm) of the top, and add a pinch of nutmeg.

The best method of doing this latter job I have found is by using a small metal canister used previously for containing pills or tablets. If a few holes are punched in the screw top, the nutmeg can be added by shaking on and wastage does not occur by using too much.

After filling, the custards should be baked immediately at 440°F (225°C): it is fatal to allow them to stand out of the oven. Slide the sheet tin into the oven very carefully, and I find that a stick, with a flat piece of wood nailed on the end, or, better still, fitted with a sun-blind 'hook', is ideal.

When using the peel, it is so fatally easy to 'rock the boat' and spoil a whole tray.

Place the sheet in a position where it will remain undisturbed and, when baking is almost complete, the custard itself will take on a slightly 'domed' appearance. Using the hook, draw gently to the mouth of the oven, and a gentle 'nudge' will ascertain whether they are ready.

It will be noted that no egg colour is included in either of these recipes, for it will be found that the quantities of egg used in both are sufficient to give a true colour, and a vivid yellow should be avoided.

Large Custards

Always popular, they do need a great measure of care, especially during baking, to produce the correct article.

Line the cleaned tins carefully, using a small piece of scrap paste as a 'dabber' to ensure that no air is trapped between the paste and the tin.

Trim the edge, thumb up and hand-notch, allowing if possible about an hour's rest to enable a skin to form. Fill as for the small custards, keeping the filling constantly agitated, and add a good pinch or shake of nutmeg. Place these directly and individually on the oven sole—round the corner and out of the way is ideal—and bake at 420°F (215°C). When set and baked, draw from the oven and allow to cool thoroughly before attempting to empty them.

To do this, place a piece of clean cardboard over the custard and reverse on to the left hand, removing the tin with the right hand. Then place the right hand on the paste and reverse again, placing the custard carefully in position on to a tray. The knack is soon acquired, but the first attempt certainly causes qualms.

Here we have the ideal situation for the use of foils, and where the necessity to empty the tins does not arise. It is to be regretted that costs prevent the production on a widespread scale. Perhaps salvation of the large custard lies with the caterer, where a higher price may be obtained.

Fruit Squares

Extremely quick to produce, many variations of the fruit square can be used. Currant, sultana, apple, or a combination of any is most common, but there are also date squares, using date paste moistened with water, fig, using fig jam, peach, incorporating peach pulp stewed with sufficient sugar to sweeten, besides the more conventional jams such as raspberry, strawberry, apricot, and pineapple.

Where necessary, a pre-gelatinised starch should be added, to assist the 'set' and to prevent fruit seepage.

Again, costing for these lines is extremely simple, for a set amount of paste may be weighed and used, as with the filling, and a seven-wheel pastry cutter or stick of correct width will facilitate regular sizes. In all, a very simple, quick and constant line with many variations.

I well remember in one establishment being asked repeatedly for date squares by one customer. This I dismissed as a fad, for its general popularity had not occurred to me. However, having resisted for quite some time, I decided to give these a trial, and was quite surprised.

For currant squares, clean a sheet tin thoroughly, paying particular attention to the corners. Scale sufficient of the paste, pin out, and line the tin carefully and thinly. For a sheet measuring 30 × 18 in (76 × 46 cm), weigh $4\frac{1}{2}$ lb (2050 g) cleaned and picked currants, $1\frac{1}{2}$ lb (680 g) sugar, castor, soft brown, or a combination of the two, and $\frac{3}{4}$-pt (430 g) water. Mix in a suitable bowl, turn on to the pastry-lined sheet and spread level. Pin out another piece of paste, scaled at the same weight as the former, roll round a long rolling pin, transfer to the prepared sheet, and unroll over the fruit, making certain that all is covered, and finishing by pinching the ends together at the open end.

Roll gently with a rolling pin to secure adhesion, and mark by using the roller docker. Wash with water, and bake at 420°F (215°C), drawing to the mouth of the oven and dusting with castor sugar, then returning for a few moments to enable the sugar to set.

When baked, allow the first heat to leave the slices, mark the predetermined size with a seven-wheel cutter or knife and measuring stick, and cut with a sharp knife.

Chorley Cakes

These are very much a local speciality.

The paste used in various establishments, to my knowledge, has been anything from fresh shortpaste to scrap and cuttings of piepaste, to which has been added fat and sugar to remove the toughness.

However, the traditional paste seems to be basically a bread dough, properly fermented, and to this is added enrichment in the form of fat and a little sugar, followed by flour to produce a shortpaste.

The paste consists of:

1 lb (450 g) bread dough	2 oz (57 g) sugar
14 oz (400 g) flour (approx.)	10 oz (280 g) fat

Place the dough, sugar and fat into a machine bowl fitted with either hook or beater, and mix well together. When clear, add the flour to produce the paste.

Size, of course, is entirely up to the individual, but generally a scaling weight of pastry of 8 oz (230 g) is usual. Mould round, allow to recover, then pin to a circle approximately $\frac{3}{16}$ in (4·5 mm) thick.

The filling comprises two-thirds currants and one-third brown sugar, well mixed together.

Chorley cakes—very much a local speciality

Place sufficient of this in the centre of the paste and wrap as for an eccles cake, having first washed the perimeter with water. Roll flat, reverse and place on to a clean baking sheet. Make one or two steam escape holes.

Two finishes are illustrated. In the first, the cakes are washed with water, then dredged with castor sugar before baking. The second (right) shows the cakes egg washed before baking and dredged with icing sugar afterwards.

In either case, bake at 420–430°F (215–220°C).

Chapter 5

SWEETPASTE AND SHORTBREAD

German Paste

German paste is a stepping stone between short and sweetpaste and is quite successful for the great majority of goods generally made solely with sweetpaste. The following recipe has the advantage of being suitable for hand or machine blocking, and is somewhat cheaper than sweetpaste, which is a point not to be overlooked in these days of high costs. The recipe is:

Group 1:

| 2½ lb (1140 g) margarine | 2½ lb (1140 g) flour |
| 2½ lb (1140 g) shortening | |

Group 2:

| 8 lb (3720 g) flour | 1 oz (28 g) baking powder |

Group 3:

| 1 lb 6 oz (620 g) water | 1½ oz (42 g) salt |
| 1½ lb (680 g) sugar | egg colour |

Made by the same method as that given for second quality shortpaste in Chapter 4, the ingredients of Group 1 are creamed together quite lightly, using the machine fitted with cake beater and warming as necessary, adding any scrap at this stage.

When the indicated lightness has been achieved, stop the machine, add the sieved baking powder and flour and restart the machine on first speed until the consistency of fine bread crumbs has been achieved. Pour in the dissolved ingredients of Group 3 and clear, using second speed, when the paste will be ready for use. If desired for hand working, it will generally be found necessary to rub down slightly before use.

For those who desire recipes for the usual sweetpaste, both the following have been well tried and proved satisfactory in every way, and both are produced by the normal rubbing-in method.

Perhaps the most popular of all sweetpaste confections is the Fruit Flan. The tins or foils are lined with the paste, docked and baked at 410–420°F(210–215°C). On cooling, the inside of the case is brushed with a quick set jelly, and may be followed with cold, well beaten, vanilla custard, after which the chosen fruit is placed neatly in position. To preserve the appearance, the fruit should be masked with quick set jelly, after which the flan may be completed with whipped fresh cream

Sweetpaste 1

4 lb (1820 g) weak flour	8 oz (230 g) egg
2¼ lb (1140 g) butter or cake margarine	egg colour
1½ lb (680 g) sugar	

Sweetpaste 2

4 lb (1820 g) flour	1 lb (450 g) sugar
2 lb (910 g) cake margarine	8 oz (230 g) egg

One very simple use for sweetpaste is in the production of biscuits which can be incorporated into a range of fancies or sold as individual biscuits.

Of the latter, perhaps the greatest appeal comes from the production of these biscuits, using fancy-shaped cutters appropriate to a festive season and which, for individuality, may be made to order at quite reasonable prices.

Those that I have in mind are, for example, rabbit and chicken cutters for Easter, and 'quarter-moon' cutters, fir trees, etc., for Christmas. These latter biscuits, carefully made and tipped with bakers' chocolate, sold complete with ribbon, find a ready sale for hanging on Christmas trees.

Care should be exercised in rolling out the paste to ensure even thickness, and to this end a marble slab and good rolling-pin should be used. Having ensured even thickness, roll over, using a marzipan roller to give added interest, and cut. Transfer carefully to a scrupulously clean sheet tin, space evenly for correct baking, and bake at 410°F (210°C).

Variety can be introduced to the all-the-year-round types by including into the paste various flavours and ingredients, such as roasted ground hazelnuts or almonds, finely-chopped lemon, orange or mixed peel, cherries, coconut, ginger crush, and so on, giving added variety by using differently shaped cutters.

Variety of finish may be obtained by washing with milk or leaving plain, dredging with castor sugar either before or after baking, or washing with milk and dipping in medium or fine desiccated coconut for this variety.

Like the larger flans, the paste is blocked in tins or foils of required size, before baking empty. Fill the small cases with beaten cold vanilla custard or Crème pâtissière, afterwards setting the fruit neatly on top. The flans may be presented for sale with no further finish, or may be completed with a whorl of fresh, whipped cream. In both cases use of foils prevents loss by breakage

Shrewsbury Biscuits

For shrewsbury biscuits the following recipe will be found to be satisfactory:

4 lb (1820 g) flour
1¼ oz (36 g) baking powder
1 lb (450 g) butter
1 lb (450 g) margarine
1¼ lb (570 g) castor sugar

10 oz or ½-pt (280 g or 0·28 litres) egg
1 lb (450 g) currants
¼-oz (7 g) nutmeg
egg colour

Produced by the rubbing-in method, the dough should be pinned out evenly to slightly less than $\frac{1}{4}$-in (6 mm) thick, and cut with a $2\frac{1}{2}$–3 in (6·4–7·6 cm) fluted cutter. Taking care to retain the correct shape, place on a clean sheet tin and bake at 400°F (205°C).

When practically baked, draw to the mouth of the oven, dredge liberally with castor sugar, and return for a few moments to enable the sugar to set.

Shortbreads

The following recipe is suitable for the production of shortbreads:

2 lb (910 g) flour	8 oz (230 g) sugar
2 oz (57 g) ground rice	egg colour
1 lb 6 oz (620 g) butter	

Mix by creaming together the butter, sugar and colour until light, afterwards adding to the sieved flour and rubbing down to a clear dough.

For smaller sizes requiring hand-notching, scale at $1\frac{1}{2}$–2 oz (43–57 g), mould round, pin out either round or oval, and notch. If desired, a final decoration of cherries and angelica may be used. Bake carefully at 400°F (205°C), dredging with castor sugar.

Shortbread rolled in strips, nipped and forked (left and right) and cut to size before baking. Note the effect of the wooden block (centre)

For the larger size, scale at 8 oz (230 g), mould round, and pin to approximately $\frac{3}{10}$ in (8 mm) thick. Hand-pinch neatly, and transfer to a clean sheet tin, preferably lined with greaseproof or silicone paper. Dock the centre portion of the shortbread and mark lightly into four with a scotch scraper, afterwards baking carefully at 380°F (195°C), sugaring prior to withdrawal from the oven.

An alternative to hand-pinching is to use marzipan nippers, with which many excellent effects can be obtained.

Wooden block

Another method is, of course, the use of the wooden block. For this, scale off the dough at the required weight, pin to the size of the block, and press carefully into position, afterwards reversing the block and tapping gently on the bench to release, then transferring very carefully to the sheet tin. If desired, a finish may be added by flooding the top centre portion with fondant or water icing, and decorating very simply with cherries and angelica.

Shortbread, produced with the aid of wooden blocks

Machine blocking

With the accent today so much on speed of production and standardisation, a quick method of producing small shortbreads is by the use of block and die attachments for the blocking machine. If specially made, they may be purchased so that the name of the firm is embossed on the finished article, thus adding distinction and individuality to the goods.

For these, the following recipe will be found to give every satisfaction:

4 lb (1820 g) flour
$\frac{1}{2}$-oz (14 g) baking powder
2 lb (910 g) butter

1$\frac{1}{2}$ lb (680 g) sugar
1 lb (450 g) egg

Cream the butter and sugar quite light, add the egg to produce a light batter, finally adding the sieved flour and baking powder, and clearing. To avoid undue waste, calculate the amount required and cut on the dough divider. Mould the cut pieces round, place in position, and operate the blocking machine in the usual manner, afterwards transferring the shortbread on to the prepared sheet tin.

Bake at 400°F (205°C) dredging with castor sugar.

Rock Shortbread

Rather similar in appearance to rock cakes, this shortbread has a character all its own, is quick to produce, and finds ready favour:

3 lb (1360 g) flour
$\frac{3}{4}$-oz (21 g) baking powder
1$\frac{1}{2}$ lb (680 g) butter
1$\frac{1}{2}$ lb (680 g) castor sugar
12 oz (340 g) egg

1$\frac{1}{2}$ lb (680 g) currants
12 oz (340 g) mixed peel
$\frac{1}{4}$-oz (7 g) cinnamon
egg colour
lemon oil or paste essence

Mix as for the blocked shortbreads, finally adding and distributing the fruit evenly throughout the dough. Scale off at 2$\frac{1}{2}$ lb (1140 g) and cut in the 36-piece divider. Place the cut portions on to a lightly-greased sheet tin, fork lightly, and bake at 420°F (215°C).

Viennese Tarts

2 lb (910 g) butter
8 oz (230 g) sieved icing sugar
2 lb (910 g) flour

egg colour
vanilla essence

Place the butter and sugar into a machine bowl and cream until light, warming as necessary. Add the colour and essence, beat in, add half the flour, and again beat well. Scrape down the bowl and beater, add the remainder of the flour, and again beat up quite light. Remove the bowl and beater, transfer part of the mixing to a savoy bag fitted with a large star tube. Pipe into papered bun tins or custard cups in spiral fashion, leaving a depression in the centre. Allow a period of rest for the tarts to set, afterwards baking at 400°F (205°C).

When cold, remove from the tins, dredge with icing sugar, and into the depression pipe a reasonable amount of raspberry jam, lemon cheese, or piping jelly.

Viennese tarts

Viennese Shells

The mixing previously given for tarts is too short in character for the production of these goods, and the following is recommended:

3 lb (1360 g) shortening	1 oz (28 g) salt
2 lb (910 g) butter or margarine	5 oz (140 g) milk
2½ lb (1140 g) castor sugar	egg colour
1½ lb (680 g) egg	vanilla essence
7¼ lb (3360 g) flour	

Cream fats, sugar, and salt until light, using sufficient heat to ensure maximum volume. Add the eggs in four or five portions, followed by the milk, still using heat as necessary. Add the colour and essence, and disperse throughout the batter, finally adding the flour gradually, whilst still beating, for the finished mixing should be quite light, creamy, and easily piped.

This may be done by using a star tube and savoy bag, piping the shell shape directly on a greaseproof or silicone-papered sheet tin. Bake at 400°F (205°C) and, when cold, remove from the paper, sandwich together with buttercream or apricot jam, and dip the pointed tips in bakers' chocolate or couverture.

An alternative shape to the shell would be to pipe out the mixing in rows on to the sheet tin, bake and, upon withdrawal from the oven, cut into fingers of the desired length, afterwards joining together in pairs, and dipping each end in bakers' chocolate.

Viennese fingers, orange discs and viennese shells—three varieties from one mixing

Orange Discs

This mixing is also satisfactory for use with the continental idea of rubber stencils. For these, the rubber 'mat' is laid on to a greaseproof papered sheet tin, the mixing spread level, and the stencil removed, leaving the biscuits.

Bake at 400°F (205°C), allowing the discs to just become tinged with colour.

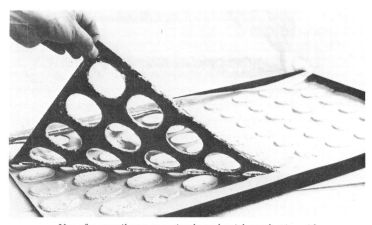

Use of a stencil mat as a simple and quick production aid

When cold, sandwich in threes with buttercream, well flavoured with orange paste, and appropriately coloured. Complete by dredging with icing sugar.

Orange Butters

Ingredients needed are:

3¼ lb (1480 g) castor sugar

2 lb (910 g) butter

1 lb 6 oz (620 g) shortening

1 oz (28 g) salt

1 lb 6 oz (620 g) egg

2 oz (55 g) orange paste

4 lb (1820 g) weak flour

Produce by the sugar–batter method and, using the round or oval rubber stencil mats, stencil on to greaseproof-papered sheet tins, baking at 360–370°F (180–190°C).

When cold, join together in threes, open fashion, with orange-coloured and -flavoured buttercream. Mask the top with orange cake coating and complete with an orange jelly segment.

Alternatively, pipe out the mixing on to greased and lightly-floured sheet tins, using a savoy bag and ½-in (1·3 cm) plain tube. As a certain amount of flow occurs on greased sheets, it is not wise to pipe too thickly. Bake as detailed.

Orange butters (stencilled) and .

. . . piped

To finish, using a small star tube, pipe orange-coloured and -flavoured buttercream along one side of the bottom finger. Dip the top finger lengthwise in orange-flavoured baker's chocolate and set immediately, at an angle, on the creamed finger.

Pitcaithly or Pitkeathly Bannocks

Yuletide festivities would be incomplete without a shortbread, and here is one with a difference. It is one well known in Scotland, but, south of the border, only infrequently come across.

2 lb (910 g) butter
3 oz (85 g) egg
4 lb (1820 g) flour
1 lb (450 g) castor sugar

1½ oz (43 g) orange paste
6 oz (170 g) fine orange peel
6 oz (170 g) almond nibs

Produce as for a normal shortbread, rubbing well down to produce a smooth dough. It may be worked off by use of blocks, or by hand as desired and already detailed. Baking temperature, 410°F (210°C).

Praline Fingers

Basically a shortbread, this line can be sold as such or, quite quickly, turned into an attractive, unusual eating cake.

For these you need:

2 lb (910 g) butter
1 lb (450 g) sugar
4 oz (110 g) praline paste

4 oz (110 g) almond nibs
4 lb (1820 g) weak flour
4 oz (110 g) egg

Having produced the shortbread dough in the normal way, divide into two. Taking the first portion, roll out to approximately $\frac{3}{8}$-in (9 mm), transfer to a clean sheet tin, levelling off the dough and placing a stick across the open end to prevent flowing.

Plain or fancy praline fingers

Mask the top with pineapple jam, roll out the second portion, placing in position and pinning lightly to level and secure adhesion.

Dock the top well and bake at 380–390°F (195–200°C).

If no finish is desired, then the shortbread may, on withdrawal from the oven, be dredged with castor sugar.

The simple finish consists of masking with praline buttercream, followed by roasted, flaked almonds.

Cut the shortbread into $2\frac{1}{2}$ in (6·4 cm) lengths, place a stick in the centre, lengthwise, dredge with icing sugar, and cut into 1 in (2·6 cm) fingers.

Shortbread Almond Slice

1 lb (450 g) margarine or butter	$2\frac{1}{4}$ lb (1020 g) flour
14 oz (400 g) icing sugar	9 oz (260 g) egg

Produce the above into a sweetpaste in the usual manner, afterwards rolling out to $\frac{1}{4}$-in (6 mm) thick. Cut into $2\frac{1}{2}$ in (6·4 cm) strips and place on a clean sheet tin. Now dilute marzipan to spreading consistency with egg whites, adding a spot of oil of lemon to flavour. Mask half of the strips of paste with this.

Using this slightly softened marzipan, pipe strips on the treated sweet-paste, alternating with lines of raspberry jam, starting and finishing with the almond paste and piping lengthwise along the strip.

Bake carefully at 360–370°F (180–190°C), and when cold sandwich an untreated strip with one treated, using apricot jam as the adhesive medium.

Brush with boiled apricot purée, followed by thin, white fondant and, when set, cut into 1 in (2·6 cm) fingers.

Ginger Linzer Torte

The normal linzer torte comprises a layer of linzer paste, raspberry jam with a lattice-work finish of linzer paste, thus showing the jam in the finished torte.

Ginger Linzer torte

Using this same paste, however, two very interesting and tasty lines may be produced. First, produce linzer-type paste from:

1¼ lb (570 g) flour	6 oz (170 g) egg
10 oz (280 g) butter	¼-oz (7 g) nutmeg
10 oz (280 g) castor sugar	1 oz (28 g) lemon paste
10 oz (280 g) roasted ground almonds	½-oz (14 g) cinnamon

Produce by either rubbing in or by the creaming method, though if using the latter it may be necessary to refrigerate the paste to harden off before use.

Using clean sandwich tins or foils of the desired size, pin out sufficient of the paste to approximately $\frac{3}{16}$ in (5 mm) thick and line in the usual way. For the filling, spread a liberal layer of ginger jam or, if not available, add chopped stem ginger or ginger crush to apricot jam.

Pin out paste for the lids to the same thickness, moisten the edges and lid in the normal way, completing by notching. Dock well, egg wash, and bake at 360–370°F (180–190°C).

Ginger Walnut Slice

Using the same pastry, line the trough-shaped frangipane tins but this time, to the filling, add chopped walnuts. Lid, dock and bake as detailed, emptying from the tins and allowing to go quite cold.

To finish, mask with couverture or baker's chocolate, allow to set, re-mask and comb. Complete with good walnut halves.

Ginger walnut slice

This may then be sold either by the piece or by weight, cut to customers' requirements.

Linzer Squares

Pin the linzer paste to $\frac{1}{8}$-in (3 mm) thick and cut out with a square 2 in (5·1 cm) fluted cutter. Place into paper-lined sheets and bake off at 370–380°F (190–200°C). When cold, sandwich together with lemon buttercream. Mask the tops with the same medium and pipe across a diagonal line of coffee buttercream, using a star tube. Into this place a roasted split almond and a pinch of green almond nibs at either side.

In the second variety both sandwich and mask the biscuit with coffee buttercream, finishing with a paddling motion. Place a good half walnut in the centre and dredge half diagonally with icing sugar.

Two varieties of Linzer squares

Linzer Biscuits

For these produce linzer paste from:

1 lb (450 g) sugar	10 oz (280 g) sieved cake crumbs
1 lb (450 g) butter or margarine	10 oz (280 g) roasted ground almonds
1 lb (450 g) flour	6 oz (170 g) egg

Cream together the butter and sugar and add the egg, meanwhile sieving together the dry ingredients, and make a bay. Place the batter in this and rub down to produce a biscuit dough, placing this on one side in a cool place overnight to set.

To work off, rub well down and pin out as for the navette biscuits, this time cutting out into oval and crescent shapes. Bake as detailed.

To finish, sandwich in pairs with coffee-flavoured, well-beaten ganaché and mask the tops with boiled apricot purée. Pipe round the perimeter with the coffee ganaché by using a star tube, afterwards flooding the centre with coffee-coloured and -flavoured fondant.

Linzer biscuits

Chocolate Fingers

In taste, these are an almost indefinable cross between shortbread and cake, yet, in their own way, very attractive.

$4\frac{1}{2}$ lb (2040 g) castor sugar
2 lb (910 g) shortening
$1\frac{1}{4}$ lb (570 g) liquid chocolate couverture
$1\frac{1}{2}$ oz (42 g) salt
$\frac{1}{4}$-oz (7 g) bicarbonate of soda

1 lb 14 oz or $1\frac{1}{2}$ pt (850 g or 0·85 litres) egg
3 lb 2 oz or $2\frac{1}{2}$ pt (1420 g or 1·42 litres) milk
$2\frac{1}{4}$ oz (64 g) cream of tartar
$7\frac{1}{2}$ lb (3480 g) weak flour

Place the sugar, shortening, chocolate, salt and soda into a machine bowl fitted with beater and cream lightly. Add the egg gradually, beating well in between each addition, then break in half the milk. Add the sieved flour and cream of tartar, partially clear, add the remainder of the milk and clear well.

Using a large star tube and savoy bag, pipe out in finger shapes on a well-cleaned, greased and very lightly floured sheet tin. Allow to stand for several hours, preferably overnight, otherwise the fingers will flow during baking.

Flash at 450°F (230°C) on wires, and when cold sandwich in pairs with vanilla buttercream. Complete by dipping both ends neatly in couverture or baker's chocolate.

Hazelnut Fruit Triangles

Of American origin, this line reflects the taste of that country in that it is rich, sweet and full of flavour. Nevertheless, it is tasty and can be popular and is well worth a trial.

For this you need:

3 lb (1360 g) Barbados sugar	½-oz (14 g) cinnamon
12 oz (340 g) egg	1 lb (450 g) sultanas
1½ lb (680 g) butter or margarine	1 lb (450 g) roasted flaked hazelnuts.
1 lb 2 oz (510 g) flour	

To the student of recipe balance, this could look very unbalanced, almost 'odd', but it does conform with the opening remarks.

Hazelnut fruit triangles

Produce by the sugar–batter method, transferring the mixing to a greased and floured sheet tin, 30 × 18 in (76 × 46 cm) and fitted with a stick to prevent flowing. Spread level and bake on wires at 370–380°F (190–200°C).

When cold, and to finish, cut into strips of the desired width, spread with praline buttercream and mask this with roasted flaked hazelnuts. Place in a refrigerator to harden, prior to cutting into the desired triangular shape.

Dobos Slice

One of the fascinating aspects of our trade is the ease by which one can, by only slight variation in recipe or method, produce something entirely different. One example of this is the Dobos slice.

Using a recipe of 1 lb (450 g) all round and scaling into round tins or hoops, one produces a madeira cake. The same recipe, scaled on to a sheet tin, will produce a heavy genoese, whilst using it still again with icing sugar replacing castor and spreading quite thinly, one has produced a type of shortbread or Dobos slice.

1 lb (450 g) butter	1 lb (450 g) egg
1 lb (450 g) icing sugar	1 lb (450 g) weak flour

Beat the butter and sugar very lightly, add the egg, beat in, and finally add the flour, clearing well. Spread on to greased and very lightly floured sheet tins to about $\frac{1}{4}$-in (6 mm) thick, baking off at 420°F (215°C), only a few minutes being required. Immediately on withdrawal from the oven, cut into strips of $2\frac{1}{2}$ in (6·4 cm) wide, using the six-wheel cutter or stick of correct width and a sharp knife.

In the first finish illustrated, five strips are sandwiched together, using buttercream flavoured by the addition of lemon cheese. Dredge with icing sugar and, using the cutting trough and a sharp knife, cut into 1 in (2·6 cm) fingers.

For the second finish, sandwich as detailed and mask the top with the lemon cream, placing in the refrigerator to harden. When this is achieved, mask a second time and comb with the comb scraper. Cut into fingers and complete by placing a lemon jelly segment at one end and piping a shell of lemon buttercream at the other.

Dobos slices, with the traditional finish of dredged icing sugar

A more elaborate finish for the dobos slice

Lemon Butters

This line is, of course, basically a shortbread. Here again, though, it has a 'difference' about it that warrants the trouble necessary in producing another line.

Mix together:

1¼ lb (800 g) weak flour   4 oz (110 g) honey
12 oz (340 g) shortening   4 oz (110 g) milk powder
8 oz (230 g) butter

Cream the above, warming as necessary, but do not cream too lightly.

Then whisk together to a firm meringue 8 oz (230 g) castor sugar, 8 oz (230 g) egg whites, and vanilla essence, and fold into the creamed mixture.

Using a savoy bag and star tube, pipe out on to sheet tins, previously covered with greaseproof paper, in the form of rings, leaving an indentation in the centre. Bake at 380–390°F (195–200°C).

When baked and cold, join together in pairs with lemon buttercream, using either lemon cheese or lemon paste and colour as the flavour/colour medium.

Dip the base and sides in lemon cake coating, pipe a good button of lemon cheese in the indentation on top and complete by 'scribbling' across the top the lemon cake coating.

The shortbread base may be coloured and flavoured, as desired. Substituting orange for lemon, for example, will produce a very nice fancy.

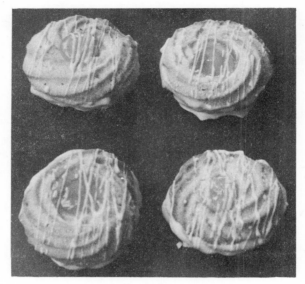

Lemon butters

Crispnuts

Here is a really delicious, crisp, biscuit-type base.

2 lb (910 g) shortening	1 oz (28 g) salt
4 lb (1820 g) castor sugar	1 oz (28 g) lemon paste
5 oz (140 g) milk powder	egg colour

Cream the above lightly, then add and beat in 1 lb 7 oz (650 g) egg. Break in 2 lb 6 oz (1070 g) water. Sieve together, add and clear well 3 lb (1360 g) weak flour, 6 lb (2730 g) fine coconut and $4\frac{1}{2}$ oz (130 g) baking powder.

Using a $\frac{1}{2}$-in (1·3 cm) plain tube and Savoy bag, pipe out in approximately $1\frac{1}{2}$ in (3·8 cm) diameter circles on to greased and floured sheet tins, leaving space for the flow that occurs with this mixing. Bake on wires or upturned sheet tins at 380–390°F (195–200°C). If necessary, when baked, trim with the appropriately-sized plain cutter.

To finish, join together in pairs with lemon-coloured and lemon-flavoured buttercream. Complete by sprinkling plain chocolate in one direction and milk chocolate at right angles, with a pinch of green nib almonds in the centre.

Coconut Shortbreads

The marrying of two different bases can quite often create a line so unique and different to the palate that it immediately becomes a firm favourite. So it is with this particular line.

Using a stencilled shortbread join with a crispnut using orange-coloured and -flavoured buttercream. Immerse base and sides in chocolate.

Complete by piping on the top a button of orange fondant, into which place in position a piece of orange jelly segment.

Maraschino Cookies

One base, three finishes and all popular, if allowed the opportunity. Maraschino cherries seem to be almost entirely ignored by the British confectioner which is a pity, for the flavour is quite delightful.

The biscuits are produced from:

3 lb 6 oz (1530 g) weak flour
¾-oz (21 g) baking powder
¼-oz (7 g) salt
10 oz (280 g) shortening
6 oz (170 g) butter

1 lb 9 oz (710 g) castor sugar
10 oz or ½-pt (280 g or 0·28 litres) egg
3 oz (85 g) maraschino cherry juice
8 oz (230 g) maraschino cherry quarters

Produce as for a sweet-paste, using the creaming method. If necessary, chill after mixing, until the paste may be handled quite easily.

Pin out and cut with hexagonal clover- and diamond-shaped cutters, placing on to cleaned sheet tins and baking at 400°F (205°C).

Maraschino cookies, No. 1

No. 1

Join the hexagonal biscuits together in pairs with apricot jam. Brush the tops of the biscuits with boiled apricot jam, and press six marachino cherry halves to adhere. Complete by enrobing with pink, maraschino-flavoured fondant.

Maraschino cookies 2 and 3

No. 2

Join two of the diamond-shaped biscuits together with maraschino-flavoured, pink buttercream into which has been incorporated some chopped cherries. Mask the top with boiled apricot jam, followed by a diamond of pink marzipan, impressed with fancy roller before cutting. Immerse base and sides in chocolate.

No. 3

The clover-shaped biscuits are paired together with apricot jam. Mask top with maraschino buttercream, once again dipping base and sides in chocolate. Complete with a half maraschino cherry on top.

Coconut Shapes

One biscuit here gives four different fancies, the difference being introduced mainly by flavour.

You need:

1 lb 14 oz (850 g) Barbados sugar
15 oz (430 g) shortening
4 oz (110 g) egg
$\frac{1}{4}$-oz (7 g) salt
$3\frac{3}{4}$ lb (1700 g) flour
$\frac{1}{4}$-oz (7 g) ginger

$\frac{1}{4}$-oz (7 g) bicarbonate of soda
5 oz (140 g) treacle
5 oz (140 g) golden syrup
10 oz or $\frac{1}{2}$-pt (280 g or 0·28 litres) water
12 oz (340 g) medium coconut

Produce by the creaming method, afterwards refrigerating for several hours. Roll out to approximately $\frac{1}{8}$-in (3 mm) thick, cut out as later detailed, place on to cleaned sheet tins before baking at 380°F (195°C). A slight lift occurs in baking, but no appreciable flow.

Coconut shapes—hearts . . .

No. 1

Heart-shaped biscuits are joined together in pairs with raspberry-coloured and -flavoured buttercream. Mask the top with boiled apricot jam and place in position an open, marzipan heart, cut from pink, ribbed marzipan with the two cutters illustrated on previous page. Fill in the centre with raspberry piping jelly.

... triangles, ovals and diamonds

No. 2

Triangular-shaped biscuits are joined together with lemon cheese, and an open whirl of lemon buttercream piped on the top. Fill the centre with lemon fondant, and sprinkle with chocolate.

No. 3

Diamond biscuits are joined together with orange curd, a whirl of orange-coloured and -flavoured buttercream, with an angelica diamond, completes.

No. 4

The top biscuit of the oval shape is cut and raspberry-coloured and -flavoured buttercream piped down the centre. The top biscuit is placed on at an angle and the joint hidden with piped raspberry buttercream, completed with cherry and angelica.

Clover Shortbread

Here the reader may notice a familiarity with a previous line, but this is entirely erroneous.

Cream together:

1¼ lb (570 g) castor sugar	½-oz (14 g) salt
1¼ lb (570 g) compound	1 oz (28 g) lemon paste
¼-oz (7 g) bicarbonate of soda	

Add and beat in:

5 oz or ¼-pt (140 g or 0·14 litres) egg

Dissolve and add:

6 oz (170 g) milk	½-oz (14 g) vol.

Add and clear:

2½ lb (1140 g) weak flour

Allow to refrigerate for several hours, before rolling out to about ⅛-in (3 mm) thick. Cut out with the clover-shaped cutter, wash with egg and sprinkle with any ancillary material such as coconut, streusel, etc., desired. Place on to clean sheet tins and bake at 380°F (195°C).

When cold, join together with praline buttercream and half dip in coffee-flavoured baker's chocolate.

Raspberry Slice

This line is very simple to produce, assists in keeping the crumb problem to reasonable limits, and is always popular. It is one where neatness of finish is of paramount importance.

8 oz (230 g) ground almonds	1 lb (450 g) castor sugar
1½ lb (680 g) sieved cake crumbs	6 oz (170 g) egg yolk

Make the above into a paste, adding a little apricot jam as moistening agent if necessary. Divide the paste into two, pin down the first portion to approximately ⅛-in (3 mm) and transfer to a clean, lightly greased sheet tin, paying particular attention to the corners.

Spread with raspberry jam, pin out the remaining paste and place on top of the prepared half, rolling gently to secure adhesion. Place a stick at the end and bake on wires or upturned sheet tins at 400°F (205°C).

Raspberry slices

When cold mask with boiling apricot jam and follow with pink, raspberry flavoured fondant. Cut neatly into slices of $2\frac{1}{2} \times 1$ in (6·4 × 2·6 cm).

Vienna Jam Slice

Two slices, similar in name, yet what a vast difference in their flavour! For these, vienna paste is required. The recipe is:

5½ lb (2500 g) butter or margarine	12 oz (340 g) roasted ground hazelnuts
3¼ lb (1480 g) castor sugar	7¼ lb (3360 g) weak flour
1¼ lb or 1 pt (570 g or 0·57 litres) egg	2 oz (57 g) salt

The quantities given for this may appear to be rather large for the smaller confectioner, but, once the paste is made it will keep, unbaked, for at least two weeks if stored in a cool place. It thus assists to even out production.

If produced by machine, only slow speed should be used throughout.

Blend the butter or margarine and sugar, but do not cream lightly. Add the egg gradually, incorporate, and finally add the remaining ingredients, the paste at this stage being very soft. Set aside in a cool place overnight and when required for use rub down well. It will be very easy to handle.

Pin out sufficient of the paste to approximately $\frac{1}{8}$-in (3 mm) thick and transfer to cover a sheet tin, pinning lightly to ensure that the paste is well bedded down.

Set the seven-wheel cutter to cut widths of $2\frac{1}{2}$ in (6·4 cm) and divide the paste lengthwise into strips of this width, removing the scrap from the end of the sheet tin, baking off at 400–410°F (205–210°C). When cold, sandwich three together with any chosen jam, like strawberry, pineapple or raspberry, and cut into neat 1 in (2·6 cm) fingers. Once the type of jam to be used is decided upon it must be used regularly, so that the customer can be certain of an article of a particular flavour.

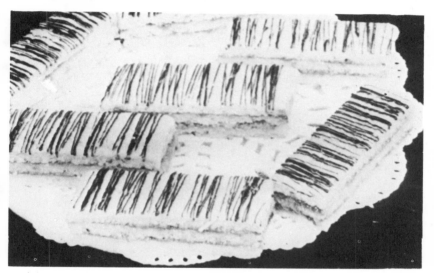

Vienna jam slice

The original vienna jam slice calls for a lattice work of royal icing, piping this on what is to be the top slices before baking. Whilst it undoubtedly has an attractive finish, it is one that will stand very little handling without becoming dislodged and thus spoiling the appearance of the fancy. The finish adopted is shown in the illustration; bakers' chocolate is scribbled, using a small piping bag with fine aperture, the hand being held high and the bag waved from side to side.

Praline Cups

To the many customers who want large quantities of nicely flavoured butter-cream, this line is a delight.

Using the vienna paste, pin quite thinly and line up the required number of small custard cups or, if these are not available, small round pie tins.

Pin out more paste, slightly thicker this time, and cut small round biscuits with a plain cutter, slightly smaller than the top of the cup, and allowing one biscuit for each of these. Bake at 400–410°F (205–210°C). If so desired the bases may be stored for at least two weeks under dry conditions before finishing.

Praline cups

To do this, dredge the cups with icing sugar, and pipe in each a good whirl of buttercream, definitely well flavoured with praline paste. Use a savoy bag and star tube for the purpose. Coat the surface of the biscuit that has been in contact with the sheet tin with either couverture or bakers' chocolate and place, when set, in position at an acute angle on the buttercream.

Walnut and Raisin Fingers

Using vienna paste pin out to approximately $\frac{1}{8}$-in (1·5 mm) thick and transfer to a clean baking sheet. With the seven-wheeled cutter cut into strips $2\frac{1}{2}$ in

(6·4 cm) wide and bake at 410°F (210°C). After allowing the paste to cool, ice one-third of the strips produced with water icing and flash in a hot oven, cutting, when cool, into 1 in (2·6 cm) fingers.

To make up, sandwich two strips together with a mixture comprising pineapple jam, well-chopped walnuts and raisins. Mask the top also with the mixture, place the prepared fingers in position and cut through to complete.

Walnut and raisin fingers

Cherry Marshmallows

4 lb (1820 g) flour
¼-oz (7 g) baking powder
12 oz (340 g) sugar
1 lb 2 oz (510 g) cake margarine
6 oz (170 g) compound

4 oz (110 g) ground rice
10 oz (280 g) egg
8 oz (230 g) chopped cherries
cherry essence and egg colour

Produce a normal sweetpaste or shortbread dough by the rubbing-in method, finally adding the cherries and clearing. Pin out to slightly less than ¼-in (6 mm) thick, cutting out with a fluted 2 in (5·1 cm) square cutter and transferring the shapes carefully with a palette knife to a greaseproof-papered sheet tin. Bake off carefully at 410°F (210°C), and avoid allowing the biscuits to take on too much colour.

Care must be exercised that the biscuits are all of one thickness, and to this end sticks of the correct thickness may be placed on either side of the paste being pinned out, with the rolling pin resting on these. Should any dusting be required, this should take the form of rice flour.

No. 1

For finishing, whisk together 4 lb (1820 g) stock marshmallow and 1 pt (0·57 litres) egg whites or albumen to stiff piping consistency.

Using a $\frac{1}{2}$-in (1·3 cm) savoy tube and bag, pipe a generous bulb on to the biscuits, finishing by releasing pressure and removing the tube from the marshmallow bulb by a circular, round, up and off movement to prevent leaving a 'peak'.

Dip two-thirds of the bulb into baker's chocolate, allowing the surface tension of the chocolate in the pan to draw off the surplus and thus prevent any untidy finish. Complete with a seasonal motif, in this case a duckling of sugarpaste purchased from one of the allied traders.

No. 2

For the all-year-round trade, the bulb is masked entirely with coconut and a half cherry placed in position on the top.

No. 3

In this case the biscuit is cut out with a fluted oval cutter measuring $2\frac{1}{2} \times 1$ in (6·4 × 2·6 cm), and the marshmallow piped on with the same tube as for the previous two lines, but this time horizontally. Complete by piping across fairly thick lines of baker's chocolate, with a sprinkle of coloured almond nibs in the centre.

Cherry marshmallows—No. 3

Coconut Crisp Fingers

This is an unusual line, finished when removed from the oven and which, very successfully, relies upon palate-appeal. Even so, it is quite attractive in appearance, which, unfortunately, the camera is unable to capture. The following recipe is sufficient for an area of sheet tin 15 × 18 in (38 × 46 cm).

1 lb (450 g) cake crumbs	10 oz (280 g) castor sugar
8 oz (230 g) ground almonds	2 oz (57 g) roasted gound hazelnuts
4 oz (110 g) flour	4 oz (110 g) egg

Make all up into a tight dough, the consistency of which will depend upon the type of crumbs used. Pin to ¼-in (6 mm) thick and line a clean sheet tin, placing a stick at the end. Mask with apricot jam.

1½ lb (680 g) medium or fine coconut	2 lb (910 g) sugar
2 oz (57 g) roasted ground almonds	12 oz (340 g) egg yolk

Bring the above to macaroon consistency in a suitable handbowl. Warm to blood heat in a water bath, place on the paste, level and bake on wires or up-turned sheet tins at 350°F (175°C) When baked and cool, cut into 2½ × 1 in (6·4 × 2·6 cm) fingers.

Coconut crisp fingers

Apple Crunch

Perhaps one of the most popular of our raw materials is the apple, the only drawback being that generally goods produced using these have only a very limited shelf-life.

Such is the case with apple crunch but, delicious and unusual to eat, it has the added attraction of using up a considerable amount of crumb, so is well worth a place on the production list.

Providing production is carefully watched and limited, public demand will make it a regular feature.

Line the required number of fluted frangipane tins with a good sweetpaste, and three-quarters fill with chopped and sweetened apples or apple pie filling, flavoured with a little cinnamon and nutmeg. Prepare the streusel topping by creaming together:

2 lb (910 g) castor sugar	$\frac{1}{2}$-oz (14 g) cinnamon
1 lb (450 g) shortening	2 oz (57 g) lemon paste
$\frac{1}{2}$-oz (14 g) salt	

Next add:
2 oz (57 g) water and finally 3 lb (1360 g) cake crumbs.

Mix well together. Place in a coarse crumb sieve and rub through the sieve on to the prepared tarts, ensuring that all the apple is well covered.

Bake at 390–400°F (200–205°C), ensuring that the apple boils thoroughly. When cool, remove from the tins, dredge with icing sugar and place in paper cases ready for sale.

Raspberry Strips

Here is a shortbread with a different flavour that is well worth a trial.

2 lb (910 g) weak flour	1 lb (450 g) margarine
1 lb (450 g) castor sugar	1 lb (450 g) ground hazelnuts
1 lb (450 g) butter	Raspberry essence

Produce the dough by creaming together, (but not too lightly) the fats and the sugar, then adding the flour and ground hazelnuts, clearing well.

Divide the paste into two, roll out to approximately $\frac{1}{4}$-in (6 mm) place on to sheet tins, dock well and bake at 370°F (190°C). When baked and cold, sandwich the two sheets together with raspberry jam, mask the top with boiled apricot purée, followed by pink, raspberry flavoured fondant. After allowing the fondant to set, cut into strips $2\frac{1}{2}$ in (6·4 cm) wide then slices of 1 in (2·5 cm) wide. To further enhance the flavour, the ground hazelnuts may be partly, or wholly, roasted.

Strawberry Bars

Although the illustration may suggest that No. 2 finish here is a duplicate of the raspberry strip, the eating qualities and actual appearance are entirely different.

Cream lightly:

6 oz (170 g) golden shortening

6 oz (170 g) butter

Then sieve together and add:

1½ lb (680 g) castor sugar
¼-oz (7 g) cinnamon

¼-oz (7 g) bicarbonate of soda
½-oz (14 g) salt

Break in:

6 oz (170 g) egg

Then mix in:

4 oz (110 g) water

8 oz (230 g) malt extract
vanilla essence

Finally add and clear:

2 lb (910 g) weak flour

1 lb (450 g) oatmeal

After the paste has been mixed, it will be found that, if possible, a short rest in the refrigerator will considerably assist in working off. Divide the paste into two, take the first portion and pin down to approximately ¼-in (6 mm), then place on to a cleaned sheet tin, levelling with a rolling pin.

Two different finishes for strawberry bars

Make up the filling from:

1 lb 14 oz (850 g) strawberry jam
1 lb (450 g) cake crumbs

cold water to achieve a reasonable spreading consistency, as required

Spread on to the prepared paste, then roll out the remaining portion of the paste. Place over the filling, pin lightly to adhere, dock well and bake at 370°F (190°C) having placed a stick at the end of the sheet to prevent flowing.

When baked and cold, cut into 3 in (7·6 cm) strips and, for the first finish, mask with strawberry-coloured and -flavoured buttercream. On to this sprinkle a covering of roasted, flaked almonds, followed by chocolate sprinkled from a fine aperture at right angles to the slice.

Cut into 1 in (2·6 cm) bars.

For the second finish, proceed as for raspberry strips, using this time, of course, strawberry-coloured and -flavoured fondant.

Peanut Fancies

These nuts are very seldom found in bakeries and then only as substitutes for the more expensive almond. This is rather a pity. However, these two lines will prove sufficiently popular to warrant the purchase of a small quantity to give yet a different line and flavour. Two entirely different finishes all add up to a greater variety.

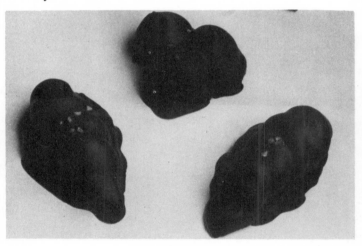

Peanut fancies 1 . . .

Mix together:

1 lb (450 g) Barbados sugar	12 oz (340 g) egg
1 lb (450 g) castor sugar	2 lb 8 oz (1140 g) weak flour
15 oz (430 g) shortening	8 oz (230 g) roasted flaked peanuts
14 oz (400 g) butter or margarine	vanilla essence
¼-oz (7 g) salt	

Produce a sweetpaste-type biscuit mixing from the above recipe and leave in the refrigerator a short time before working off. Then roll out to approximately ⅛-in (3 mm) and cut with cutters to the desired shape and size. Place on to greaseproof-lined sheet tins and bake at 370–380°F (190–195°C).

No. 1

When cold, using savoy bag and tube, follow the shape of the biscuit with beaten marshmallow. Enrobe with baker's chocolate or couverture and finish with a small pinch of green almond nibs.

. . . and 2

No. 2

Join the biscuits in pairs with a small amount of peanut butter, placing the biscuits 'top to top'. Mask the sides with praline buttercream and roll in roasted, flaked peanuts. On one side of the top of the biscuit pipe praline buttercream using a small star tube and, at an angle, place a piece of cut chocolate of the same shape as the biscuit.

Prune Tarts

The reader with wartime memories may well raise his eyebrows askance at the title, for prunes, generally, may not be a popular fruit. Used in conjunction with pineapple, as detailed below, however, it produces one of those tasty lines to guarantee repeat orders, with the joint flavours of prunes and pineapple combining deliciously.

You need:

1½ lb (680 g) stoned, chopped prunes	3 oz (85 g) prune juice
10 oz (280 g) chopped, tinned or fresh pineapple	¼-oz (7 g) cinnamon
6 oz (170 g) brown sugar	⅛-oz (3·5 g) ginger
3 oz (85 g) pineapple syrup	⅛-oz (3·5 g) nutmeg
	¾-oz (21 g) cornflour

Place the stoned prunes in a suitable pan, cover with water, cook gently to 'plump', and drain, afterwards chopping, using some of the juice as shown in the recipe.

All ingredients are then placed in a pan and cooked gently, stirring constantly until clear and thickened. When slightly cooled, fill into ready-baked sweetpaste cases and level off.

Prune tarts—delightfully different

Produce a cold meringue and, using savoy bag and star tube, pipe a ring round the perimeter. Dredge with castor sugar, sprinkle with fine flaked almonds and bake at 325°F (160°C) for 10–12 min until lightly tinged.

Complete with either chopped glacé pineapple, or a spoonful of pineapple jam in the centre.

Cherry Biscuits

It would be only fair to say that this particular line seems to evoke delight or displeasure, with no 'in betweens'. The answer, of course, lies in the recipe, where the appearance of cheese in a sweet cake or biscuit will immediately react upon the reader's personal taste and place him in one or the other category.

Cherry biscuits

You need:

12 oz (340 g) cream cheese	1 lb (450 g) weak flour
1 lb (450 g) margarine or butter	$\frac{1}{8}$-oz (3·5 g) salt
8 oz (230 g) chopped maraschino cherries	9 oz (255 g) sugar

Produce by the creaming or, rather, blending method, then chill to facilitate easier working.

Then, using dusting flour as necessary, pin to approximately $\frac{1}{8}$-in (3 mm) thick, cutting into 3 in (7·6 cm) squares. Fold over two opposite corners to the centre and decorate with a half maraschino cherry.

Alternatively, mould to a fairly thin rope, and coil as in the illustration.

In either case, place in cleaned, ungreased sheet tins, bake at 350°F (180°C) for 15–17 min, dredging with castor sugar before baking is complete.

Rice Cookies

Rice flour is one of the lesser used of our bakery commodities, yet incorporated in certain types of confectionery is doubtless quite popular.

For these you need:

1 lb (450 g) castor sugar

1 lb (450 g) butter or margarine

$\frac{1}{8}$-oz (3·5 g) salt

2 oz (57 g) milk powder

2 oz (57 g) glycerine

1 lb (450 g) egg

1 lb 14 oz (850 g) rice flour

vanilla essence

Produce by the sugar–batter method, piping out the mixing on to well-greased and lightly-floured sheet tins, using star tube and savoy bag. For the whirls, place a half cherry in the centre of half the number, whilst finger shapes may be piped 'straight' or with a 'crinkling' motion. As this is a 'heavy' type of

Rice cookie whirls

Rice cookie fingers and drops

mixing, care should be taken not to pipe out too large. Bake at 360–370°F (180–190°C).

Join the whirls together when cold with apricot purée, cherry uppermost, and sprinkle with chocolate. For the finger shapes, join together with butter-cream flavoured nicely with lemon cheese and dip either end in chocolate.

Raisin Fingers

The use of raisins in the preparation of Christmas goods prompts one to consider how sadly these deliciously flavoured fruits are neglected during the year. Deserving of wider use, the following three lines will prove to command a ready sale in all seasons.

Raisin fingers

Pour 4 oz (110 g) warm water over 1 lb (450 g) chopped raisins and allow to stand whilst the mixing is being produced.

5 lb (2270 g) Barbados sugar
2 lb (910 g) shortening
12 oz (340 g) eggs
1 lb (450 g) chopped walnuts

3 lb (1360 g) weak flour
$\frac{1}{2}$-oz (14 g) bicarbonate of soda
$\frac{1}{2}$-oz (14 g) cinnamon
1 oz (28 g) salt

Produce by the sugar–batter method, though obviously the weight of sugar as against fat will preclude a light cream being formed. Finally add the chopped and dampened raisins and clear well.

Using a savoy bag and large plain tube, pipe into $2\frac{1}{2}$ in (6·4 cm) fingers on to greased and floured sheet tins, baking at 390–400°F (200–205°C).

When cold, and to finish; set the fingers out on the bench, the right way up, and on the top of each pipe a line of well-beaten ganaché liberally flavoured with rum. Allow to become firm before enrobing with chocolate and completing with a walnut half.

Pikfeen

Several different types of fancies are possible using sweetpaste cases baked empty, or 'blind' as they are usually termed. Care should be taken that the paste is of good quality, and the lining kept as thin as possible, yet will not collapse with reasonable handling. Small frangipane tins are the ideal size, baking the empty cases at 410°F (210°C).

A continental favourite—pikfeen

Pikfeen are, of course, a well-known Continental fancy, but are, nevertheless, popular here.

The base is usually an empty sweetpaste case, but there is no reason why a very small amount of frangipane should not be baked in it, to prevent the finish being too sickly.

Into the bottom of each case drop a few sultanas, previously well soaked in liqueur rum. Fill with well-beaten ganache, level off and dredge with a mixture comprising equal quantities of cocoa powder and icing sugar. Mark into the dust a triangular pattern, using a palette knife or other suitable knife held at an angle of 45°. Complete by piping on the top a rosette of well-beaten ganache and on each rosette place a silver dragée.

Lemon Cups

Providing the round, crinkled frangipane tins in which the bases are baked are of reasonable size, the base may simply take the form of sweetpaste, baked empty. If veering to a larger size, then it is advisable to pipe in a very small amount of frangipane filling without jam, to prevent the fancy becoming too rich and sickly.

To finish, flavour neutral buttercream lemon by adding sufficient lemon cheese or curd to give the required colour and flavour, fill the cups and level off with a palette knife.

Now pin out sufficient marzipan or almond paste of good golden colour fairly thinly, using castor sugar to prevent sticking. When of the right thickness mark with the basket roller and cut into discs, using a fluted cutter the same size as the top of the base. Using a $\frac{1}{2}$-in (1·3 cm) plain cutter or savoy tube remove the centre of each, taking care not to spoil the shape.

Place the cut-out in position on the base, pipe into the centre a small amount of lemon cheese, and complete by placing the small 'plug' in position, which is off centre.

Ganache Tarts

This utilises a similar base to the previous variety, either an empty sweetpaste cup, or one containing a very small quantity of frangipane, certainly not much more than $\frac{1}{4}$-in (6 mm) thick when baked.

Fill the cup with well-beaten ganache and level off with a palette knife. Allow a few moments to set, then mask the top with green fondant and when dry pipe in the centre a chocolate fondant 'button', keeping the fondant neat, for 'icicles' dripping down the sides and smears of chocolate fondant will ruin the appeal of this fancy.

To the reader who queries the use of green fondant, I would qualify it by stressing that a blue green should be avoided and a nice spring yellow green used. This line, in an assortment of fancies, is attractive, gives colour and sells well.

An alternative is to flavour the ganache with rum and add a sprinkling of washed, plump sultanas and roasted almonds or chopped walnuts. In this instance, mask the tops with coffee-coloured and -flavoured fondant and again finish with the chocolate 'button'.

Marzings

Unique in that this line is a cross between a viennese tart and an almond macaroon, they are simple to produce, delicious to eat, and could be classed as either biscuit or fancy.

Marzings

1½ lb (680 g) marzipan or persipan	1 lb (450 g) butter or margarine
6 oz (170 g) castor sugar	1 lb (450 g) weak flour

The marzipan and butter should be well rubbed down, or beaten if made by machine, followed by the sugar, well creamed in, and finally the flour, ensuring that the mixing is well cleared.

Using a savoy bag and star tube, pipe out in rings on to greased sheet tins or siliconed papered sheets, and allow to stand overnight.

The next day, flash in an oven of 470–480°F (245–250°C) and immediately on withdrawal from the oven brush with thin water icing, completing with a sprinkle of fine, roasted, flaked almonds.

Praline Fingers

1 lb (450 g) brown sugar
1 lb (450 g) castor sugar
15 oz (430 g) butter or margarine

1 lb (450 g) shortening
$\frac{1}{4}$-oz (7 g) salt
$\frac{1}{4}$-oz (7 g) vanilla essence

Cream the above well together; then add $1\frac{1}{2}$ oz (43 g) egg and beat well in. Add and well clear 2 lb 6 oz (1080 g) weak flour and 8 oz (230 g) roasted ground hazelnuts.

Allow to stand in a cool place overnight, re-beat and pipe out on to greased and lightly floured sheets, using a savoy bag and $\frac{3}{8}$-in (4·5 mm) plain tube. Sprinkle with flaked hazelnuts and bake at 370–380°F (190–195°C).

When baked and cold, finish by joining together in pairs with praline butter-cream and complete with a pinch of mauve almond nibs.

Nutmeal Diamonds

Cream lightly:

2 lb (910 g) Barbados sugar

$1\frac{3}{4}$ lb (800 g) shortening

Add to above:

2 egg whites

Sieve together, add to above and clear:

1 lb (450 g) fine coconut
1 lb (450 g) medium oatmeal

$1\frac{1}{2}$ lb (680 g) flour

Nutmeal diamonds

After mixing and well clearing, place on to a well-greased 30 × 18 in (76 × 46 cm) sheet tin. Pin level to cover the sheet, place a stick at the end to prevent flowing, and bake at 360–370°F (180–190°C) on wires or upturned sheet tins, ensuring that the sheet is thoroughly baked.

When cool, and using a sharp knife, cut the sheet into two equal pieces, sandwiching with pineapple jam. Then cut, first into strips of the required width and, finally, into diamonds.

An alternative recipe to give a similar-type article, yet with a vastly different flavour, is:

Coconut Munchette

Cream well together:

$1\frac{1}{4}$ lb (570 g) castor sugar	$\frac{3}{4}$-oz (21 g) salt
4 oz (110 g) butter or margarine	$\frac{3}{4}$-oz (21 g) lemon paste
8 oz (230 g) shortening	

Break into the above:

6 oz (170 g) honey	10 oz or $\frac{1}{2}$-pt (280 g or 0·28 litres) milk

Blend together and add to above:

12 oz (340 g) castor sugar	$2\frac{1}{2}$ lb (1140 g) fine coconut

Sieve together, add and well clear:

$2\frac{1}{2}$ lb (1140 g) weak flour	$\frac{1}{2}$-oz (14 g) baking powder

From this stage on, proceed as already detailed for the nutmeal diamonds.

Hollywood Tarts

Line foil, cardboard or tin plates with sweet paste in the usual manner, trimming off neatly or, if available, blocking them on the machine. Into a suitable pan place:

$2\frac{1}{4}$ lb (1020 g) crushed pineapple	$1\frac{1}{2}$ oz (42 g) leaf gelatine, previously soaked
2 lb (910 g) sultanas	until flabby in cold water
12 oz (340 g) castor sugar	8 oz (230 g) chopped walnuts
8 oz (230 g) glucose	

Stand on the gas and, stirring constantly, bring to the boil (just); allow to cool, then place a reasonable quantity in each of the lined plates.

In place of the usual lid, a type of viennese is piped on the top, and this is prepared from:

12 oz (340 g) butter	1 oz (28 g) baking powder
12 oz (340 g) shortening	7 oz (200 g) milk
10 oz (280 g) castor sugar	vanilla essence
1 lb 14 oz (850 g) flour	egg colour

Cream together the fats and sugar quite lightly, adding colour, essence and the milk, luke-warm and in small quantities, until all has been incorporated. Add the flour and clear well, though not too lightly. Transfer the mixing to a savoy bag, fitted with star tube, piping on to the filled tart in an attractive pattern that will allow the filling to be seen.

Bake to the colour of normal viennese at 380°F (195°C) when the filling will be seen to be boiling. Complete by dredging with icing sugar.

Hollywood tarts

Fruited Nut Slices

2½ lb or 1 qt (1140 g or 1·14 litres) egg white	1½ lb (680 g) chopped or broken walnuts
6 lb (2720 g) castor sugar	1½ lb (680 g) sultanas
2 lb (910 g) desiccated coconut	

Method

Line a 30 × 18 in (76 × 46 cm) sheet tin with sweetpaste, which will require approximately 4 lb (1820 g), then spreading this with raspberry jam.

Place the egg whites, castor sugar, coconut and walnuts into a suitably sized copper pan. Heat on the gas, stirring constantly until the mass comes to the boil, then remove from the heat and stir in the sultanas. Pour on to the prepared sheet tin, spreading evenly with a trowel pallette knife. Bake at 360°F (180°C) until the top surface takes on a golden brown colour, which will take something like 20 min.

Fruited nut slices

Leave until the following day before slicing with a sharp knife into suitably sized pieces. If desired, the fingers may be partially dipped in bakers chocolate.

Coffee Chocolate Bars

This is another line with an unusual flavour and one that has the advantage of using up a large amount of crumbs.

Mix together:

3½ lb (1530 g) castor sugar	1½ oz (43 g) baking powder
4 lb (1820 g) weak flour	6 lb (2730 g) cake crumbs
1 oz (28 g) bicarbonate of soda	1 lb (450 g) cocoa

Then add 8 oz (230 g) honey and 1 lb (450 g) eggs with sufficient milk to form a medium-soft dough.

Finally, add and mix in 2 lb (910 g) chopped walnuts.

Roll out in 2 in (5·1 cm) wide strips, approximately ½-in (1·3 cm) thick, and place on greased sheets with sticks between each strip to prevent flowing, ensuring that a stick is at the end of the sheet. Bake on wires or double trays at 370°F (190°C) and allow to cool thoroughly before finishing.

Type No. 1

Mask the strips with coffee-flavoured baker's chocolate and allow to set. Remask, comb with a comb scraper and place a roasted hazelnut or pinch of green decor in the centre of each 1 in (2·6 cm) slice.

Type No. 2

Mask the slices with coffee-flavoured baker's chocolate and, while still wet, grate on the tops of each coffee-flavoured baker's chocolate, hardened by placing in the refrigerator to assist in the grating.

Place a stick along the centre of each slice, dredge with icing sugar, and cut into 1 in (2·6 cm) slices.

Currant Walnut Tarts

This is an interesting tart, packed with fruit (which at once ensures its popularity) and is different in that no flour is used in the filling.

Line the required number of foil or cardboard plates with sweetpaste, trimming off the edges neatly. Produce the filling by creaming together:

1¼ lb (570 g) butter	2 lb (910 g) castor sugar (quite lightly)

Then add in four stages:

1¼ lb (570 g) egg yolk

Now add:

6 lb (2730 g) currants	12 oz (340 g) chopped walnuts

Mix in to the batter and clear well. Divide amongst the prepared plates, spreading level, using strips of sweetpaste as top decoration. These may be from a piece of paste rolled out or, more quickly, paste softened to piping consistency with water, and piped into the lattice pattern. Bake at 370°F (190°C) until firm to the touch. The tarts may be sold as they leave the oven or, preferably, be glazed with boiling apricot purée, followed by thin water icing or hot, thin fondant.

Currant nut tarts

Engadiner Torten

Line suitably sized sandwich tins with sweetpaste, then prepare the filling by placing into suitable pan:

2 lb (910 g) castor sugar   4 oz (110 g) butter
2 oz (57 g) glucose   10 oz or ½-pt (280 g or 0·28 litres) cream

Place on to medium gas, and stirring gently but constantly, bring to the boil, then add:

10 oz (280 g) chopped or broken pecans   12 oz (340 g) chopped, mixed fruit, i.e. mixed or citron peel, cherries, pineapple, etc.

When the mixture is fully amalgamated, allow the first heat to leave, then fill the prepared tins. Lid with a thin sweetpaste lid and bake at 400–410°F (205–210°C). Any filling not used may be stored in a cool place until required, when it will, in all probability, have set fairly stiff. In that case, the addition of a small quantity of milk will bring back to the original consistency. This is a line that can be produced in large sizes as an after dinner sweet or small sizes as a fancy.

Florentine Cookies

2½ lb (1140 g) weak flour   1 lb 6 oz (625 g) castor sugar
1 oz (28 g) baking powder   8 oz (230 g) egg
½-oz (14 g) salt   10 oz or ½-pt (280 g or 0·28 litres) milk
5 oz (140 g) shortening   1½ oz (42 g) lemon paste
5 oz (140 g) butter or margarine

Produce a short biscuit paste by the creaming method and, after mixing, allow to stand for a few hours in the refrigerator, or a cool place, overnight.

To work off, rub well down and pin to approximately $\frac{3}{16}$ in (5 mm) thick, cutting out with a $1\frac{3}{4}$ in (4·5 cm) plain cutter. Transfer the discs carefully to a sheet tin previously covered with greaseproof paper. On to half the biscuits spread a thin layer of florentine mixing and bake at 380°F (195°C).

Allow to go cold, then join together in pairs with pineapple jam, one florentine biscuit with one plain. Dip base and sides in chocolate and allow to set on greaseproof or wax paper, finally 'scribbling' with chocolate.

Alternative finish for Florentine cookies

An attractive and tasty alternative can be produced by baking the biscuits plain, then joining together with lemon buttercream. Complete by piping 'buttons' of chocolate on to either greaseproof or wax paper and affixing a half walnut to the centre of each. When set, lift from the paper with pallete knife and place on to a whirl of lemon cream previously piped on the top of the fancy.

Malted Lemon Walnuts

Mix together:

1¼ lb (570 g) castor sugar	¼-oz (7 g) salt
8 oz (230 g) malt extract	1 oz (28 g) lemon paste
8 oz (230 g) shortening	

Add to the above: 4 oz (100 g) egg

Dissolve together:

4 oz (110 g) milk $\frac{1}{2}$-oz (14 g) vol

and add to the above.

Then add and clear:

2 lb (910 g) weak flour $\frac{1}{2}$-oz (14 g) baking powder

Allow the paste a few hours rest in a refrigerator, then pin out to $\frac{1}{8}$-in (3 mm) thick and cut with a 2 in (5·1 cm) plain cutter. Transfer the discs to a greaseproof-papered sheet tin and bake at 380–390°F (195–200°C).

When baked and cold, join together in pairs with lemon buttercream and dip base and sides in chocolate, placing on greaseproof or wax paper to set.

To finish, pipe a neat button of chocolate on to greaseproof or wax paper, and, when still wet, place a half walnut in the centre. When set, lift from the paper with a palette knife and affix to the top of the fancy with a spot of lemon buttercream. It is, of course, possible to pipe the chocolate 'button' directly on to the cake but, unfortunately, this often leads to a 'messy' finished appearance.

Hazelnut Rings

One recipe, two cutters, two finishes and two entirely different lines, both in appearance and taste.

3 lb (1360 g) Barbados sugar $1\frac{1}{2}$ oz (42 g) salt
3 lb (1360 g) high-ratio shortening $4\frac{1}{2}$ lb (2040 g) weak flour
$1\frac{1}{2}$ lb (680 g) egg   3 lb (1360 g) roasted, flaked hazelnuts

Hazelnut rings

Mix in the usual way to produce a smooth sweetpaste-type dough. Pin out to slightly less than $\frac{1}{4}$-in (6 mm) thick and cut out with a vol-au-vent cutter of suitable size. Place on a clean sheet tin and bake at 390–400°F (200–205°C).

When cold, and to finish, pipe a ring of beaten ganaché, flavoured with rum, on top of the biscuit. Set into this four whole roasted hazelnuts and enrobe with coffee-flavoured baker's chocolate.

Ginger Rings

Using the previous recipe, pin out the paste rather thinner and cut out with a 2 in (5·1 cm) cutter. Bake as detailed then, when cold, join in pairs with apricot jam.

Ginger rings

Pipe a ring of vanilla buttercream on the top biscuit, and into the centre place a small amount of chopped ginger. Complete with a sprinkle of chocolate.

Yuletide Kups

Small frangipane tins are used for this line, being blocked with sweetpaste and baked empty.

Into the bottom of the baked cases place a sprinkling of cleaned raisins or sultanas, followed by a small piece of sponge, genoese or crumbs. Moisten sufficiently with a simple syrup well flavoured with rum, then fill the pastry case level with a well flavoured coffee buttercream. Place a good walnut half in the centre, and dip the whole of the top in a quick setting neutral jelly.

It is important that the crumb filling is soaked sufficiently without being sodden, and in this respect it may be found more simple to moisten cake and raisins in a bowl prior to placing in the cases. Produced this way, the job is undoubtedly speeded up.

Cinnamon Cookies

Cream together:

1½ lb (680 g) brown sugar   8 oz (230 g) shortening

Add and beat in:

4 oz (110 g) egg

Mix together and add:

1½ lb (680 g) golden syrup   1 oz (28 g) bicarbonate of soda
1 lb (450 g) water

Add and clear:

1½ lb (680 g) cake crumbs   1 oz (28 g) cinnamon
3 lb (1360 g) weak flour   ¼-oz (7 g) mixed spice

This mixing, as the student of recipe-balancing will readily notice, produces a fairly soft paste. This should be placed in a refrigerator, preferably overnight, to allow to firm.

Tendency to Spread

To work off, pin to ⅛-in (3 mm) or less, and cut out with a cutter of the desired shape and size, using both round and square fluted cutters. Lift carefully and place on greaseproof paper-lined sheet tins, baking at 400–410°F (205–210°C). The paste will be found to have quite a fair amount of lift and with a tendency to spread, hence the papered sheet tin.

In the first variety, two round biscuits are sandwiched together with pineapple jam, and a ring of buttercream, similarly flavoured, is piped round the perimeter. In the centre is placed a liberal amount of pineapple jam.

The second variety, square this time, is very simply joined with apricot jam and with two opposite corners dipped into chocolate.

Strawberry Mallows

Using a good-quality sweet paste or shortbread pin out to approximately $\frac{1}{8}$-in (3 mm) thick, cut with a 2 in (5·1 cm) fluted cutter, place on papered sheet tins and bake at 380–410°F (195–210°C).

Strawberry Mallows

When baked and cold, whisk together the desired quantity of marshmallow, used at the rate of 4 lb (1820 g) stock marshmallow to 1 pt (0·57 litres) egg white or albumen. When almost at piping consistency, drop in 2 lb 8 oz (1140 g) cleaned and dried strawberries with a spot of colour, continuing to whisk until the desired consistency is reached.

In the centre of each biscuit pipe a spot of strawberry jam, and follow this with a bold bulb of the prepared marshmallow. Enrobe completely with a suitably coloured fondant into which a spot of strawberry essence has been added.

Russe Tarts

Even though the shelf life of this line is not long, it is delicious to eat, reasonable in cost and fairly quick to produce. In short, well worth a trial.

1 oz (28 g) leaf gelatine
1 lb 14 oz or 1½ pt (850 g or 0·85 litres) water
12 oz (340 g) castor sugar
6 oz (170 g) melted chocolate
pinch salt
pinch cream of tartar

8 oz (230 g) whipped cream
10 oz (280 g) chopped maraschino cherries
vanilla essence
6 oz (170 g) egg yolk
6 oz (170 g) egg white

Soak the gelatine until flabby in a bowl of cold water.

Place into a suitable pan the water stated in the recipe, salt, chocolate and approximately half the sugar, cooking over the gas whilst stirring constantly, until the mixture is brought to the boil.

Russe tarts, with simple fresh cream finish. Obviously, larger sizes could be produced with advantage for after dinner sweets

Beat the yolks slightly, add a little of the boiled mixing, blend, add to the remainder of the chocolate mixing and, stirring constantly, bring back to the boil. Remove from the gas, add the now flabby gelatine and stir in. Allow to cool, then chill until slightly thickened.

Produce a meringue with the egg white and remaining sugar, add to the chocolate mixing and amalgamate, along with the cherries, into the chocolate mixture. The cream of tartar will, of course, have been used in the production of the meringue.

Pour into pre-baked tart shells and chill until set. A simple finish consists of piping on the tops of the tarts whipped fresh cream, with small pieces of maraschino cherry to complete.

Navettes

Biscuits can be extremely useful as bases, for, not only are they generally popular, but they may be made in quantity and stored, to be brought out and finished as required. Such is the navette biscuit of the unusual flavour.

1 lb 2 oz (510 g) butter or margarine	3 oz (85 g) milk
1 lb 10 oz (740 g) praline paste	1 lb 14 oz (850 g) flour
12 oz (340 g) cake crumbs	oil of lemon or lemon paste

Blend all the ingredients to produce a biscuit dough and pin to something slightly less than $\frac{1}{4}$-in (6 mm) thick, again using two sticks to ensure uniformity. Cut out with 2 in (5·1 cm) square cutter.

Place on to a clean, lightly greased sheet tin and bake off on wires at 370–380°F (190–195°C).

When baked and cold, sandwich together in pairs with a reasonable quantity of lemon buttercream.

The first finish is one of extreme simplicity, with a good half walnut placed in one corner and the remainder covered with a sprinkling of chocolate.

In finish No. 2 the biscuits are masked with coffee buttercream followed by roasted, flaked hazelnuts. Completion is by placing a metal hot-cross-bun cross from corner to corner and dredging with icing sugar.

Pineapple Tarts

Line sufficient patty tins with sweetpaste, dock and bake empty at 410–420°F (210–215°C). When cold lightly mask the inside of the case with buttercream or quick-set jelly before filling to the top and levelling off with cold, well-beaten vanilla custard. Around the perimeter pipe a ring of white vanilla-flavoured buttercream, using a star tube, and inside the ring place a dessertspoonful of tinned, drained, crushed pineapple, completing with a tinned cherry. No quick-set jelly is used here in order to preserve the 'tang' of the pineapple.

As the reader will very readily appreciate, these, as flans, are purely a one-day line, so production should, to avoid waste, be kept very carefully on the short side.

Brazil Delights

Although this line does call for brazil nuts, if none is available then other types may be used, with a corresponding change of name.

Ingredients needed are:

2 lb (910 g) sugar	$4\frac{1}{2}$ lb (2040 g) flour
$1\frac{1}{2}$ lb (680 g) shortening	$\frac{1}{8}$-oz (3·5 g) vol
$1\frac{1}{4}$ lb or 1 pt (570 g or 0·57 litres) egg	1 lb (450 g) chopped brazil nuts
10 oz or $\frac{1}{2}$-pt (280 g or 0·28 litres) milk	$\frac{1}{2}$-oz (14 g) salt

Produce by the sugar–batter method, taking care not to get the batter too light. It will be an advantage if the dough is refrigerated before use.

Roll out to $\frac{1}{8}$-in (3 mm) thick, cut out with a 2 in (5·1 cm) fluted cutter, dipping half the number of biscuits into finely chopped brazil nuts. Place on sheet tins carefully so as not to disturb the shape and bake at 390—400°F (200–205°C)

To finish, join together in pairs, a plain biscuit to a nutted one, with pineapple jam, completing with chocolate 'scribble' if desired.

Brazil delights

Coffeenut Drops

Cream together:

2 lb (910 g) castor sugar	2 oz (57 g) glycerine
4 lb (1820 g) margarine	$\frac{1}{4}$ oz (21 g) salt

Add and beat in:

8 oz (230 g) egg	coffee essence

Sieve together, add and clear:

5 lb (2270 g) weak flour	1 lb (450 g) fine coconut

Using a plain tube and savoy bag, pipe out in rounds on to greaseproof-papered sheet tins, baking at 410–420°F (210–215°C).

When baked and cool, release from the paper, join together with lemon cheese and half dip in coffee-flavoured baker's chocolate, completing with a pinch of violet décor.

Coffeenut drops

Honey Almonds

Basically of American origin, the method of mixing may appear somewhat unusual to us.

Place on the machine fitted with beater and mix together on slow speed:

1½ lb (680 g) castor sugar	1 oz (28 g) bicarbonate of soda
12 oz (340 g) shortening	¼-oz (7 g) salt
12 oz (340 g) nib almonds	¼-oz (7 g) ginger
12 oz (340 g) chopped raisins	½-oz (14 g) cinnamon

Next add:

6 oz (170 g) egg

Add and break in:

12 oz (340 g) honey	4 oz (110 g) milk
4 lb (1820 g) weak flour	

Roll out the paste to approximately ⅛-in (3 mm) thick and cut out with a 2¼ in (5·7 cm) fluted cutter, placing the shapes on to a greaseproof-papered sheet tin. Using a star tube, pipe a ring of rout paste on to half the biscuits produced, baking all off at 410–420°F (210–215°C).

Immediately on withdrawal from the oven, wash over the rout-pasted biscuits with a gum-arabic solution. To finish, join in pairs with lemon cheese, piping lemon fondant into the centre of the rout paste.

Honey almonds

Walnut Butters

One recipe with two distinctly different finishes, both of which are delicious, make this an extremely useful base.

1½ lb (680 g) butter	¼-oz (7 g) salt
10½ oz (300 g) brown sugar	1¼ lb (570 g) chopped walnuts
10½ oz (300 g) separated egg	vanilla essence
1½ lb (680 g) weak flour	

Produce the above mixing by the sugar–batter method, using only yolks of the eggs.

When mixed, transfer to a tray and refrigerate for 3–4 h, then scale the

Walnut butters No. 1

mixing at $1\frac{1}{4}$ oz (36 g) and mould round. Beat up the egg-whites to a froth, dip in the balls, roll into chopped walnuts and place 2 in (5·1 cm) apart on to ungreased sheet tins. Bake at 375°F (190°C) for 5 min, press a half cherry into the centre of each, and bake for a further 8 min approx.

Walnut butters No. 2

For No. 2 do not refrigerate, but stencil out the mixing on to greaseproof-papered sheet tins, using the oval rubber mat. Dress half the stencilled short-breads with chopped walnuts and cherries, baking off at 390–400°F (200–205°C).

To finish, join in pairs with orange curd, dipping base and sides in coffee-flavoured baker's chocolate.

Mochas

For the customer looking for a line with an intriguing flavour and 'something chewy', this is it.

Cream together:

4 lb (1820 g) brown sugar	$\frac{1}{2}$-oz (14 g) salt
2 lb (910 g) shortening	

Add and beat in:

1 lb (450 g) egg

Break in:

8 oz (230 g) milk	1 oz (28 g) coffee essence

Add and partially clear:

6 lb (2730 g) weak flour	1 oz (28 g) baking powder
8 oz (230 g) cocoa	

Add and clear:

1 lb (450 g) lightly-chopped cherries	1 lb (450 g) nib almonds

Pin out to approximately $\frac{1}{8}$-in (3 mm) thick and cut out with an oval cutter. Place on to a greaseproof-papered sheet tin, baking at 370–380°F (190–195°C).

Mochas No. 1 . . .

No. 1

Join the biscuits together in pairs with ginger jam or, failing this, apricot jam to which has been added some finely-chopped ginger.

. . No. 2

Mask the tops with boiled apricot purée, piping round the perimeter chocolate buttercream, using a star tube. Flood the centre with coffee fondant, completing with parallel lines of piped, cool, chocolate fondant, with four dots piped within the lines.

No. 2

Join the biscuits together with lemon cheese, pipe two parallel lines $\frac{1}{2}$-in (1·3 cm) apart, lengthwise along the biscuit with chocolate buttercream, piping between the two lines lemon buttercream. Complete with a piece of cherry and angelica.

. . . and No. 3

No. 3

The biscuits here are slightly thicker and cut out with a size smaller oval cutter. Join together in pairs with coffee-flavoured baker's chocolate to which has been added some nibbed croquant. The top finish is simple, using coffee or coffee and chocolate buttercream.

German Cheese Cake

Whilst the thought of the combination of sweet and savoury may not appeal to all palates, it is certainly different and, to many, delightful.

Cream well together:

2 lb (910 g) dry cottage cheese	6 oz (170 g) strong flour
1¾ lb (800 g) cream cheese	6 oz (170 g) melted butter
9 oz (260 g) castor sugar	½-oz (14 g) salt

Whisk together, then break into the above:

2 oz (57 g) egg yolk	¾-oz (21 g) lemon paste
15 oz or ¾ pt (430 g or 0·43 litres) milk	

Whisk to meringue, then fold into the above:

12½ oz (360 g) egg white	10 oz (280 g) castor sugar

Line the required number of sandwich tins with sweetpaste and, if desired, mask the base thinly with apricot jam.

German cheese cake

Add the cheese filling to approximately two-thirds full, sprinkle with Parmesan cheese and bake at 325–330°F (160–165°C). If, during baking, the cake tends to crack rather too much, remove from the oven for about 10 min, then replace to finish baking which, as will already have been noted, is quite slow. Such additions as coconut, chopped walnuts, sultanas, almonds, etc., may all be tried to produce a local speciality.

NUT TARTS

Here is a line with a moist-eating nutty centre, guaranteed to be popular.

Line or block the required number of round, crinkled frangipane tins with sweetpaste, then prepare the following mixture:

1 lb 2 oz (510 g) castor sugar	9 oz (255 g) chopped roasted hazelnuts
11 oz (310 g) cream	9 oz (255 g) chopped walnuts
7 oz (200 g) milk	

Melt the sugar in a copper pan over a low gas, stirring constantly; then slowly add the milk and cream, boiling to thread degree 225°F (105°C). Remove from the gas, add the nuts, stir well in and allow to cool. The cream should be unwhipped and may be either fresh or artificial.

A larger version of the nut tarts, suitable for catering

Fill the lined tarts two-thirds full and roll out further sweetpaste quite thinly for the lids. Roll with the basket roller prior to cutting out with a crinkled cutter the size of the tart.

Moisten and place in position in the usual way prior to baking off at 380–390°F (195–200°C). When baked, remove from the tins and dredge with icing sugar.

An alternative for catering readers is to produce the above in sandwich tins finishing, as shown, by dredging with icing sugar after placing strips of cardboard or wood in position.

For the reader desiring this to appear more decorative, then reverse and mask the base with baker's chocolate, marking into segments and, upon each, placing a half walnut.

The filling, when prepared, will keep indefinitely under proper storage conditions and, if thick after standing, should be placed in a water bath for a short time before use and, if required, bringing back to original viscosity with a spot of milk.

Lemon Nuts

1¼ lb (570 g) castor sugar	⅛-oz (3·5 g) bicarbonate of soda
9 oz (255 g) Barbados sugar	½-oz (14 g) salt
12 oz (340 g) butter or margarine	¾-oz (21 g) lemon paste
8 oz (230 g) shortening	

Cream to maximum volume, then add:

5 oz (140 g) egg yolk	2 oz (57 g) fresh cream

beating well in. Now add:

8 oz (230 g) finely chopped almond nibs	1¾ lb (795 g) weak flour
6½ oz (180 g) fine coconut	

Delicious and unusual lemon nuts

Clear thoroughly and allow to stand in refrigerator overnight. For use, rub well down, pin to slightly less than ¼-in (6 mm) thick, and cut with a 2 in (5·1 cm) fluted cutter, placing the discs on to a greaseproof-papered sheet tin.
For the topping, whisk together:

10 oz or ½-pt (280 g or 0·28 litres) egg white	pinch of cream of tartar
10 oz (280 g) castor sugar	

to soft peak. Now add and clear:

1 lb (450 g) finely chopped almond nibs	12 oz (340 g) coconut

Place a collar of the topping round the perimeter of the biscuits and bake at 370–380°F (190–195°C) to an attractive golden brown, using biscuit wires to minimise bottom heat. Complete by piping in the centre a liberal quantity of lemon cheese.

Pineapple Centres

2 lb (910 g) castor sugar	¾-oz (21 g) salt
12 oz (340 g) shortening	vanilla essence

Cream the above quite lightly, then add and beat in:

8 oz (230 g) egg

Break in:

8 oz (230 g) milk,

Then add:

3 lb (1360 g) weak flour	1½ oz (42 g) baking powder

previously sieved together, and mixing all to a smooth dough.

Allow to remain in a cool place for a short time before rolling out to slightly less than ¼-in (6 mm) thick, and cutting out with a 2 in (5·1 cm) fluted cutter. Place the discs on a sheet tin previously lined with greaseproof paper and into the centre of each pipe a reasonable quantity of pineapple jam to which has been added a few jap crumbs to prevent flowing. Moisten the lids and place in position, sealing with the reverse edge of a 1¼ in (3·2 cm) cutter.

Bake at 410°F (210°C) and, on withdrawal from the oven, mask with boiled apricot purée followed immediately by brushing on warmed, softened, white fondant.

Complete by placing a half walnut on the top of each.

Coconut Honeys

15 oz (430 g) shortening	10 oz or ½-pt (280 g or 0·28 litres) water
1 lb 14 oz (850 g) Barbados sugar	3¾ lb (1700 g) weak flour
4 oz (110 g) egg	¼-oz (7 g) salt
10 oz (280 g) honey	⅛-oz (3·5 g) ginger
¼-oz (7 g) bicarbonate soda	12 oz (340 g) fine coconut

Cream the shortening quite lightly, add the sugar gradually and cream together until light. Add the eggs and honey and beat well in. Dissolve the bicarbonate of soda in the water and add to the mixing alternately with the sieved flour, salt and ginger, a small amount at a time, beating well in after each addition. Clear well after the final addition, add the coconut and again clear well.

Roll carefully to ⅛-in (3 mm) thick, cut with a fluted oblong biscuit cutter, place on lightly greased, or silicone papered sheet tins, baking at 370°F (190°C).

When cold, sandwich together in pairs with a good quality lemon cheese, dipping either end in bakers' chocolate or, alternatively, dip diagonally to give a clean, neat finish.

Peach Flans

A filling that is different for flans. Although this only mentions peaches, practically any other fruit could be employed.
Drain and lightly chop:

6¾ lb (3070 g) sliced peaches

Then bring to the boil:

1¼ lb (680 g) peach juice and water	¼-oz (7 g) salt
1 lb (450 g) castor sugar	

Dissolve:

3½ oz (100 g) cornflour	5 oz (140 g) water

Add to the mixture and cook until thickened.

Add 1 lb (450 g) granulated sugar and ½-oz (14 g) lemon paste to the above, cook until clear, remove from the heat and add peaches. Add egg colour as desired.

Divide out into sweetpaste-lined sandwich tins, decorate with pastry strips, as desired, and bake at 400–410°F (205–210°C).

When cold, decorate with whipped and sweetened cream.

These flans cut well, whilst the flavour, by virtue of the small amount of lemon paste, is really excellent.

Apple Crumble

As a change from the normal apple tart, this can be highly recommended.

Line the required number of tin or foil plates with a good sweetpaste, then add sufficient of the filling which will have been previously produced.

For the filling you need:

2½ lb (1140 g) apples (tinned or fresh)	12 oz (340 g) castor sugar
5 oz or ¼-pt (140 g or 0.14 litres) water	1½ oz (42 g) butter
pinch cinnamon	¼-oz (7 g) salt

Place the above into a suitable pan and simmer gently until the apples fall. Then add 1 oz (28 g) cornflour dissolved in 5 oz or ¼-pt (140 g or 0.14 litres) water and cook to thicken, stirring constantly. Remove from the gas and add ¾-oz (21 g) lemon paste. Allow to cool before filling the prepared plates.

Pass the crumble through a coarse crumb sieve, well cover the apples and bake at 400°F (205°C) until the crumbs are golden brown.

For the crumble you need:

1¼ lb (570 g) brown sugar	4 oz (110 g) butter
1 lb (450 g) shortening	

Cream the above lightly together.

Add and cream in 2 lb 8 oz (1140 g) weak flour and $\frac{1}{16}$-oz (1.7 g) cinnamon. Dredge lightly with icing sugar to complete.

Out of season especially, mincemeat is an extremely popular change from apple.

Strawberry Krunch Tarts

The very mention of the word 'strawberry' conjures up visions of hot summer days, but, thanks to deep freeze, use of these luscious fruits is not only confined to summer. Always popular, these tarts could also be usefully employed as a sweet by the catering confectioner. The shelf-life here must obviously be limited, so care should always be exercised in the number produced.

Sandwich tins or foils of fair depth are to be recommended, as the filling does lift during baking.

Line the required number with sweetpaste, then add sufficient of the following fruit mixture to nicely cover the bottom:

2¾ lb (1250 g) fresh or frozen strawberries	12 oz (340 g) sugar
2 oz (57 g) cornflour	

Having well mixed the ingredients together without squashing the fruit, produce a streusel topping as given on page 126: then spread over the fruit as thinly as possible. Bake at 425–430°F (215–220°C) until the streusel is quite golden brown.

Allow the tarts to go cold, remove from the tins and pipe cold, well-beaten vanilla custard, spiral fashion, on the top, finishing with a sprinkle of croquant.

For variety, blackberries could very well replace the strawberries, to which could also be added a pinch of nutmeg and cinnamon to give that 'little extra' flavour.

Chapter 6

PUFF PASTE

Possibly no other range of goods that we produce enjoys such widespread popularity as those coming under this heading, for both sweet and savoury varieties are ever-popular and for them we find a steady demand all the year round. A drawback in their production is the time required for resting, but this can be overcome by the judicious use of refrigeration and deep freeze, this equipment being ideal for the confectioner to institute long production runs, thereby ironing out production peaks. A further aid, and one used both extensively and very successfully by the larger producer, is the use of a fungal enzyme in the dough. This has the effect of mellowing and softening the gluten fairly rapidly, so that resting periods are virtually eliminated. By overcoming these resting periods, the work can be so arranged that the goods can be produced and ready for sale first thing in the morning, when time is so valuable.

First, let us consider the production of the paste. Pre-war, it was common for confectioners to produce three lots, half, three-quarter, and full puff, each required for different tasks and each name indicative of the total amount of fats used in proportion to flour. Whether this resulted in any actual saving, taking time into consideration and the fact that a much thicker piece of half or three-quarter puff had to be used to produce a particular article of comparable lift, is a very moot point. It is much wiser, to my mind, to produce a full puff, rolling the varieties rather more thinly for those jobs which previously employed the puff containing less fats.

Now a word regarding the ingredients. Flour should be of fair strength. Some recipes call for the addition of cream of tartar or cream powder to strengthen the gluten, but I find that as the optimum is so fine and as it is so simple for an operative to add 'about' the right amount rather than weigh it, a more regular puff is produced without its addition, for too much will toughen the paste, making it 'wild' during baking, even after giving the necessary resting periods. A small amount of salt is added to give the necessary flavour.

The butter must be of a good, tough character and the choice of pastry margarines and fats, now very wide, can produce a very good article. However, for superior eating quality a proportion of the fat should be butter.

For producing the paste, it is very convenient to make up the total required for a week in units of 3 lb (1360 g) flour, which, after turning, is placed in large slab tins lined with greaseproof paper. Two such pieces of paste separated and covered by greaseproof paper or polythene fit comfortably in one tin, and, if kept in a refrigerator, will not skin and are always on hand. Made regularly on the slack day each week, it is a simple matter, when required, to take out the amount required and work off, rather than produce daily.

Unit Recipe

The unit recipe, then, is:

3 lb (1360 g) flour	5 or $\frac{1}{4}$-pt (140 g or 0·14 litres) egg yolk
6 oz (170 g) butter or cake margarine	$\frac{1}{4}$-oz (21 g) salt
1 lb 9 oz or $1\frac{1}{4}$ pt (710 g or 0·71 litres) water	2 lb 10 oz (1190 g) butter/pastry margarine

Place the flour, salt, and a small amount of butter in the machine bowl fitted with a dough hook and start the machine on slow speed. Add the water and egg yolks—or egg colour if replacing the yolks with water—and mix to a smooth dough. Remove from the machine and replace with the butter and pastry margarine, running the machine on slow speed until a smooth plasticity is obtained.

If more than the above unit is being produced, scale the dough at 5 lb 4 oz (2390 g) and mould round. Scale off the butter/pastry margarine at 2 lb 10 oz (1190 g) and form into a cube shape, using a small amount of dusting flour as required.

Reverse the dough, and with a french knife cut a cross half-way through and open out to form a cross with a thick centre portion and thin edges. Place the cube of butter in the centre and fold over the edges, envelope fashion, to enclose totally. Roll to a rectangle of approximately 18 × 12 in (46 × 30 cm), cover with a piece of polythene and allow a short period—$\frac{1}{2}$-h is ideal—to rest.

After this period has elapsed, roll out the dough to a large rectangle and fold each end to meet in the centre, making certain that the corners in all cases are square, otherwise uneven lift in the various articles to be produced will result. Now fold the right-hand half over to cover the left-hand half. Roll out the pastry again to a large rectangle and fold as already indicated, afterwards leaving in a cool position, covered with the cloths or polythene, for a period of at least 1 h. The pastry will now have had what we may call one full book turn, each individual roll and fold being known as one half-turn. Dusting flour will, of course, be necessary during rolling, but this should be well brushed off before folding.

Storing the paste

After the period of rest, the pastry should be given one more full turn, and, if the idea mentioned of producing sufficient to last the week is adopted, then the paste should be placed in the large, lined, slab tins, separated and covered by polythene until required.

When this time comes during the busy part of the week, it is a simple matter to take as many pieces as required, give one further half-turn, a rest of 1 h if fungal enzymes are *not* used, and the paste is then ready for working off.

The method just described is merely one way of making puff paste, and is the one I prefer simply because it does save a little time in that it needs only five half-turns to the six half-turns required by the methods now to be described. Whilst the time saved may appear to be infinitesimal, all these odd minutes throughout the day do count, and where the results are exactly similar, then I feel that preference must be given to the quicker method, even if the saving of time is quite small.

English method

Using the recipe already given, produce the dough as detailed, afterwards scaling at the unit weight, moulding round and allowing a period to recover: meanwhile working down the butter/margarine to a smooth plasticity.

Roll out the dough to an oblong, ensuring that the corners are square, and place the butter over two-thirds of the surface in 'dabs'. Fold the untreated third over half the treated two-thirds and fold over again so that now there are three layers of dough enclosing two layers of butter. Pin out to a large rectangle, brush away surplus dusting flour and fold into three in the manner previously described, repeating the procedure so that one full turn has now been given.

Allow a resting period of at least 1 h in a cool position, covering to prevent skinning. Give one further full turn, followed by the resting period, again give a further full turn, and allow at least another hour's rest before working off.

French or continental method

Proceed as already detailed to mix, scale and mould the dough, and work the butter to a smooth plasticity, afterwards moulding to a cube as for the first method. Now, take the dough and pin out to a cross, once again with a thick centre and thin edges, placing the cube in the centre and totally enclosing, envelope fashion.

Proceed as detailed for the English method, to give three full turns, together with the necessary resting periods.

Scotch method

Place flour, salt and total fats (previously cubed) in the machine bowl fitted with the hook, and allow the cubes of fat to become coated with flour. Add the liquid and produce a rough dough, afterwards stopping the machine. Mould to a ball, allow a short rest, and then pin out as detailed for the English method until three full turns have been given. Allow the usual period of rest before working off.

Further points

Any of the methods which is adopted will produce consistently good results but, apart from the correct choice of ingredients, attention to the small details such as brushing away surplus dusting flour, ensuring that at all times the corners are correctly squared, are necessary. Again, with the rolling, the pastry must be rolled quite thinly, otherwise some of the butter will remain in too thick a layer, thus causing uneven rising.

Finally, strict attention must be paid to the resting periods, unless a fungal enzyme product is being used.

It will be, perhaps, most convenient to deal first with puff-paste varieties suitable for use to accompany savouries.

Small Vol-au-vent or Patty Cases

Correctly made and served warm with a tasty savoury filling, these are always acceptable, although, perhaps, the production of really good patty cases with even lift is the greatest test of any puff paste variety. For use as a cocktail savoury the cases must be small and in keeping with the size of the remainder of the savouries, but if intended as a course in a meal then they will have to be correspondingly larger.

Take a piece of virgin puff and, to assist even lift, trim off the edges and pin out to slightly less than $\frac{1}{8}$-in (3 mm) ensuring even thickness of the paste, and afterwards cutting with the appropriately sized cutter, which, for these lines, should be fluted. Pick up the discs carefully so as not to disturb the shape, reverse, and set out on a clean sheet tin previously covered with a sheet of greaseproof or silicone paper.

Vol-au-vent cases, the size to be produced depending upon the use

For the tops, roll out another piece of paste to the same thickness and cut with the same sized, fluted cutter, afterwards removing the centre with a smaller sized, plain cutter. The sizes recommended are $1\frac{3}{4}$ in (4·4 cm) for the outer and 1 in (2·6 cm) for removing the centre.

Here, and as an aid to speedy production, I would recommend that two cutters of the appropriate size be soldered together so that the cutting of the tops can be accomplished in one operation. The price of cutters is very cheap, and it is a simple matter to solder across the two a strip of metal, so that the time taken is reduced by half. It is possible now to purchase a tool to do this job.

Egg-wash the discs which are to form the bottoms, and carefully place the tops in position, the fluted edges on the former corresponding with those on the latter. The practice of using egg-wash to join the two halves together may seem unusual, and indeed wrong, for the line of egg-wash may be visible in the finished case. However, the reason for the use of this will be apparent later.

As stated previously, it is possible to produce goods to be ready for sale first thing in the morning, hence the reason for setting out the patty cases on greaseproof paper, for, if cut out in the afternoon, they can be left overnight in a retarder and thus have a sufficient period of rest before baking in the morning. The paper is necessary to prevent any discoloration of the bottoms, which often occurs through the contact with the metal of the sheet tin.

When required for baking off, egg-wash the tops very carefully, ensuring that no egg-wash runs down either inside or outside, for if this occurs it will hold down that part of the puff and thus cause uneven lift.

Bake off carefully at 400–420°F (205–215°C), depending on size, until thoroughly baked, but do not allow the cases to take on too much colour, for the goods generally have to be warmed again.

It is sometimes necessary to hurry along the production of patty cases, and bake off before sufficient rest has been given. In these cases it will be found a help if, after the final egg-wash, three or four holes are made by inserting the blunt end of a cocktail stick through the two pieces comprising the patty case. These form what we may term a 'lock', and thus assist even rise of the puff. The small holes thus made reseal during baking, and become visible.

Finishing off

The typically English method of finishing is to produce a lid from puff paste, using a cutter somewhere between the inner and outer sizes, and then decorating with a small puff paste leaf, but I must express preference for the continental method, accepting that the filling is the whole point of the case, and consequently the latter should be as thin as possible.

When cold, then, the centre of the patty case should be removed with a small, sharp knife, and this portion used as a lid—the reason for egg-washing the top to the bottom now becoming apparent.

Now for the filling. If to be consumed on the premises the cases may be warmed and the filling added, afterwards setting the goods out on silver dishes and garnishing with parsley, cut tomato, etc. If purchased for use later, the filling should be made, put into a jar, and instructions given to the customer to immerse the jar in hot water for approximately half an hour or so, before filling the already warmed cases.

Producing the filling

To produce the filling, take 1 pt (0·57 litre) fresh milk, use a small amount to dissolve 2 oz (57 g) cornflour, and boil the remainder with 2 oz (57 g) butter. Season with salt and pepper, add the boiling milk to the cornflour paste and return to the gas if necessary, stirring constantly to prevent burning, in order to thicken to the required consistency: finally add the meat or fish desired.

This may take the form of finely-chopped chicken, ham or other cooked meats, salmon, lobster, crab or shrimps, and for these latter varieties any bone or skin should be removed and a spot of pink colour added, together with a very small quantity of vinegar to bring out the flavour.

Further varieties can include mushrooms lightly fried in butter, and cheese, using one of good flavour, finely grated, preferably bakers' cheese.

Cheese Straws

Using sufficient virgin puff, roll to approximately $\frac{1}{4}$-in (6 mm) thick, wash with weak egg-wash, and liberally grate cheese of full flavour over two-thirds of the surface. Fold the untreated third half-way over the treated portion, fold over again in a manner similar to giving the paste one half-turn, and pin out to a rectangle $\frac{1}{8}$-in (3 mm) thick and approximately 6 in (15 cm) wide, afterwards cutting into $\frac{1}{4}$-in (6 mm) wide strips. Place on a clean sheet tin, allow the period of rest; bake at 400°F (205°C) after egg-washing carefully. Complete by dredging with celery salt.

Alternative method

An alternative method of production, and possibly one with rather more eye appeal, is, after proceeding to the stage of adding the cheese and giving one half-turn, pin out to rather less than $\frac{1}{8}$-in (3 mm) and egg-wash. Sprinkle the surface again with grated cheese, pin lightly to secure adhesion, and cut into $\frac{1}{2}$-in (1·3 cm) wide strips.

With a strip flat on the bench, place the flat of the hands, one on each end of the straw, drawing the left hand towards the body and at the same time pushing away the right hand, thus twisting the strips. Fix on to the cleaned sheet by pressing each end down with the thumb, rest for 1 h, apply a very light egg-wash, and bake until crisp at 400°F (205°C).

As with all savoury varieties, the seasoning is all important, so, whilst still warm, sprinkle the straws with celery salt and rub it lightly through the hands to ensure an even distribution.

Sausage Rolls

If desired for a cocktail party order, the size, of course, should be in keeping with the rest of the goods. After producing with puff paste, allow the normal resting period of at least 1 h before egg-washing and baking off at 400°F (205°C).

Large Savoury Vol-au-vent

These can be produced as already detailed for the smaller varieties, but for ease of production I think the one-piece variety far superior.

Roll out sufficient virgin puff to the required thickness, which will depend on the finished size required, but generally will be somewhere in the region of $\frac{1}{2}$ to $\frac{3}{4}$-in (1·3–1·8 cm). Cut with the desired cutter, either round or oval—usually the latter—and place the disc upon the cleaned sheet tin. Now, using a smaller cutter of the same shape, cut another disc about 1 in (2·6 cm) smaller, place carefully in position so as to leave a $\frac{1}{2}$-in (1·3 cm) width all the way round, and press carefully so as to cut half-way through the disc.

Using a good strong egg-wash, wash carefully the whole surface, ensuring that no egg-wash runs into the cut, and decorate the centre portion with thin puff paste leaves.

Allow a period of rest of at least 1 h, preferably, if convenient, overnight on a silicone papered sheet tin; egg-wash again and bake carefully at 380–400°F (195–205°C), changing to a slightly cooler oven if necessary to ensure complete drying out.

During the baking process it will be observed that the whole of the vol-au-vent rises, and just before baking is completed the cut centre portion will collapse into the case. After baking and allowing to cool thoroughly, it will be a simple matter to follow the cut carefully with a small sharp knife and to lift out the decorated centre portion, which will now serve the purpose of a lid.

Remove any surplus paste still remaining within the case and prepare the filling as already detailed for the smaller cases. A final garnish of parsley, cut tomato, beetroot, cucumber and so on may be added.

A further method of producing this line is of continental origin and illustrates full well the belief that the case must be as thin as possible to hold the maximum amount of filling. Whilst it does take rather more time to produce than the methods previously detailed, the result is quite different—and I may say unusual—to the customer more used to our British variety.

The base and domed top are produced from well-rested puff cuttings or, if none are available, virgin puff should be chopped up to approximately 1 in (2·6 cm) cubes, gathered together, allowed a short rest, and pinned out very thinly. The reason for using cuttings is to keep the amount of lift to a minimum, thus giving crispness to the case. After rolling very thinly, cut out with a cutter or, if none is available, with a sharp knife, round the outer perimeter of a tin of the required shape and size, reversing the disc and placing in position on a clean sheet tin, afterwards docking well.

To produce the shape, some method of packing must be employed to keep the upper part and base of the case separate, and this is usually done by taking a double thickness of greaseproof paper, filling with a handful of clean straw or paper shavings, screwing up the 'neck' of the 'bag', and tying securely with string.

Having made the ball of packing, pin out sufficient cuttings, again very thinly, to slightly larger than the base. Egg-wash a $\frac{1}{2}$-in (1·3 cm) circle round the outer edge of the latter, place the packing in the centre, string uppermost, and lay the top over neatly, thumbing to join with the egg-washed portion of the base.

Trim off to the correct shape and size, and complete by thumbing up the edge and notching with a knife at $\frac{1}{2}$-in (1·3 cm) intervals. Egg-wash carefully and, using a plain cutter of appropriate size, mark half-way through the puff forming the domed top.

Decorate the case with strips, circles and fancy-cut pieces of virgin puff, the idea being, of course, that the virgin puff will stand out against the case. Egg-wash again, allow a rest of 2 h; egg-wash yet again and bake at 420°F (215°C).

When baked, remove from the oven and, using a small, sharp knife, carefully remove the centre portion previously marked, and lift clear. Now cut the string, open the ball of packing and remove the straw or paper shavings a little at a time, finally removing the paper forming the 'bag'; make sure that all packing has been removed.

Now return the case, with lid removed, to a slightly cooler oven and dry out thoroughly to ensure maximum crispness.

Add the desired filling and garnish as already detailed.

Ham Crescents

Here is a further variety which is always popular as a cocktail savoury.

Pin out sufficient virgin puff to slightly less than $\frac{1}{10}$-in (2 mm) and, using the seven-wheel cutter, cut into horizontal strips $2\frac{1}{2}$ in (6·4 cm) wide. Cut the strips into triangles having a base of 3 in (7·6 cm) and in the centre of the base place a small amount of lean, cooked, chopped ham. Moisten the paste with water, roll and make into a crescent shape, place on a clean sheet tin, with the apex of the triangle now underneath.

Egg-wash, rest for a period of 1 h, egg-wash again and bake at 430°F (220°C).

SWEET VARIETIES OF PUFF PASTE

Though now rarely seen, the sweet vol-au-vent may be produced round, oval or oblong, and, with a combination of tinned fruits, can be made most attractive to assist firstly in a window display, and secondly as an after-dinner sweet, some customers preferring the base produced from puff paste rather than sweet paste.

Large Sweet Vol-au-vent

To produce the case, roll out virgin puff quite thinly for the base, dock with the roller docker, and cut with the appropriate cutter, afterwards transferring the piece carefully to a sheet tin.

Roll out further virgin puff to approximately $\frac{1}{4}$-in (6 mm) thick, cut with the same sized cutter, and remove the centre with another cutter of similar shape but approximately 1 in (2·6 cm) smaller.

Wash round the edges of the base with egg whites or water and place the cut-out carefully in position. Egg-wash the ring or, alternatively, wash with a mixture of egg whites and water, and dust with castor sugar, afterwards leaving in a cool position for a rest of 1 h. Egg-wash again, if this finish is desired, and bake at 400°F (205°C), ensuring thorough baking, afterwards leaving until cold.

To finish, pour a small amount of quick-set jelly into the case and allow to set: this takes only a very few minutes. This is necessary because, should the fruit be placed direct on to the puff, a certain sogginess will be apparent and make for poor eating.

Arrange the chosen, drained fruit neatly in position, and here a wide choice gives plenty of scope for variety—peaches, apricots, pineapple, etc. Having patterned the fruit attractively, add further jelly to cover, and complete with a few whorls of sweetened, whipped, fresh cream.

Vanilla Slices

Continental Method

Easier to produce in quantities, better to handle and travel, daintier to eat, this consists of two layers of vanilla custard enclosed in three thin, crisp layers of puff-paste.

For use with sheet tins measuring 30 × 18 in (76 × 46 cm) weigh 1½ lb (680 g) puff cuttings or, if none are available, virgin puff should be cubed before use, for in this method crispness and not lift is required.

Pin the first piece of puff out to the size of the sheet tin, which will, of course, mean that the puff is rolled out very thinly. When this state has been reached, roll the piece of puff round a long rolling-pin, place on the cleaned sheet tin and unroll, pinning again as lightly as is necessary to ensure complete flatness. Using the wheel cutter or 'jigger', trim off the edges, leaving a 1 in (2·6 cm) margin all round.

Dock well all over by using the roller docker, and continue until sufficient pieces have been rolled out, allowing three pieces of puff for each 'set' of slices. After the required period of rest, bake at 400°F (205°C) until crisp. The test here is when lifted up on end the whole piece should be rigid, for if insufficiently baked a sogginess will result.

'Better to handle, easier to produce and daintier to eat'—vanilla slices by the continental method

The vanilla custard should now be produced and when the custard has attained the required consistency, sprinkle castor sugar quite liberally over the surface, which will turn into a syrup and thus prevent the formation of a thick skin.

To finish the slices, take one of the sheets of puff, flat side down, and spread on it a layer of cold, beaten vanilla custard. On top of this place another sheet of puff, press down lightly, and spread a further layer of the custard. Take now a third piece of puff and place in position, this time with flat side uppermost.

Now place on top a clean board or tin and press lightly to secure adhesion, afterwards icing with fondant of the correct consistency or water icing.

After allowing a short period for this to set, mark with the seven-wheel cutter or stick of the correct width, and cut into slices of the required size, after neatly trimming the edges.

English Method

Again using puff cuttings, roll out sufficient to $\frac{1}{8}$-in (3 mm) thick to cover a sheet tin completely, which has, of course, been previously well cleaned with particular attention paid to the corners.

Vanilla slices, English method

Using the seven-wheel pastry cutter, or stick of correct width, cut into strips $3\frac{1}{2}$ in (8·9 cm) wide, which, if using a sheet tin 30 × 18 in (76 × 46 cm) will just give five strips. Dock well down the centre of each strip, allow the usual period of rest, and place in oven at 420°F (215°C) until thoroughly baked and, again, for this the test previously described should be carried out.

To finish the slices, reverse one strip, flat side uppermost, and ice with either fondant or water icing, afterwards placing on one side to allow to set.

Fit a $\frac{1}{2}$-in (1·3 cm) plain tube to a savoy bag, fill with cold, well-beaten vanilla custard, and pipe this along the hollow, formed by docking, of a second strip, taking care to keep the custard away from the edge, which would make the finished slice look messy.

Returning now to the strip that has been iced, cut carefully into $1\frac{1}{4}$ in (3·2 cm) widths, and it is a simple matter to mark the divisions with the seven-wheel cutter, afterwards cutting through with a sharp knife. Slide a long palette knife under the cut pieces, and transfer to the strip previously treated with vanilla. Complete by cutting through, using a cloth as necessary to wipe the knife, thus preventing any custard appearing on the iced top.

Third Method

By no stretch of imagination could this particular method be termed a slice, for each piece is made individually, but for the wholesale trade, where the goods are required to withstand a fair amount of vibration in transit, or where a large force of unskilled labour is utilised, this method can be used to ensure uniformity.

Individually produced vanillas, ensuring uniformity when using unskilled labour

The puff should be rolled out to the same thickness as for the previous method, namely $\frac{1}{8}$-in (3 mm) thick, and cut with a plain, oval cutter measuring approximately $2\frac{1}{4}$ in (5·7) long by $1\frac{1}{2}$ in (3·8 cm) wide at the widest point. In a large bakery with corresponding output, uniformity is a simple matter to achieve by passing the puff through the pastry rollers set with the dial. Allow the cut pieces, after tinning up, the normal resting period and bake off at 420°F (215°C).

After cooling, reverse, and ice the flat tops with either water icing or fondant, allow to set, then split each one through the centre, adding the required amont of vanilla.

This method was followed very successfully in a large bakery, water icing being used, and the whole process accomplished by entirely unskilled labour on the belt system, each operative being solely responsible for one job.

A complaint did arise from the van salesmen that, due to vibration, the iced tops cracked. This trouble was obviated by adding 4 oz (110 g) soft oil or melted fat to 7 lb (3150 g) water icing and mixing in well.

Cream Slices

This line can be produced by either of the first two methods given for making vanilla slices, the difference, of course, being in the finish.

If employing the continental method, the sandwiching will be three layers of puff enclosing two layers of raspberry jam and two of whipped and sweetened fresh cream. Cut into slices and dredge with icing sugar.

For the English method, produce the strips of puff as already detailed, and in place of vanilla spread a layer of raspberry jam, followed by piping along the hollow surface the whipped cream. Cut the top strip into the required slices, place in position on the creamed base and cut through, finally dredging fairly heavily with icing sugar.

Sugar Squares

Here, again, is a line which lends itself to quick production.

Using a sheet tin which has been scrupulously cleaned with special attention paid to the corners, pin out sufficient puff to slightly more than $\frac{1}{8}$-in (3 mm) thick, roll round a long rolling-pin, place in position on the sheet and unroll, using the end and edges of the tin to cut off any unwanted puff. Using a stick or seven-wheel cutter, mark in $2\frac{1}{2}$ in (6·4 cm) squares and trim off edges.

Wash over the whole of the surface with egg whites and water, or water alone, and dredge with castor sugar, afterwards cutting into squares as previously marked. Make two small holes in the centre of each square with the point of a french knife, allow the usual resting period, and bake at 420°F (215°C).

After cooling, finish by slitting open and piping in a small quantity of jam, followed by a liberal whorl of fresh whipped and sweetened cream.

Sugar squares

Puff Tarts

These are produced in a similar manner to the savoury patty cases, except that, in this case, the bases are rolled rather more thinly and docked twice with a pointed french knife.

Egg-wash the tops or wash with water and dip into castor sugar. After baking, and if egg-washed, the cases should be dusted with icing sugar and the centres filled with apricot or raspberry jam or good quality lemon cheese.

Eccles Cakes

Originally very much a local speciality, the popularity of these goods in all areas can never be open to question. It is a line which lends itself admirably to pre-packing in either fours or sixes in transparent cellulose, thus adding to sales appeal.

Again, they may be made up on the afternoon previous to the day they are required, placed on greaseproof-papered boards, each layer separated by greaseproof, and baked off the following morning, thus ensuring the perfection of absolute freshness daily.

The production of these goods, however, is not quite as simple as may first appear and, to my mind, the first snag to be overcome, especially in the larger bakery, is that of uniformity, for constant variation in the size of any article sounds the death knell so far as sales are concerned.

The ideal, then, for bakeries so equipped, is a pastry-roller incorporating a thickness indicator, the pastry always being passed through at the correct thickness as set by the dial; after cutting with a 3 in (7·6 cm) cutter this will give individual discs of pastry somewhere in the region of 1–1½ oz (28–43 g). After costing, it is then a simple matter to weigh so many pieces at intervals to ensure that the amount of paste is constant.

As an alternative, for a bakery not so equipped, the paste may be weighed and cut on the hand dough-divider, each piece then being rolled out to the correct size.

The pastry may be well-rested cuttings and a proportion of fresh virgin puff.

The filling

The filling requires a little thought, as many recipes for this are in existence, some incorporating mincemeat, cake crumbs and various spices. These, I feel, spoil the article, for the taste of an eccles cake should be the crispness of the puff, with the flavour of the fruit in the form of currants only, mellowed by the soft brown sugar and butter.

My recipe for the filling is:

2¼ lb (1140 g) currants   6 oz (170 g) butter or cake margarine
8 oz (230 g) soft brown sugar

Mix the cleaned fruit and sugar, melt the butter and pour over, afterwards rubbing well through the hands to ensure even distribution. The immensely improved flavour when using butter as compared with margarine is one that has to be tasted to be fully appreciated.

To fill, take one of the discs of puff in the left hand, add the correct quantity of filling, and commence wrapping by gathering the edges together to form a purse, completing by just pinching together. The danger here is that, if incorrectly wrapped, a large piece of paste may be forced inside the cake and remain unbaked, thus forming an indigestible core.

After all the pieces have been so treated, using a plain cutter of the correct size, somewhere in the region 2–2½ in (5–6·5 cm) place each cake in the cutter, joints uppermost. Now, using a tin or block of slightly smaller diameter than the cutter and dusting flour as necessary, press lightly until the cake reaches the size of the cutter, thus, once again, ensuring uniformity.

Allow to recover or stand overnight as previously indicated, reverse with the smooth surface uppermost, wash with a mixture of egg whites and water or just water, dip into castor sugar and place in position on a clean sheet tin.

Make a small steam escape hole with the point of a french knife and bake at 420°F (215°C).

Banbury Cakes

Closely related to the eccles cake the difference here, apart from the shape, is a slight variation in the filling, which is that as previously given, plus the addition of $\frac{1}{2}$-oz (14 g) nutmeg and the zest and juice of two lemons or 1 oz (28 g) lemon paste.

Eccles and Banbury cakes

Prepare and cut the puff as for eccles cakes, afterwards adding the required amount of filling, this time leaving the discs flat on the bench. Pinch the edges together to form the well-known oval shape, afterwards tapping lightly with the small pie-block, or rolling level with the rolling-pin.

Reverse the shapes, joints downwards, and after the requisite period of rest wash with egg whites and water, dip into castor sugar and place in position on a clean sheet tin. Make two cuts in the centre of each with scissors, and bake at 420°F (215°C).

Puff Mince Pies

Pin out well-rested puff cuttings quite thinly and cut with the appropriately sized fluted cutter, afterwards picking up and carefully reversing the pieces so as not to disturb the shape before placing them in position on a cleaned, water-splashed sheet tin.

Place a small amount of mincemeat in the centre of each disc, and roll out sufficient puff to slightly less than $\frac{1}{8}$-in (3 mm) thick, afterwards cutting with a fluted cutter slightly larger than that used for the base.

Fold a small piece of clean cloth to form a pad and place in a cottage pan, afterwards filling with water. Moisten the cut tops by contact with the pad, place in position on the bases, and press the centres down with the reverse end of a small cutter. Wash the tops with egg whites and water and dredge with castor sugar. Bake, after rest, at 420°F (215°C).

Fruit and Other Squares

Quick to produce in infinite variety, this line was dealt with in the chapter on 'Short Paste Goods' (Chapter 4). However, these are equally popular using puff paste.

Jam Puffs

Roll out virgin paste to slightly more than $\frac{1}{16}$-in (1·5 mm) thick and cut with an oval fluted cutter measuring somewhere in the region of $4\frac{1}{2}$ in (11·5 cm) long by $2\frac{1}{2}$ in (6·4 cm) at the widest part. Place the cut portions in rows on the bench and wash over half the surface with water.

Using a savoy bag fitted with plain tube, pipe in the centre of each a reasonable amount of raspberry jam, afterwards folding over, ensuring that the fluted edges of top and bottom correspond. Wash with egg whites and water, dip in castor sugar and place in position on a cleaned sheet tin. Make two cuts with a pair of scissors as for banbury cakes. Allow the usual period of rest and bake at 420°F (215°C) ensuring thorough baking.

Cream Crescents

To all intents and purposes, these are very similar to jam puffs, so proceed as already indicated, with the omission of the jam. After baking, and when cool, split the rounded edge in the centre with a sharp knife. Pipe in a small amount of raspberry jam followed by piping in sufficient whipped and sweetened fresh cream.

The ever popular jam puffs, which, with slight variation, can be cream crescents

Coventry Cakes

Well-rested puff cuttings are eminently suitable for this line. Roll the pastry to approximately $\frac{1}{8}$-in (3 mm) thick, and cut out with a 3 in (7·6 cm) cutter, afterwards rolling out each individual disc quite thinly. Pipe slightly off centre sufficient jam or lemon cheese in each, wash round the outer edges with water, and fold three times to form the familiar triangular shape.

The secret of the folding is to enclose totally the jam to ensure that it does not boil out, thus leaving an empty shell. Therefore, the first fold should be from the side nearest the jam, and taken over to enclose it completely, afterwards ensuring that the second and third folds overlap the first.

As each is folded, reverse, finally washing with egg whites and water, dipping into castor sugar and placing in position on a cleaned sheet tin. Make a small steam escape hole and, after the usual rest period, bake at 420°F (215°C).

Lemon Cream Ovals

Actually a variation of sugar squares, the combination of lemon cheese, cream and crisp puff paste is unusual and quite popular.

Roll out virgin puff to a thickness of $\frac{1}{8}$-in (3 mm) and cut with an oval cutter of approximate size, 3 × 2 in (7·6 × 5·1 cm). Wash each disc with egg whites and water, dip into castor sugar, and bake at 420°F (215°C).

After baking and when cold, split, pipe in a liberal amount of good quality lemon cheese, followed by a whorl of whipped and sweetened fresh cream, afterwards replacing the top.

Coconut Cream Batons

Roll out a rectangle of virgin puff to $\frac{1}{8}$-in (3 mm) thick, then, using the seven-wheel pastry cutter or measuring stick of the correct width, cut into strips $3\frac{1}{2}$ in (8·9 cm) long × $1\frac{1}{4}$ in (3·2 cm) wide. Wash with egg whites and water, dip into medium or fine desiccated coconut, afterwards placing in position on a clean sheet tin. After the usual resting period, bake at 420°F (215°C).

When cold, finish by splitting and piping in a line of raspberry jam, followed by whipped and sweetened fresh or synthetic cream.

Cream Horns

Using well-rested puff cuttings, pin out very thinly in the form of a rectangle, afterwards cutting into strips of approximately 18 × 1 in (46 × 2·6 cm).

Taking a cream horn tin, place the tip on to the end nearest to you and rotate away, ensuring all the time that each turn neatly overlaps the previous one, until the wide end of the tin is reached. Here, two turns should overlap, with the joint of the puff on the underside of the tin, with the puff moistened with water to secure adhesion.

A word of warning

A word of warning here—ensure that the last turn of the paste is approximately $\frac{1}{4}$-in (6 mm) away from the open end of the tin, otherwise, during baking, it is possible that the puff will expand over and into the tin, thus causing breakage.

When all have been completed, wash the tops with egg whites and water, dip into castor sugar and place on to a clean sheet tin, pressing slightly on the inside of the tin to prevent rolling. After the usual resting period, bake at 420°F (215°C) and then, when the first heat has left the goods, remove the tins.

When cold, complete by piping inside a line of raspberry jam, followed by a whorl of fresh cream.

Cream horns

Baton Glacé

Roll out sufficient virgin puff to ¼-in (6 mm) and cut into strips 4 in (10·2 cm) wide. Place on the bench with the strip running parallel to the edge and spread quite thinly with royal icing, to which a few spots of cold water have been added, together with a small amount of cornflour, to act as a binding agent. A dry palette knife should be used for this operation, for any water applied will, of course, reduce the consistency of the royal icing, and an excess will give the appearance of a sugar-dipped finish.

Using a good cutting knife dipped constantly into flour to prevent sticking, cut into slices 1¼ in (3·2 cm) wide, afterwards using a broad-bladed palette knife to transfer the pieces carefully to a clean sheet tin.

Give the usual resting period of 1 h longer if possible, and bake at 380–400°F (195–205°C), the latter temperature being the maximum, otherwise caramelisation will occur, thus detracting from the finished appearance. After baking and when cold, split through the centre with a sharp knife and pipe in a line of raspberry jam, followed by a line of whipped and sweetened synthetic cream, or, if costs will allow, fresh cream.

These goods must be handled with very great care for the tops are extremely brittle and, unlike the puff, do not shrink during baking, therefore protruding over the edge. Rough handling will, in consequence, break these tops and give them an untidy appearance.

Cream Coronets

These goods are very similar to baton glacé, the puff here being cut into 3 in (7·6 cm) squares and spread with royal icing as already detailed. After placing in position on the sheet tin, two thin strips of puff are placed across from corner to corner. After baking at 380–400°F (195–205°C) finish as for baton glacé.

Cream Crisps

This is a line that has suffered very badly from the craftsmanship point of view, for far too often are the 'crisps' anything but, the paste being cut far too thickly, with the result that the article eats rather like stale bread.

Our continental friends often use these to form a variety of biscuit, the finished crisp being thin and very delightful to eat.

Roll out virgin puff in the form of a rectangle of 16 in (42 cm) wide, the length being immaterial, using castor sugar for dusting in place of flour. Wash over the surface with a mixture of egg whites and water, dust very lightly with castor sugar, and starting at the top, make a fold of $2\frac{1}{2}$ in (6·4 cm), repeating the procedure at the bottom. Now make a further fold of $2\frac{1}{2}$ in (6·4 cm) top and bottom, which will cause both folds to meet in the centre. Now fold the top half on to the bottom, taking care to ensure that the top fold lies evenly and neatly over the bottom.

Trim the edge and cut into strips of something less than $\frac{1}{4}$-in (6 mm) afterwards spacing at least 2 in (5·1 cm) apart on heavily greased sheet tins, turning whilst in the hands through 90° to expose the cut surface, for these goods are to expand outwards, not upwards.

Cream crisps, finished ready for display and sale. Single crisps may be used in a variety of dessert biscuits

Allow the usual resting period before baking at 380–400°F (195–205°C), reversing with a palette knife when set, afterwards returning to the oven to complete baking and caramelise the sugar.

When cold, the crisps may be sold singly, or can be finished off by joining together with raspberry jam and a whorl of fresh cream, afterwards lightly dredging with icing sugar, or, alternatively, icing the tops with fondant or water icing.

Another method of finishing—continental in origin—is to join the two pieces together with a small amount of buttercream, afterwards just dipping the closed end of the crisps into bakers' chocolate or couverture. This method has much to commend it if the goods have to be transported, for it does hold the top firmly to the bottom.

Orange Crunch Squares

From puff-paste produced in the normal manner, pin out a piece of virgin puff to $\frac{1}{8}$-in (3 mm) thick and cut with a $2\frac{1}{2}$–$3\frac{1}{2}$ in (6·4–8·9 cm) square fluted cutter.

Place the pieces side by side on the bench, wash with a mixture of egg whites and water, and sprinkle heavily with crunch topping. Then place on to

A delightful combination to eat—orange crunch squares

cleaned sheet tins, allow the usual resting period and bake thoroughly at 400–410°F (205–210°C). Allow to go quite cold, split, pipe in a reasonable quantity of orange curd and follow with a whirl of whipped and sweetened fresh whipping cream. Afterwards replace the top.

Orange crunch topping
For this you require:

1 lb (450 g) fine dessicated coconut	8 oz (230 g) castor sugar
9 oz (260 g) nib almonds	5 oz or ¼-pt (140 g or 0·14 litres) egg
¼-oz (7 g) salt	

Mix these thoroughly together, place on to a cleaned sheet tin and dry thoroughly in an oven at approximately 300°F (150°C). The ingredients should be occasionally turned to prevent over-colouring. Finally, add and rub well through 2 oz (57 g) orange paste. This can, of course, be stored over reasonable periods and used as desired.

Marianas

All lines of puff-paste seem to enjoy steady popularity and this one is no exception, using a filling with a difference.

Marianas—a puff paste filling with a difference

Using full virgin puff-paste, pin out to ⅛-in (3 mm) thick and cut with a 2½–3 in (6·4–7·6 cm) square cutter. Transfer half the shapes to a clean sheet tin, wash round the edges with water and pipe a reasonably-sized portion of the following filling in the centre of each square:

10 oz (280 g) macaroon paste	1 lb 14 oz or $1\frac{1}{2}$ pt (850 g or 0·85 litres) egg
1 lb (450 g) butter	12 oz (340 g) flour
1 lb (450 g) castor sugar	12 oz (340 g) cornflour
2 oz (57 g) lemon paste	

Produce by the sugar–batter method, including the macaroon paste along with the butter and sugar.

Place the top in position, coinciding the flutes and pressing to adhere. Decorate the top with a cross of puff-paste, eggwash and allow to stand for approximately 1 h to recover. Re-eggwash, bake at 390°F (200°C) and, immediately on withdrawal, glaze with boiling apricot purée, following immediately with either thin water-icing or warm, thin white fondant and a sprinkle of roasted, flaked almonds.

Apple Frangipane

This line can be produced either as a slice, or it can be made individually in small fluted frangipane tins, but from the point of view of time taken, the former idea is the most practicable. If trough-shaped tins are available they will be found ideal, otherwise the slices can be made on ordinary sheet tins.

Pin out well-rested puff cuttings to $\frac{1}{8}$-in (3 mm) and lay out on the sheet tins in 3 in (7·6 cm) wide strips. Finely chop and sweeten sufficient apple to set along the centre of each strip.

Prepare the frangipane required, mixing by the sugar-batter method and using 1 lb (450 g) each of castor sugar, butter or margarine, egg and ground almonds and 1 oz (28 g) flour. Should this prove uneconomic, cake crumbs for part or all of the ground almonds may be substituted, but only white crumbs should be used, and in this case a spot of lemon and almond flavour will be necessary.

Using a savoy bag and $\frac{1}{2}$-in (1·3 cm) plain tube, pipe on top of the apple two parallel lines of frangipane, afterwards pinning out sufficient virgin puff to a thickness of $\frac{1}{8}$-in (3 mm) and cutting into strips $3\frac{1}{2}$ in (8·9 cm) wide.

Now egg-wash the edges of the first strip, and roll the top carefully round a rolling-pin, placing one end in position and unrolling over the strip. Trim the edges neatly, afterwards notching with knife or thumb to seal firmly. Dock lightly along the centre, egg-wash, allow the usual resting period and bake at 380–400°F (195–205°C), ensuring thorough baking.

On withdrawal from the oven, brush with hot apricot, followed by water icing or thin fondant heated to the correct temperature. When cold, cut into $1\frac{1}{4}$ in (3·2 cm) slices and the goods are ready for sale.

Stars

Pin out virgin puff to $\frac{1}{8}$-in (3 mm) thick and cut out with one of the special cutters made for the purpose. Alternatively, using a sharp knife, cut into $2\frac{1}{2}$ in (6·4 cm) squares, then cut each corner at an angle of 45° to a depth of approximately $\frac{3}{4}$-in (1·9 cm) to form a maltese cross, afterwards moistening the centre with egg. Taking each alternate corner, fold over to the centre and press lightly to secure adhesion, and, when each is completed, place in position on a clean sheet tin. Now roll out further virgin puff quite thinly, and cut out 1 in (2·6 cm) discs. Moisten the centre piece and place the discs in position to cover the joints. Egg-wash the completed pastries and bake at 420°F (215°C).

When cold, dredge lightly with icing sugar and complete by piping on alternate corners a star of whipped and sweetened cream, and on the other two corners a spot of raspberry jam.

CONTINENTAL VARIETIES

Many and varied are the continental lines using puff paste, and I propose to conclude the puff paste section with just three typical varieties. Each is capable of great variation in the type of filling used, thus adding even more variety and, possibly most important today, each has proved a good saleable line, the continental flavour not being too pronounced for the British palate.

Last, but by no means least, these three lines are, unlike many continental lines, very quickly produced and are, therefore, a commercial proposition for the British confectioner.

Mandel Gipfel

Essentially an almond crescent, this is quite easy to produce and, if eaten fresh, enjoyed immensely.

Roll out virgin puff to approximately $\frac{1}{16}$-in (1·5 mm) thick in the form of a large rectangle and then, using the seven-wheel pastry cutter, or stick of the correct width, cut into horizontal strips approximately $4\frac{1}{2}$ in (11·5 cm) wide, although this will, of course, depend on costings.

Now cut the strips into triangular shapes, and place on the base of each triangle a small portion of the filling, comprising 1 lb (450 g) ground almonds, 1 lb (450 g) fine castor sugar and sufficient cold water to produce a stiff paste. It should be stressed that the paste, when produced, should be quite firm, otherwise, during baking, the filling will leave the crescent.

Dab the apex of the triangle with egg-wash and start to roll from the base, thereby totally enclosing the filling. After rolling, place the pastry in a slightly crescent shape, apex underneath, on to a clean, water-splashed tray, and flatten slightly with the heel of the hand. Egg-wash, allow the usual period of rest, egg-wash again, and bake at 400–410°F (205–210°C).

Apfel Strudel

That our industry has few facets upon which one may be dogmatic is indisputable, and an illustration of this occurred some years ago.

In answer to a readers query in the 'Answers to Correspondence' column of *'The British Baker,'* this recipe and method were given. Very soon, a lively correspondence was started, with several disagreeing that this was an 'Apfel Strudel'. Recipes and methods were produced to support the theory that it should be produced from a thin strudel paste, which enclosed a large quantity of apples and other fruits, the whole being rolled up, swiss roll fashion, and baked. True, this is the type produced in Austria, and possibly the one that our catering contemporaries would produce.

As always, the customer had the last word. The original inquirer finally wrote to say that he had produced them all, and both he, and his customers, preferred the one given below, which is of Swiss origin.

This line is basically an apple tart, but as will be seen, the number of possible varieties are again large.

Roll out to $\frac{1}{8}$-in (3 mm) thick either virgin puff, or well-rested cuttings, to a large rectangle, afterwards cutting into smaller rectangles, the size depending on costings.

In the centre of each place sufficient finely-chopped apple, to which the necessary amount of sugar has been added, and to this mixture may be added any of the following, keeping a careful eye on costings and local tastes: Juice and zest of lemon, cinnamon or nutmeg, rough cut hazelnuts or almonds, cleaned currants or sultanas.

Wash the perimeter with egg, fold to rectangular shape, totally enclosing the filling, reverse, and place in position on to a clean sheet tin. Egg-wash carefully, and decorate with strips or other shapes of virgin puff. Allow the usual resting period, egg-wash again, bake at 380–410°F (195–210°C) depending upon the size.

Lemon Gateau

This is a line which, I venture to suggest, would make a change for a 'Saturday Special'.

Roll out well-rested puff cuttings very thinly and, using a hoop or tin of the required size, cut out two discs for each gateau required with a sharp knife held vertically to cut round the edge of the hoop or tin. Transfer the disc very carefully so as not to disturb the shape, to a clean, water-splashed sheet tin. Dock quite heavily, and give the maximum resting period before baking at 410°F (210°C).

To make up the gateau, take one of the baked, cold discs and spread with lemon-coloured buttercream flavoured by the addition of the juice and zest of fresh lemons. Now place on top of the buttercream a disc of either sheet sponge or thin genoese, cut to exact size, or, to prevent wastage in cutting, a half-sandwich previously baked in tins of the size used for cutting out the puff.

Using a simple syrup made from boiling together 1½ lb (680 g) sugar and 1 pt (0·57 litres) water flavoured with fresh lemon juice, soak the cake by ladling or spraying over. Follow this with another layer of buttercream, and complete the build-up with the second disc of puff, reversed this time to give a flat top, which is then brushed with boiled apricot purée. Mask the sides of the gateau with buttercream, followed by fine, roasted flake almonds.

To complete, warm sufficient lemon-coloured and flavoured fondant, and have ready a small bag of chocolate fondant. Mask with the lemon fondant, and complete by piping on lines or rings of chocolate, afterwards marbling to give the desired effect.

If any number are being produced it will, of course, be an advantage to have two or three operatives to assist in the marbling.

Fruit Slices

Roll out puff-paste cuttings to about ⅛-in (3 mm) thick, cut into strips 3 in (7·6 cm) wide and place across the cleaned sheet tin. Moisten the edges with water and along these place further strips of paste about ½-in (1·3 cm) wide. Place a stick alongside to prevent flowing and repeat until the required number have been produced.

Dock the centres well, allow the usual resting period, then bake crisply at 400–410°F (205–210°C). To finish, mask the strip with quick-set jelly, arrange fresh or tinned fruit to choice and cover well with quick-set jelly. Decorate the sides with whipped and sweetened fresh cream and cut into 1½ in (3·8 cm) slices.

Strawberries? Of course!

Chapter 7

CHOU PASTE

Where goods produced from this medium are displayed for sale, the great majority take the form of chocolate eclairs and cream buns, which admittedly are ever popular, but more variety is possible with very little more time and trouble, as I hope to show.

Many recipes exist for producing the basic paste and the majority of them, in capable hands, produce excellent articles, but whatever recipe is used some degree of craftsmanship is necessary, for the stumbling blocks causing the most trouble are obtaining the correct consistency of the paste and correct baking.

With regard to the former, the amount of egg required will depend on the strength of the flour and degree of cooking, but, generally speaking, the more eggs absorbed the lighter and more acceptable will be the finished product. The paste, when mixed, should be just stiff enough to retain its shape when piped out, but, in the case of cream buns, should be slightly softer yet still just retain the shape of the star tube used.

Baking should be carried out at the temperatures stated, preferably with a little steam introduced in the early stages, but all varieties should be quite crisp and thoroughly baked before being removed from the oven, when they are immediately slid on to a wire to cool.

The recommended recipe is:

1 lb 9 oz or $1\frac{1}{4}$ pt (710 g or 0·71 litres) water	$1\frac{1}{4}$ lb (570 g) flour
8 oz (230 g) butter or margarine	$2\frac{1}{4}$ lb (1020 g) egg

Place the water and butter or margarine in a suitable bowl or pan on to the gas and bring to the boil, meanwhile sieving the flour on to a sheet of paper. When the water and butter are boiling vigorously, add the flour and stir well with a wooden spatula, while still subjecting to heat, for approximately $1\frac{1}{2}$ min, when the mixture will be thoroughly cooked and leave the sides of the bowl or pan cleanly.

Remove from the gas, and transfer the paste to a suitably sized machine bowl fitted with the cake beater. Start the machine on second speed and commence adding the egg in small portions until the correct consistency has been obtained, scraping down bowl and beater at intervals to ensure thorough amalgamation of the eggs.

Paste for cream buns

It was the practice in former years to make up a separate paste for cream buns, but this, with increased labour costs and the fact that a good article can be produced from the foregoing recipe with the addition of a small quantity of egg and carbonate of ammonia (vol), makes the production of a separate paste unnecessary. To the recipe given, if required for cream buns, add sufficient egg—probably in the region of 4–6 oz (110–170 g)—and a quarter teaspoonful of vol, dissolved in the last of the egg and beaten well in, care being taken to ensure thorough amalgamation. In normal production, the paste required for eclairs and other varieties would first be removed, then the extra egg and vol in proportion to weight of remaining paste added.

Cream Buns

Prepare the chou paste as detailed, adding the extra egg and moistened vol until the required piping consistency is obtained.

If the special deep-lidded cream bun tins are available, pipe out the paste, using a large star tube, in bulbs of approximately $1\frac{1}{4}$ in (3·2 cm) diameter, ensuring that all are of the same size and that sufficient space is allowed for the great expansion that will take place. Should these tins not be available, pipe bulbs out on to a lightly greased sheet tin, covering each as piped with a 1 lb (450 g) bread tin to ensure correct spacing.

As stated previously, one of the greatest difficulties in producing these goods is in the baking, for if the lids covering the buns are lifted and steam allowed to escape before the goods are properly baked, the buns will collapse, and thus prove useless. How, then, can this be surmounted?

When all the buns are piped out and covered with either the deep lid or 1 lb (450 g) bread tins, pipe a $\frac{1}{2}$-in (1·3 cm) bulb in the centre of the lid, or on top of one of the bread tins in the centre of the sheet. This bulb then gives an indication of what stage the baking of the bulbs has reached, and when this 'pilot' bulb has taken on a dark brown, almost burnt appearance, then the goods can be safely removed from the oven, the lids removed, and the buns placed on a wire to cool. The baking temperature should be 430°F (220°C) and the buns will take approximately 30 min to bake.

Cream buns from chou paste of the correct consistency—icing sugar having been purposely omitted from the front two, in order that the indentations may be more clearly seen.

Completion takes the form of piping into each bun a liberal amount of fresh whipped and sweetened cream, and either of two methods may be adopted.

The first consists of splitting with a sharp knife, afterwards piping in the necessary amount of cream. This method has the advantage of being able to see that the correct quantity has been piped in, but the disadvantage of the cut showing.

The second method is accomplished by inserting a finger into the side of the bun and piping in the cream through the hole thus formed, the advantage and disadvantage being exactly the reverse of the previous method.

When all the buns are so treated, complete by dredging lightly with icing sugar.

Cheese Eclairs

Using a $\frac{1}{4}$-in (6 mm) plain savoy tube, pipe out on a lightly greased sheet tin small eclairs approximately $1\frac{1}{2}$–2 in (3·8–5·1 cm) long, but certainly of a size in keeping with the remainder of the savouries. To prevent the eclair having a tail, after piping the correct length stop pressure, lift the tube slightly upwards and, in the same motion, take the tube forwards and off, thus leaving a clean finish. Only a small point, but one that counts in neatness of the finished article.

Having piped out a sufficient number in neat rows, scatter liberally with slightly-chopped flake almonds. Any falling between the rows can be collected after baking and used for finishing various other articles. Bake at 430°F (220°C), ensuring thorough baking, otherwise the cases will soften and tend to eat tough and leathery.

When thoroughly cold, slit carefully and fill with a white sauce/cheese filling, the recipe for which is on page 168.

Chocolate Eclairs

Using a ½-in (1·3 cm) plain savoy tube, pipe out the paste in pieces approximately 3 in (7·6 cm) long on to lightly greased sheet tins, using the method previously described to preserve a neat finish. Bake at 420°F (215°C).

After thorough baking and allowing sufficient time to cool, split the cases open by using a sharp knife, making the cut rather higher than half-way up the

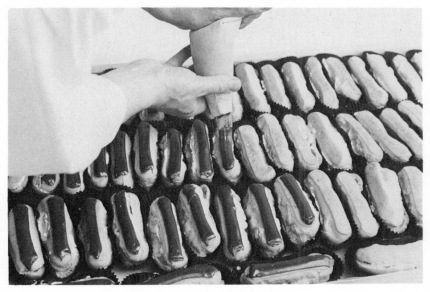

A flattened ⅝-in (16 mm) savoy tube, chocolate fondant in a savoy bag, combine to give . . .

. . . a quick, neat finish to chocolate eclairs, with the minimum of handling

side of the case, afterwards piping in a liberal amount of whipped and sweetened vanilla-flavoured fresh or synthetic cream.

Now prepare sufficient chocolate fondant by warming white fondant to 100°F (38°C), reducing with stock syrup or water to normal dipping consistency, afterwards adding approximately 25% melted, unsweetened block cocoa or bakers' chocolate, stirring well in and reheating slightly or adding further stock syrup or water as required to restore to normal dipping consistency and temperature.

Finish the eclairs neatly by icing the flat side, i.e. the part previously in contact with the sheet tin, using a small palette knife or the finger to remove any surplus. This latter is a job that calls for considerable care, for, neatly done, the finished article has a greatly enhanced appearance: we have all seen displayed for sale really messy-looking eclairs that must have repercussions on sales.

After a short time to allow the fondant to dry, place in the long paper cases, when they are ready for display and sale.

Further Varieties of Eclair

In my experience, the public remain true to the chocolate eclair, but I have no doubt that in some districts—and especially when catering for parties and dances, etc.—further varieties would be quite popular.

These consist of filling the baked case with a differently coloured and flavoured whipped and sweetened cream, e.g. coffee, raspberry, strawberry, etc., and finishing by icing with appropriately coloured and flavoured fondant.

Rognons

Using the same paste as for eclairs, pipe out in kidney shape, keeping the size fairly small, whilst using a ½-in (1·3 cm) plain tube, otherwise the finished article will be apt to look clumsy.

Rognons, with the usual finish of coffee fondant/roasted flaked almonds

Bake thoroughly at 420°F (215°C) and, when cold, slit open the cases, piping round the shape whipped, sweetened and vanilla-flavoured cream with a savoy bag and star tube.

When all the cases have been so prepared reduce coffee-coloured and flavoured fondant to the usual consistency and temperature and, holding the case in the left hand, immerse the top, removing the surplus with a small palette knife. Dip immediately into finely roasted flake almonds, and the rognons are complete.

Petits Choux

Using a very slightly softer paste than for eclairs, yet without using vol, pipe out small bulbs on to a lightly greased sheet tin, afterwards baking at 420°F (215°C) without covers.

Petits choux

After baking and thoroughly cooling, slit carefully and fill with a variety of whipped, sweetened, coloured and flavoured fresh cream, e.g. vanilla, raspberry, strawberry, coffee, etc. Afterwards complete by dipping the tops of the petits choux in appropriately coloured and flavoured fondant—chocolate for vanilla cream, pale pink for raspberry, and so on.

Swans

Not by any means a new line, this is, nevertheless, very attractive and commands attention if properly made.

Prepare sufficient bases for the number required by piping small bulbs of chou paste on to a lightly greased sheet tin, using a $\frac{1}{2}$-in (1·3 cm) plain tube, in a similar manner to petits choux, but in this case the bulbs will be very slightly smaller and oval shaped.

The heads and necks are prepared by using a $\frac{1}{8}$-in (3 mm) plain savoy tube and piping out the required number in the form of a figure '2', piping carefully to get as near as possible to the graceful arch of the swan's neck. A small flaked almond is inserted to represent the beak. These will, owing to the difference in baking time, be piped separately on a greased sheet tin, afterwards being baked at 420°F (215°C). The 'bodies' of the swans may be baked at the same temperature.

Chou paste swans

To finish, split the bases crosswise slightly above the half-way mark, remove the top portion and cut into two. Now pipe in the base sufficient fresh cream, spiral fashion, and insert the head and neck portion by putting the 'foot' of the figure '2' well into the piped cream.

Complete by turning the cut portions of the top to an angle of 45° and placing in position to represent the wings. Lightly dredge with icing sugar.

Coffee Creams

All the lines described so far consist solely of chou paste, but used in conjunction with puff or sweet pastry, the range can be further extended.

For this particular line, roll out virgin puff pastry quite thinly or, alternatively, sweet or german paste to $\frac{1}{8}$-in (3 mm) thick. Cut with a 2 in (5·1 cm) plain cutter and place the discs on a clean sheet tin, allowing a resting period of 1 h. Using a $\frac{1}{4}$-in (6 mm) plain tube, pipe rings of eclair paste round the edge of each disc, ensuring that each joint is neatly made. Bake at 410°F (210°C).

When cold, complete by dipping each chou ring in coffee coloured and flavoured fondant, and piping in the hollow a whorl of fresh or synthetic cream, surmounted with a small piece of cherry and pinch of green almond nibs.

Gateau St. Honoré

This may, of course, be made to a size to suit the customer and occasion but, generally, a size of 7 or 8 in (17·8 or 20·3 cm) diameter is acceptable.

Roll out sufficient virgin puff very thinly or sweet paste to $\frac{1}{8}$-in (3 mm) thick, and transfer the disc carefully to a clean sheet tin, care being taken to ensure that the shape is not disturbed. Dock heavily and allow a rest of at least 1 h.

Moisten the edges of the paste with egg, and pipe in a ring of chou paste just inside the edge, using a $\frac{1}{2}$-in (1·3 cm) plain tube. Using the same paste and tube, pipe on to a separate sheet tin sufficient small bulbs to cover the ring of chou paste when baked, together with one extra, which will go in the centre of the finished gateau. Egg-wash the ring carefully and bake all at 410°F (210°C) until thoroughly dry.

When baked and cool, mask the base and outer ring edges with boiled apricot purée and cover with roasted flake almonds. The centre of the ring may now be partially filled with cubes of sponge, genoese, or swiss roll, afterwards soaking carefully with a little stock syrup well flavoured with sherry or a liqueur. Follow this by a layer of cold, beaten vanilla custard.

Make an aperture in the side of each cream bun and fill with whipped cream. Have ready a small pile each of washed and chopped cherries, roasted flake almonds, green almond nibs and silver dragées.

Dipping in sugar

Now, observing the normal sugar boiling rules, boil a small quantity of sugar and water to 285°F (140°C). On attaining that temperature immerse the base of the pan in cold water for a few seconds to prevent a further rise in temperature. Dip the tops of the buns first in the prepared sugar and then into the decorative materials prepared, ensuring that sufficient of each are produced to go alternatively round the side of the gateau. When all are completed, attach the buns to the ring of chou by first dipping the base into the sugar, and then placing in position, following in sequence until this part of the decoration is completed. Just one bun—the one dipped into silver dragées, should be left, and will be placed in the centre after fresh cream has been piped over the vanilla, when the gateau is completed.

Further adornment may be added in the form of spun sugar, which certainly greatly enhances the appearance of the gateau, but such is our atmosphere that it is very questionable if this added touch is worth the time spent on it, for all too soon does it disappear.

Chapter 8

GINGER GOODS

It is often said that the ways of the general public are strange, and nowhere do we find this more true than in the sale of goods under this heading. Some shops find a steady demand for ginger goods of all sorts and varieties, whilst others find just the reverse to be the case. Indeed, I can quote several instances of confectioners having branch shops in town centres within several hundred yards of one another where a ready sale in one shop is just the reverse in another. Why this should be so I just do not know.

However, goods under this classification are worth the effort, both in production and salesmanship, for all are relatively easy and quick to produce, finishing time is non-existent in most cases and, therefore, they are low in production costs. Raw material costs are also relatively low and, in some instances, cake crumbs are found a useful outlet, so that we are able to offer a tasty article of good food value to the slender-purse holder.

To the confectioner who does not find a ready demand for these goods. I would suggest choosing one or two fancied lines and trying small mixings, giving the shop manageress instructions to display the goods to advantage and trying to introduce them diplomatically. Peak sales of these goods can be expected in autumn and early winter, so make the most of it.

All the recipes and methods given are well tried, good commercial lines and, in all cases, the amount of ginger stated is variable. I have purposely, as local tastes vary, kept these quantities to the minimum. It is a simple matter to increase this in subsequent mixings, whereas too much initially may be sufficient to ruin a promising start.

There are two types of ground ginger, black and white, the former being much stronger in flavour and odour than the white. The amounts in the following recipes, then, are approximately the minimum required using white ginger.

Ginger Nuts

Ever popular as a biscuit variety, these can prove to be a good line if the shop is situated in a busy position, such as near to a long-distance bus station, or has a snack bar attached. In any case, pre-packing in small amounts should pay handsomely, but it will be very necessary to ensure regularity in thickness. To this end the dough should be pinned out on a marble slab or a perfectly smooth, level bench with two sticks of correct thickness employed to support each end of the rolling-pin.

4¼ lb (2040 g) flour	1½ lb (680 g) fats
¾-oz (21 g) baking powder	2¼ lb (1020 g) castor sugar
1 oz (28 g) ginger	1 lb 14 oz (850 g) golden syrup
½-oz (14 g) mixed spice	

Sieve the flour, baking powder, ginger and spice on to the bench and rub in the fats, which can take the form of lard, golden shortening or a mixture of these.

Make a bay and add the sugar and syrup; the best way of measuring the latter, I find, is to warm the tin of syrup, rinse out a measure in cold water, weigh the correct quantity and immediately reverse the measure over the bay. Done in this manner the syrup will be found to leave the measure quite cleanly. Alternatively, of course, it is a simple matter, after weighing the sugar, to adjust the weights accordingly, make a bay in the sugar on the scale end, and weigh the syrup on top of the sugar.

Dissolve the sugar in the syrup and work all together, afterwards rubbing well down to produce a clear dough.

Pin out the dough in small quantities, using rice flour for dusting, as indicated, to ⅛ in (3 mm) thick, and cut with a 2 in (5·1 cm) plain cutter, afterwards using a broad-bladed palette knife to transfer the shapes to a clean, lightly greased sheet tin. Wash with milk and bake at 350°F (175°C) to a golden brown, employing upturned sheet tins or biscuit wires if necessary to guard against undue bottom heat.

Ginger Biscuits

3 lb (1360 g) flour	12 oz
¾-oz (21 g) ginger	1½ lb (680 g) castor sugar
¼-oz (7 g) baking powder	12 oz (340 g) liquid egg
12 oz (340 g) butter or cake margarine	

Ginger biscuits, with simple pre-packing to preserve crispness

Sieve together the flour, baking powder and ginger, rub in the fats to the consistency of fine bread-crumbs, make a bay, and add the sugar and egg. Dissolve the former in the latter and rub down well on the bench to produce a dough of smooth consistency. Pin out as previously detailed, once again using rice flour for dusting purposes. Cut with a $2\frac{1}{2}$ in (6·4 cm) plain cutter, and transfer to a lightly greased sheet tin, spacing evenly and allowing room for slight expansion during baking at 350°F (175°C).

Parkin Biscuits

Method 1

The name 'Penny Parkin' still clings to this line.

$4\frac{1}{4}$ lb (2040 g) flour
$4\frac{1}{2}$ lb (2040 g) medium oatmeal
5 oz (140 g) baking powder
12 oz (340 g) margarine
12 oz (340 g) compound

1 lb 2 oz (510 g) castor sugar
2 oz (57 g) ginger
$\frac{3}{4}$-oz (21 g) mixed spice
$5\frac{1}{4}$ lb (2390 g) syrup

Sieve together the flour, baking powder, ginger and spice, rub in the fats finely, afterwards adding the oatmeal and mixing all well. Make a bay, add the sugar and syrup, dissolve, and mix to a clear dough.

Scale off at $2\frac{1}{2}$ oz (70 g) split into two and mould round, afterwards spacing well apart on greased sheet tins to allow for flowing. Flatten slightly with the palm of the hand, egg-wash and place a split almond in the centre of each, afterwards baking at 340–350°F (170–175°C).

Care should be exercised in the ordering of oatmeal, small quantities at regular intervals being the rule, otherwise, should the meal be at all rancid, the inevitable soapy taste will be apparent, giving just cause for complaint.

Parkin biscuits with the characteristic 'crack'.

Method 2

A biscuit containing less oatmeal may find greater favour, and the following can be recommended:

4½ lb (2040 g) flour	1 lb (450 g) margarine
2¼ lb (1020 g) oatmeal	8 oz (230 g) compound
1½ oz (42 g) cream powder	1½ lb (680 g) sugar
1½ oz (42 g) bicarbonate of soda	3 lb (1360 g) syrup
1¾ oz (50 g) ginger	1 lb 2 oz (510 g) liquid egg
1 oz (28 g) mixed spice	

The method of mixing and details for working off are as previously given, the egg being added to the sugar and syrup in the bay.

Ginger Buns

1 lb (450 g) soft brown sugar	2 lb (910 g) syrup
8 oz (230 g) castor sugar	4 lb (1820 g) flour
1½ lb (680 g) cake margarine	2 oz (57 g) baking powder
8 oz (230 g) shortening	1¼ oz (36 g) ginger
1 lb 14 oz or 1½ pt (850 g or 0·85 litres) egg	½ oz (14 g) spice

Well grease sufficient small bun tins and place a split almond in the bottom of each tin.

Cream together fats and sugar until light, then gradually add the egg until all is incorporated, scraping down the bowl and beater as necessary. Finally, add the warmed syrup and mix in well.

Remove the bowl from the machine, clean off the beater, clear by hand and add the sieved flour, baking powder and spices, mixing carefully to a clear batter. Now transfer the batter to a savoy bag fitted with large plain tube, and fill the tins three-quarters full.

Bake at 360–370°F (180–190°C), afterwards reversing the bun for sale to show the almond. This recipe may be used to produce larger units.

Gingerbread Squares

6 lb (2720 g) flour	1 lb (450 g) soft brown sugar
2 oz (57 g) baking powder	4 oz (110 g) castor sugar
2 oz (57 g) ginger	1 lb (450 g) sieved cake crumbs
$\frac{3}{4}$-oz (21 g) mixed spice	10 oz (280 g) milk
1 lb (450 g) cake margarine	2 pt (1·14 litres) syrup
8 oz (230 g) shortening	

Prepare a sheet tin, 30 × 18 in (76 × 46 cm) by cleaning and well greasing, afterwards fitting a greased stick across the end to prevent flowing.

Sieve together the flour, baking powder and spices, rub in the fats, make a bay and in it put the sugar, syrup and milk. Dissolve the sugar in the liquids and mix to produce a clear dough, afterwards transferring to the prepared sheet tin. Roll out level and dock well all over, using the roller-docker. Egg-wash and bake at 340–350°F (170–175°C), approximately $\frac{1}{2}$-h being required.

Allow to cool thoroughly before cutting into squares of the required size, predetermined by costing. Use the seven-wheel pastry cutter or a stick of correct width to ensure regularity.

If desired, the slab may be iced with white fondant before cutting.

Honey Gingerbread

Very similar to the previous line, honey does give this a rather unique flavour and, therefore, produces a useful alternative line.

7 lb (3150 g) flour	2 oz (57 g) bicarbonate of soda
4 oz (110 g) margarine	2 lb (910 g) honey
1 lb (450 g) compound	2 lb (910 g) syrup
2 oz (57 g) ginger	1½ lb (680 g) soft brown sugar
2 oz (57 g) mixed spice	1½ lb (680 g) castor sugar
1 oz (28 g) nutmeg	

Prepare one sheet tin as already detailed, and grease a second, placing the greased stick in this instance across the middle of the sheet.

Mix as for the previous recipe to a smooth dough, afterwards dividing in the proportions of two-thirds and one-third for the prepared one and a half sheets. Roll out, dock and egg-wash. Bake at 320–330°F (160–165°C) allowing to cool before cutting into the required sizes.

Parkin Slab 1

On Guy Fawkes night, the demand for the traditional bonfire refreshments of parkin slab and treacle toffee should be at its height. An excellent recipe for the former, to produce six 8 lb (3600 g) slabs baked in 16 × 12 in (42 × 30 cm) slabs tins, is as follows:

3 lb (1360 g) soft brown sugar	1½ oz (42 g) mixed spice
6 lb (2730 g) shortening	9 oz (255 g) ginger
2½ lb or 1 qt (1140 g or 1·14 litres) egg	6 lb 14 oz or 5½ pt (3120 g or 3·12 litres)
7 lb (3150 g) medium oatmeal	milk
11 lb (5000 g) wheatmeal or wholemeal	16 lb (7270 g) syrup
3¼ oz (105 g) baking powder	

Place the sugar and shortening in the machine bowl fitted with cake beater and commence creaming, warming as necessary to produce a light batter.

Meanwhile, prepare the slab tins in the usual manner by lining with a double thickness of greaseproof paper—cap paper is unsuitable for this purpose for, after baking and when the paper is being removed from the slab, cap paper is apt to stick, causing inevitable wastage and untidy appearance.

When the fat and sugar have achieved the required lightness, commence adding the egg in four quantities, creaming well in between each addition, and scraping down bowl and beater as necessary. Stop the machine, add the oatmeal, wheatmeal, baking powder, spice, and ginger, and start the machine on slow speed, mixing until a consistency of fine bread-crumbs is achieved. Stop the machine, add the warmed syrup, and restart the machine, first on bottom speed and then on top speed, again beating light, scraping down the bowl and beater at intervals.

Again reduce to bottom speed, adding the milk in three quantities, and beating on top speed in between each addition. The finished batter should be light, yet reasonably easy to scale at 8½ lb (3830 g) per slab.

Many of the parkin recipes one follows often give a batter of such soft consistency that scaling in the normal way is practically impossible and the only means of trying to transfer batter to slab tin is by a quart measure, which is both messy and unsatisfactory. In addition, the majority of parkin slabs are displayed usually with a pronounced sinking of the centre, and quite often with scorched edges and sides, giving a bitter after-taste.

Mixed as indicated, and baked for approximately $2\frac{1}{2}$ h at 330°F (165°C), none of these faults will be apparent.

When exposed for sale, it is, of course, traditional to cut and divide into the required weights by means of a household fork.

Alternative scaling weight would be 5 lb (2270 g) into 10 × 8 in (25 × 20 cm) or 11 × 7 in (28 × 18 cm) slab tins or frames.

Parkin Slab 2

For the reader requiring a real solid North Country parkin here is one that should be satisfactory.

$2\frac{1}{4}$ lb (1020 g) brown sugar	2 lb 6 oz (1080 g) flour
$\frac{1}{2}$-oz (14 g) tartaric acid	2 lb (910 g) medium oatmeal
$\frac{3}{4}$-oz (21 g) bicarbonate of soda	6 oz (170 g) glycerine
$1\frac{1}{2}$ lb (680 g) suet	15 oz or $\frac{3}{4}$-pt (430 g or 0·43 litres) egg
$\frac{3}{4}$-oz (21 g) ground ginger	10 oz (280 g) black treacle
$\frac{1}{4}$-oz (7 g) cinnamon	10 oz (280 g) golden syrup
$\frac{1}{2}$-oz (14 g) mixed spice	

Moisten the bicarbonate of soda with a little milk, then mix all the dry ingredients together in the machine bowl, using the dough hook. Add the treacle and syrup, together with the glycerine, then gradually add the egg until a smooth dough is produced.

Using 11 × 7 in (28 × 18 cm) or 10 × 8 in (25 × 20 cm) slab tins, 5 lb (2270 g) will be required with 14 oz (400 g) into 7 in (18 cm) cottage pans or 12 oz (340 g) into 1 lb (450 g) bread tins. All tins will require to be clean and well greased.

After scaling and moulding, pressing well into tins, allow to lie overnight before baking at 360°F (180°C). The correct way to cut these cakes is by using a fork.

The larger units will require a week or so to mature, so should be produced well in advance of November 5.

Ginger Fruit Cakes

$4\frac{1}{2}$ lb (2040 g) flour	8 oz (230 g) castor sugar
1 oz (28 g) baking powder	$1\frac{1}{4}$ lb or 1 pt (570 g or 0·57 litres) egg
$\frac{3}{4}$-oz (21 g) ginger	$1\frac{3}{4}$ lb (800 g) syrup
$\frac{1}{4}$-oz (7 g) mixed spice	$1\frac{1}{4}$ lb or 1 pt (570 g or 0·57 litres) milk
1 lb (450 g) shortening	$1\frac{1}{2}$ lb (680 g) sultanas
8 oz (230 g) cake margarine	12 oz (340 g) mixed peel
1 lb (450 g) soft brown sugar	

Prepare twenty-four 6 in (15 cm) round hoops or tins by lining with paper bands and placing a circle of greaseproof paper in the bottom of each.

Place fats and sugar into the machine bowl fitted with cake beater and cream until light, warming as necessary, then adding the eggs in four quantities, scraping down bowl and beater at regular intervals. When all has been thoroughly incorporated, add the warmed syrup and mix well in, afterwards adding and breaking in half the milk.

Remove bowl and beater from the machine, clean off the beater, and add the previously sifted flour, baking powder and spices. Partially clear, add the remainder of the milk, mix in, finally adding the fruit and clearing thoroughly.

Scale into the prepared tins at 9 oz (255 g). Spread level with the back of the hand moistened with water, add a sprinkling of flaked almonds and bake at 360°F (180°C).

Iced Ginger Cakes

Basically similar to the preceding mixing, this is nevertheless of rather better quality and, when iced, can be made to look quite attractive and hence assist sales:

3 lb (1360 g) flour	1 lb (450 g) castor sugar
1 oz (28 g) baking powder	1¼ lb or 1 pt (570 g or 0·57 litres) egg
¾-oz (21 g) ginger	1 lb (450 g) syrup
8 oz (230 g) margarine	10 oz or ½-pt (280 g or 0·28 litres) milk
8 oz (230 g) shortening	

Prepare fourteen 1 lb (450 g) oval bun loaf or bread tins by cleaning thoroughly and greasing very carefully with well-creamed fat, paying particular attention to the corners.

Produce the batter as previously detailed, afterwards scaling into the prepared tins at 9 oz (255 g) levelling with the moistened back of the hand, and afterwards baking at 340–350°F (170–175°C). After baking, remove carefully from the tins and leave on a clean cloth or sack until thoroughly cold.

To finish, brush on what was previously the base a thin layer of well-boiled apricot purée, and follow by carefully icing the top with white fondant warmed to the correct temperature, with consistency adjusted by water, taking particular care that none runs down the side of the cake, thus giving a messy appearance.

Complete by piping on the word 'Ginger' in cool, white fondant and, if time and costs permit, a simple border of white fondant bulbs.

Iced Ginger Slab Cake

This recipe will produce six slabs, scaled at 8 lb (3620 g), in the greaseproof-lined 16 × 12 (41 × 31 cm) in slab tins previously mentioned, or, again, scale at 5 lb (2270 g) into the 10 × 8 in (25 × 20 cm) or 11 × 7 in (28 × 18 cm) tins or frames.

Iced ginger slab cake

7 lb (3150 g) butter or cake margarine	11½ lb (5230 g) flour
4 oz (110 g) glycerine	1¼ oz (36 g) baking powder
1 lb (450 g) shortening	10 lb (4540 g) chopped, washed and drained,
8 lb (3600 g) castor sugar	preserved ginger
10 lb or 8 pt (4540 g or 4·54 litres) egg	egg colour

Mix by the sugar-batter method, ensuring that a good, light batter has been produced.

After all the eggs have been incorporated, add the sieved flour and baking powder and, when half mixed, the chopped ginger clearing thoroughly. Scale into the prepared tins, spread level with the moistened hand, baking carefully at 340°F (170°C).

Next day, when cold, remove from the tins, strip off the papers and ice with white fondant. Complete by covering the surface with thin strips of preserved ginger, dredging with castor sugar, quite heavily, to complete.

Crystallised Ginger Cakes

In many instances today we find that the slab cake has lost favour, the trend being for the smaller unit to find a better sale. This recipe is to produce a similar, though rather cheaper, type of cake to the foregoing slab:

12 oz (340 g) cake margarine
12 oz (340 g) shortening
1¼ lb (570 g) castor sugar
1¼ lb or 1 pt (570 g or 0·57 litres) egg
3¼ lb (1480 g) weak flour
5 oz (140 g) syrup

1¼ lb or 1 pt (570 g or 0·57 litres) milk
1½-oz (14 g) mixed spice
¾-oz (21 g) baking powder
2½ lb (1140 g) chopped, drained, preserved
    ginger
egg colour

Prepare eleven 6½ in (16·5 cm) round hoops or tins by papering in the usual manner. Mix by the sugar-batter method, adding the syrup after all the egg has been incorporated, beating in, and then breaking in half the milk. After the sieved flours and powders have been partially mixed, add the ginger and the remainder of the milk and clear.

Scale at 1 lb (450 g) into the prepared hoops or tins, spread level and bake at 360°F (180°C). When cold, finish as for the slab cake with fondant and crystallised ginger.

Ginger Walnut Cakes

If something 'different' is required, this may provide the answer:

1¾ lb (800 g) cake margarine
4 oz (110 g) shortening
2 lb (910 g) castor sugar
2¼ lb or 2 pt (1140 g or 1·14 litres) eggs
3 lb (1360 g) flour
½-oz (14 g) baking powder

2½ lb (1140 g) chopped, drained, preserved
    ginger
1 lb (450 g) broken walnuts
egg colour
vanilla essence

Prepare twenty 1 lb (450 g) loaf tins by lining in the usual manner with greaseproof paper or special tin liners.

Mix by the usual sugar-batter method, afterwards scaling at 10½ oz (300 g) for each cake. Smooth level, place a few walnut halves on top, and bake at 360°F (180°C).

Brandy Snaps

2 lb (910 g) syrup
2 lb 6 ox (1080 g) castor sugar
2 lb (910 g) flour
1¼ lb (570 g) shortening

½-oz (14 g) baking powder
1 oz (28 g) ginger
½-oz (14 g) mixed spice

It is questionable whether these goods are today a commercial proposition, but no chapter on ginger goods would be complete without a passing reference. Indeed, they are great favourites, especially at Fair times, and it seems a pity that economic necessity precludes them from more widespread production. One other point that has to be seriously considered is that of storage for, being hygroscopic, unless kept in airtight tins, the loss can be very considerable.

Sieve the flour and powders together, rub in the fat, make a bay, placing syrup and sugar therein. Dissolve the latter in the former and proceed to rub down to a short dough. The best results will be obtained if the dough is allowed to stand overnight in a cool place.

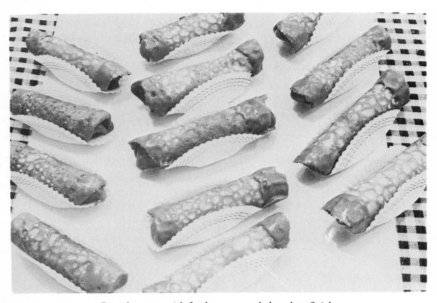

Brandy snaps with fresh cream and chocolate finish

Rolling the snaps

Drop out in ½oz (14 g) pieces on to a thickly greased sheet tin and bake at 350°F (175°C), giving each sufficient room to flow. When a rich, golden-brown colour has been reached, remove from the oven, allow the first heat to leave, reverse and roll round special rollers, removing after the snaps have set.

It was, in the past, customary to use peel handles, brush tails and other oddments of bakery furniture for rolling the snaps. Besides being unhygienic, this practice had its repercussions when these tools were required for their normal use in that hands and overalls became literally smothered in grease.

To avoid this, then, it is a simple matter to get together sufficient sticks of a diameter of 1 in (2·6 cm), measuring anything from 6–12 in (15–30 cm) in length.

A different type of finish, and one that certainly makes these goods a commercial proposition, is to fill them with whipped and sweetened fresh cream, and include them in the variety of cream cakes.

The difficulty here, of course, is the hygroscopic quality of the brandy snap, but if the base is produced in advance and stored under airtight conditions, then they may be utilised.

Fill with whipped fresh cream, and dip both ends in chocolate as soon as filled. It is a wise policy to restrict production to the amount expected to be sold by early afternoon.

Ginger Rings

It is the aim of all confectioners who have an eye on costings to keep the 'crumb' situation within reason. Quite a number of people are under the impression that crumbs and stales generally cost nothing, which is, of course, quite erroneous.

Any recipe that can reduce these and help to keep waste down to the absolute minimum is, therefore, welcome, and more so if, as is the case of the first variety, an attractive fancy can be produced.

Mix together:

1 lb 2 oz (510 g) cake crumbs — $\frac{1}{2}$-oz (14 g) ground ginger
1$\frac{1}{2}$ lb (680 g) malt extract — $\frac{1}{2}$-oz (14 g) salt
10 oz (280 g) shortening — 6 oz (170 g) egg
$\frac{1}{2}$-oz (14 g) cinnamon

Dissolve together and add:

4 oz (110 g) water — $\frac{1}{4}$-oz (7 g) vol
$\frac{3}{4}$-oz (21 g) bicarbonate of soda

Blend together and add:

2$\frac{1}{4}$ lb (1020 g) weak flour — 1$\frac{1}{4}$ lb (570 g) castor sugar

As to be expected, this recipe produces a rather tight type of biscuit dough, and may be mixed by machine, using dough hook, or beater on first speed, clearing well.

Roll out to approximately $\frac{1}{8}$-in (3 mm) thick, cut with a 2 in (5·1 cm) plain cutter, place the biscuits on a clean sheet tin and bake at 380°F (195°C).

When finishing, reverse half the number on to the bench and pipe round the perimeter, using a $\frac{3}{8}$-in (9 mm) plain tube and savoy bag, a ring of buttercream nicely flavoured with ginger syrup and chopped, stem ginger. Into the hollow thus formed, pipe a good spot of pineapple jam.

Reverse another biscuit on to the top, press gently to force the cream level with the edges of the biscuit and enrobe with couverture or bakers' chocolate.

The unusual ginger rings

Just before the chocolate has set, place a disc of stem ginger, with the top dipped into castor sugar, in position. If desired, chopped ginger and nuts may be added to the biscuit paste.

Ginger Slices

1½ lb (680 g) butter	3 oz (85 g) golden syrup
1½ lb (680 g) sugar	¼-oz (21 g) ginger
1 lb 14 oz (850 g) flour	1 lb 14 oz or 1½ pt (850 g or 0·85 litres) egg
¼-oz (21 g) baking powder	

Delicious to eat, this line has won high praise from all who have tried it—and the taste for ginger is far more widespread than many confectioners imagine.

Produce the base by the sugar-batter process, dividing the batter equally between two sheet tins, 23 × 18 in (60 × 46 cm), previously prepared by lining with greaseproof paper. The batter, really light and beautifully smooth,

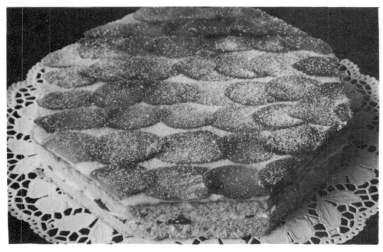

One mix, one finish, two lines. Ginger gateau and . . .

should be spread level and baked at 400–410°F (205–210°C) on biscuit wires or upturned sheet tins.

When cold, and preferably the following day, tip from the sheet tins, remove the paper and sandwich the two together with a ¼-in (6 mm) layer of buttercream into which has been added some chopped, crystallised ginger.

. . . ginger slices

Mask the top with boiled apricot jam, followed by white fondant, straight away covering the fondant with thin slices of ginger prepared beforehand. Dredge fairly heavily with castor sugar, before cutting into the desired shapes and sizes.

As shown, these may be used to produce fancies, or cut by the piece to sell as a gateau. In this latter case, of course, it would be advisable to mask the sides with buttercream, and follow this with roasted, flaked almonds.

Ginger Honey Slice

This is another slice, somewhat cheaper than the previous one which, incorporating a fair amount of crumbs in conjunction with the honey, provides a different flavour.

Ginger honey slices

Cream lightly together:

1½ lb (680 g) shortening	1 oz (28 g) salt
1½ lb (680 g) brown sugar	4 oz (110 g) milk powder

Add and well clear:

3 lb (1360 g) glucose	2¼ lb (1020 g) honey
3 lb (1360 g) cake crumbs	

Add and break in:

2¾ lb (1250 g) milk   2 oz (57 g) bicarbonate of soda

Sieve together, add and clear:

6¾ lb (3070 g) weak flour   ½-oz (14 g) nutmeg
3 oz (85 g) ginger   ½-oz (14 g) mixed spice
1½ oz (42 g) cinnamon

Scale on to well-greased and lightly floured sheet tins, scaling at 10 lb (4·5 kg) for a 30 × 18 in (76 × 46 cm) sheet, with other sizes in proportion. Spread level with a moistened scraper, bake at 375°F (190°C), and, when cold, finish as required.

For a quick, cheap finish, ice with white fondant after masking with boiling apricot purée, then cut into 2½ × 1 in (6·4 × 2·6 cm) slices. Alternatively, after icing, decorate with slices of crystallised ginger, dredge with castor sugar and cut as desired.

Ginger Fruits

Stem ginger is a commodity very little seen in confectioners' shops at the present time, having apparently been lost during the war and since been allowed to remain in Limbo. That it is a popular taste with the public is evident at Christmas time, when small jars command both a ready sale and a good price.

This line uses this raw material and will prove quick to produce and to the taste of many customers.

Clean thoroughly a 30 × 18 in (76 × 46 cm) sheet tin, then produce a sweet-paste type of mixing in the normal rubbing-in manner from:

3½ lb (1530 g) weak flour   ½-oz (14 g) baking powder
1 lb (450 g) butter or margarine   ½-oz (14 g) mixed spice
1¼ lb (570 g) castor sugar   2 lb (910 g) treacle/syrup
3 oz (85 g) ginger crush   5 oz (140 g) milk

Divide the paste into two and pin one half to line the sheet tin. Spread this with a filling comprising:

1 lb (450 g) persipan   7 oz (200 g) ginger crush
8 oz (230 g) egg   4 oz (110 g) apricot jam
4 oz (110 g) cake crumbs

Beat to a spreading consistency. Pin out the second piece of paste, lay over the prepared half and pin lightly to adhere. Place a stick at the end to prevent flowing and bake on wires or upturned sheet tins at 360°F (180°C).

On removal from the oven and after cooling, mask with boiled apricot purée, followed by thin, rather warm, white fondant. Cover the whole with thin slices of stem ginger, finally dredging heavily with castor sugar before cutting into squares or fingers as desired.

Ginger fruits, finished with stem ginger and (right) a gum arabic wash as an alternative

Ginger Fruit Cake

Well fulfilling the unusual label is this particular line. The oil referred to can be a cooking oil or fat just melted to produce an oil—but should certainly not be 'hot'. The addition of beer to the recipe is also of interest—if only to the staff! It might be suggested that this latter item be put into the care of a non-drinker!

1¼ lb (570 g) oil
1¼ lb or 1 pt (570 g or 0·57 litres) egg
8 oz (230 g) Barbados sugar
2¾ lb (1250 g) golden syrup
1¼ oz (35 g) bicarbonate of soda

1 lb 2 oz (510 g) beer
3¾ lb (1700 g) strong flour
2½ oz (70 g) mixed spice
1 lb (450 g) chopped ginger
2 lb (910 g) sultanas

Whisk together oil, eggs and sugar, to dissolve the latter. Add the syrup and whisk well in. Dissolve the soda in the beer, add and whisk in. Add the remainder of the ingredients and well clear.

Scale at 2¼ lb (1020 g) into 2 lb (910 g) sandwich loaf tins, previously papered, or into greased and floured, or lined cottage pans, 7 in (18 cm) in diameter, scaling at 360°F (180°C).

Whilst the finished cakes may be displayed for sale as withdrawn from the oven, they certainly look more attractive if iced with white fondant, then masked with thin slices of preserved ginger, finally dredging heavily with castor sugar to complete. Whilst this finish will certainly increase raw material costs, stem ginger is extremely popular with all sections of the public, who appreciate the economics, and are only too ready to purchase that which they enjoy. Thus is the producer able to ask—and receive—a much higher price than the unfinished cake alone would bring.

Chapter 9

CAKES AND CAKE-MAKING

Before commencing to give recipes and details of cake-mixing it will, perhaps, be an advantage to consider the materials required, methods of mixing, faults that may occur and consequent remedies.

CAKE-MAKING

Sugar-batter Method

The sugar-batter method is perhaps the most popular cake-making method. All ingredients should be at a temperature of approximately 72°F (22°C) and it will be convenient if a gas-ring is placed in a position near the machine so that, during cold weather, the fat and sugar can be warmed, if and as necessary, during creaming. Great care should be exercised, however, that the batter is not allowed to become oily, for, should this occur, the results will be far from satisfactory.

When the fats and sugar are sufficiently light in character—and this can easily be ascertained by observation of bulk and colour—the eggs should be added in small quantities, each addition being allowed to be thoroughly incorporated before any further egg is added. The bowl and beater should be scraped down regularly to ensure thorough incorporation and amalgamation. When this stage has been reached, colours and essences may be added and thoroughly beaten in to ensure correct distribution throughout the batter.

A small mixing of good quality should now be removed from the machine and completed by hand, but a larger mixing may be completed on the machine at slow speed, although a final clearing by hand will still be necessary.

If the recipe contains milk, half should be broken in with the machine engaged on first speed. Stop the machine, add the sieved flour and baking powder, and restart on bottom speed. When the flour is approximately half cleared, add any fruit required, pour in the remainder of the milk and clear, afterwards removing the bowl and beater and clearing by hand.

The reason for adding the milk in two stages is to prevent the development of gluten, which would occur if all the milk were added at the final stage; whilst, if it were all added immediately after the egg, it would be sufficient to break down the batter.

As already stated, in the production of top quality cakes, the flour should be blended in very carefully to prevent toughening. Indeed, we may take a step further in that a small amount of flour may be added to the fat and sugar in the initial stage of mixing, thus turning the sugar-batter method into a 'hybrid'. The amount of flour that may be added is up to half the amount in weight of the total fats used. If this idea is followed, any danger of the batter curdling when adding the eggs or milk is obviated. Again, the gluten of that amount of flour is acted upon by the fat and prevented from developing. Thus, with a reduced quantity of flour to be added in the final stage, the chances of toughening are considerably lessened.

Cheaper qualities of cakes should be mixed thoroughly in the final stage to ensure thorough and even distribution of the fats and egg—the two ingredients which control the quality.

Flour-batter Method

Certain advantages are to be gained in the use of this method when producing cakes of cheap to medium quality, but whether these outweigh the disadvantages is for the individual to decide.

Place the fats, together with an equal amount of flour into the machine bowl fitted with a beater and commence creaming on slow speed, warming as necessary. When both have been blended to form a paste, change to top speed and cream until light.

The eggs, together with an equal weight of sugar, are now whisked to slightly below full sponge in a grease-free bowl. Any sugar remaining should be dissolved in the milk, whilst the flour and baking powder are sieved together.

When both batters have reached the indicated stage, remove the sponge from the machine and add to the creamed batter in four or five quantities, beating well in between each addition and scraping down the bowl and beater several times, as necessary, after which colour and essence may be added and thoroughly dispersed throughout the batter.

Now add the milk, into which the sugar has been thoroughly dissolved, and break in, followed by the sieved flour and baking powder. For cheap quality cakes, beat thoroughly, and then add and distribute evenly any fruit required. For better quality cakes, the batter should be partially cleared prior to adding the fruit, final clearing taking place after the fruit is added.

Disadvantages

To the practical commercial confectioner, the disadvantages of this method will become obvious immediately.

More weighing of the ingredients is required, thus taking up more time and giving a wider margin for error. More equipment is required, which, besides entailing greater capital expenditure, means more work on the cleaning side: a small point, perhaps, but one that is not to be overlooked when computing labour charges on costings.

Very little, if any, advantage is to be gained by using this method with top quality cakes, but for cheap quality slab cakes, etc., a better textured cake of shorter-eating quality is produced as against the same recipe produced by the sugar-batter method.

By creaming the fat and part of the flour together, the gluten of the flour is broken down and prevented from developing, thus reducing toughness in the finished article. We can now see that a flour of rather greater strength than normal may be used by this method without adverse effect.

'Rub In' or 'All In' Method

Very seldom used—this method is confined solely to extremely cheap mixings of the 'Farmhouse Cake' type. Mixing is exactly similar to that as for powder aerated goods, dealt with in Chapter 3.

High-Ratio Cakes

This method has been so widely publicised by the service bakeries of speciality fat manufacturers and the millers producing special cake flour that I feel very much on this subject would be superfluous. Indeed, the methods and timing are so precise as given on their recipe charts as to make production almost foolproof.

Suffice to say that any production should follow these instructions to the letter and to time each stage of the process meticulously for this, in my experience, is the only loophole where mistakes may occur.

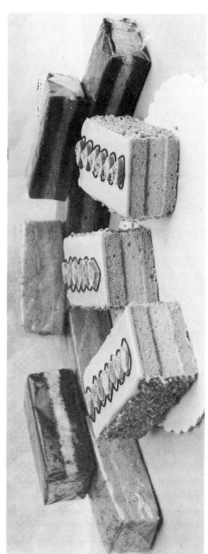

High-ratio Cakes

The tender-eating, fine, evenly-textured cakes produced from high-ratio recipes are exceedingly popular and, as shown here, can be utilised to produce a wide range of attractive 'units', especially when wrapped in transparent film

Any production troubles here are swiftly dealt with by the firms in question for, on request, the majority are only too pleased to arrange for a demonstrator to attend and so assist in ironing out any snags.

High-ratio cherry slab cakes showing the effect of omitting the small amount of acid that plays so important a part in ensuring that the cherries do not sink during baking. All three slab cakes were made from the same recipe, the acid being omitted in the top example, where it can be seen that the fruit has sunk and the texture suffered in consequence.

Recipe Balancing

In considering cake-making we must, first, define what is a good cake, for the confectioner should, by merely scanning a recipe, be able to place it in its correct category of cheap, medium or good quality. We must then have a yardstick to measure by, and to do this possess some understanding of the theory of recipe balancing.

A good cake, therefore, must possess a tempting and appetising golden brown crust, smooth rounded top and, when cut, show a bright, evenly textured crumb, with any fruit evenly dispersed. To obtain this result we must adhere in principle to the basic rules which, although there are exceptions, form an excellent general guide. They are:

(*a*) The proportion of fat to flour decides the richness of a cake, so that as the total amount of fats contained in any particular recipe approaches the weight of flour, the richness will increase. Any increase of fat over the weight of flour will produce a certain type of fault, which will be considered later.

(b) Eggs will aerate their own weight of flour. Flour in excess of the total weight of eggs must be aerated by baking powder, the amount to be used varying with the type of cake being produced, e.g. queen cakes, madeira or fruit cakes, genoese etc., and this is generally between 1 oz per lb (63 g per kg) of excess flour for smaller goods and $\frac{1}{2}$-oz per lb (31 g per kg) of excess flour in larger goods.

(c) Moisture must be added in the form of egg and milk, the top quality recipes, of course, containing only the former. The optimum weight of egg is approximately $1\frac{1}{4}$ parts of egg to 1 part of fat. As each 3 lb (1360 g) flour requires 2 pt (1·14 litres) liquor, any excess flour above that optimum must be moistened by milk and aerated by baking powder as previously detailed.

(d) The amount of sugar required in any particular recipe may be roughly calculated by adding together the total amounts of fats, eggs, milk and flour and dividing by four. The answer is generally slightly low, but it does give a guide to the confectioner thinking out new recipes.

From the above rules we arrive at what should produce a good cake, and the recipe reads:

1 lb (450 g) sugar	$1\frac{1}{4}$ lb (570 g) egg
1 lb (450 g) fats	$1\frac{1}{4}$ lb (570 g) flour

Should the reader produce this cake, using 14 oz (400 g) margarine and 2 oz (57 g) golden shortening as the fats, made by the sugar-batter method he will find that it produces an excellent madeira cake.

Suppose we try to improve it by, say, adding more fat. The balance would then be disturbed, and we would get a shiny top crust on the finished cake, and, when cut, the lower part of the crumb would be greasy to the touch and close textured, whilst the upper part would be quite open.

Two Major Faults

The two major faults in cake-making are known as the 'M' and 'X' faults, so-called because when the cake is cut the outline takes the shape of the letter denoting the fault.

'M' fault is caused by too much baking powder, excess sugar or excess fat, the presence of the latter being noted as previously mentioned.

'X' faults are caused by too much liquid being present in the mixing, and this can be clearly seen if the cake is cut—a soggy core running horizontally

Recipe Balance

The effect of increasing the sugar in a cake recipe is clearly shown here. The cake on the left is from the normal well-balanced recipe then, as sugar is progressively increased, there is a loss of volume, then the appearance of white 'sugar' spots on the top crust and eventually a sunken top with quite a sugary crust. This is known as the 'M' fault

Recipe Balance

The use of excess liquid in a cake batter produces the 'X' fault. Here the cake on the left is made from the normal well-balanced recipe whilst the others show the effect of using increasing amounts of liquid, namely, loss of volume, the eventual collapse at the sides, and the production of a 'core' near the bottom crust through the cake. This should not be confused with a core caused through under-baking, for in this instance the core remains just under the top crust.

It is interesting to note that 'M' and 'X' faults do not appear simultaneously in any one cake or mixing, for these two faults cancel each other out.

'M' faults can be corrected by reducing the baking powder or sugar, increasing the milk or reducing the fat. 'X' faults can be corrected by reducing the milk, increasing the baking powder or increasing the sugar.

Other minor faults are sometimes apparent, such as a tray of cakes being knocked in the oven before being properly set; the use of unsuitable materials such as too strong a flour, too coarse or too fine a grain of sugar, baking in too cool or too hot an oven, failure to wash the syrup from cherries or dry other fruits thoroughly and so on, but, in my experience, these latter faults are due to thoughtlessness or carelessness, and do not so often appear.

Preparing tins

The more frequent faults I find are due to bad preparation of the tins and wrong baking. Often the former is the result of the everyday rush of the bakery, but an extra few minutes spent in preparing the tins correctly is well worth the effort. A badly lined tin produces a badly shaped cake and, similarly, a tin carelessly greased and floured produces stuck and broken cakes, with the inevitable wastage and loss.

For tins requiring papers, the latter are easily purchased at a reasonable cost in the form of bands and circles, and, besides the convenience, they do save time in cutting up sheets of papers, with consequent wastage. Boxes should be obtained to store these, for far too often, unless carefully preserved, they are to be found scattered far and wide.

Greased and floured tins should be prepared by carefully washing and drying, or wiping out thoroughly, before greasing with well-creamed fat, paying particular attention to the corners, and afterwards dusting with flour kept specially for the purpose, ensuring that the surplus is knocked thoroughly from the tin. To save time, some confectioners prefer to mix the fat and flour, thus accomplishing the operation with one handling of the tins. This should be in the proportion of $\frac{2}{3}$ fat and $\frac{1}{3}$ flour, well creamed together. Admittedly, this does save time, but I do feel that a much better 'skin' is given to the cake by doing both tasks separately.

The baking of the cakes needs quite a fair amount of skill, allied to a careful knowledge of the oven used, for quite often in the commercial medium and small bakeries a job has to be done whether oven temperature is correct or not, and this applies especially to ovens heated by solid fuels.

However, as far as possible, the oven should be filled and, if this is impracticable, pans or bowls of water introduced to provide the humid atmosphere needed. With a full oven, of course, sufficient steam will be provided by the cakes themselves during baking. The oven door should, as far as possible, remain closed during baking, and the baking time be carefully noted, for far too many cakes are left in for 'just another minute', which often runs to another 10 min, thus drying out what would otherwise have been an excellent batch. We have all tasted cake which brings on a bout of coughing, through having been left in that few minutes too long, with a consequent coarse, dry, crumb.

GENERAL PURPOSE MIXING

This can be one of the most useful mixings in the bakery, and it must have the advantages of being reasonable in price and lend itself to a variety of productions ranging from the small bun weighing approximately 1 oz (28 g) to bases suitable for larger type sandwiches and, with the requisite colour and flavour, gateau bases. A keeping quality of a minimum of one week is necessary, and the following recipe will be found to satisfy these requirements. Arranged for the sugar-batter method, it will read:

2 lb (910 g) sugar	2 lb 14 oz (1310 g) flour
1 lb (450 g) margarine	1¼ lb or 1 pt (570 g or 0·57 litres) milk
4 oz (110 g) golden shortening	2¼ oz (64 g) baking powder
1½ oz (43 g) glycerine	egg colour
1¼ lb or 1 pt (570 g or 0·57 litres) egg	vanilla essence

This mixing will be found perfectly satisfactory made by the sugar-batter method, but for the reader desiring to try it by the flour-batter method, the rearranged recipe reads:

Group 1

1 lb (450 g) margarine	1¼ lb (570 g) flour
4 oz (110 g) golden shortening	1½ oz (43 g) glycerine

Group 2

1¼ lb or 1 pt (570 g or 0·57 litres) egg	1¼ lb (570 g) sugar

Group 3

12 oz (340 g) sugar	egg colour
1¼ lb or 1 pt (570 g or 0·57 litres) milk	vanilla essence

Group 4

1 lb 10 oz (740 g) flour	2¼ oz (64 g) baking powder

Full details of the methods of mixing were given earlier in this chapter.

Small Buns

Using a savoy bag and large plain tube, pipe out the batter into small custard or bun tins, previously papered with a crimped paper case, two-thirds full or approximately $1\frac{1}{4}$ oz (36 g). Those required for decorating afterwards should be left plain, whilst others may be decorated prior to baking with a sprinkle of flaked almonds, currants, cherries, etc., afterwards baking at 410°F (210°C).

Buns finished by top decoration before baking

After baking, allow to cool thoroughly, then the buns may be finished in a variety of ways.

Using Fondant

Brush the tops of those buns to be decorated with boiled apricot purée. Warm a pan of white fondant, using stock syrup or water as required to obtain the correct consistency and temperature, and commence decorating one-third of them by dipping the tops into the fondant and removing the surplus with the finger or a small palette knife. The aim should be to keep the buns neat, and to prevent any of the fondant from dribbling down the side of the paper case.

When one-third has been so treated, colour the fondant palé pink, restoring to correct consistency and temperature as necessary, and complete half of the buns remaining in a similar manner, always aiming for a clean finish.

To the remaining fondant add sufficient warmed baker's chocolate and chocolate colour and flavour to give the required rich colour and flavour, warming and adding stock syrup or water to bring the fondant back to the correct consistency before completing the remaining one-third of the buns.

Complete the decoration by placing half a cherry on the white fondant, a neat piece of crystallised pineapple on the pale pink, and a quarter walnut on the chocolate fondant.

Further varieties may be produced by icing with white fondant and masking immediately with fine or medium coconut, or icing with lemon or orange coloured and flavoured fondant and decorating with a piece of lemon or orange jelly slices as appropriate. Another variety would be to ice with coffee fondant, using a whole roasted hazelnut to complete.

Using vanilla custard or cream

Allow the bun to cool thoroughly before removing the centre carefully with the point of a sharp knife, afterwards reversing this on to the bench. Using a small plain cutter of appropriate size, cut the centres neatly, afterwards piping in the depression of the bun sufficient beaten, cold vanilla, using a savoy bag and $\frac{1}{2}$-in (1·3 cm) plain tube. For cream buns, using a star tube and savoy bag, pipe in a neat whorl of cream. Replace the tops and dredge liberally with icing sugar.

Cream Shells

These shell tins are obtainable singly, or in trays containing four or six, similar to the housewife's patty tins. Greased carefully, approximately $\frac{3}{4}$-oz (21 g) of batter is piped in, before baking at 410°F (210°C). After baking, remove immediately from the tins and leave reversed on a clean cloth or sack to cool. When cold, split horizontally with a sharp knife approximately two-thirds up from the base, pipe in a whorl of cream, replace the top and dredge with icing sugar to complete.

Currant Lunch Buns

Oval-shaped bun tins are cleaned and greased, with a few currants sprinkled on the bottom of the tin. Pipe into the tins approximately $1\frac{1}{4}$ oz (36 g) batter, or two-thirds full, and make at 410°F (210°C). When baked, remove immediately from the tins, and leave reversed for display.

Simple finishes to give variety

Bakewell-type Tart

Line fluted 6 in (15 cm) tart tins with sweet or german paste (see Chapter 5) and pipe in the bottom a liberal amount of raspberry jam. Scale, or pipe in, 4 oz (110 g) of the batter and spread level with the back of the hand moistened with water. Bake at 400°F (205°C) and, when cold, remove from the tins and mask with apricot purée. Ice with white fondant, and complete with a half cherry.

Cream Sandwiches

In latter years the public taste has veered from the deeper type sandwich to one of greater circumference, giving a greater number of slices per sandwich. Probably, whilst the thinner type does appear better value for money, it makes very little difference from our point of view, as long as our customers are satisfied.

A cake that is reasonable in price and can be readily consumed by a small family at one sitting always finds favour, and for this $2\frac{1}{2}$ oz (70 g) of batter is piped or scaled into greased 3 in (7·5 cm) tins. For 6 in (15 cm) tins a scaling weight of 6 oz (170 g) is satisfactory whilst, for the larger size sandwich tin of 8 in (20 cm) a weight varying between 9 oz (255 g) for sandwiches and 12 oz (340 g) for gateau bases is satisfactory.

Bake in greased tins; the oven temperature should be 400°F (205°C) for the small and 390°F (200°C) for the large sandwich.

After baking, empty immediately on to a clean cloth or sack to cool thoroughly before splitting carefully, masking with raspberry jam and piping in sufficient cream.

An alternative to cream, which often finds favour, is, of course, vanilla custard. Complete by dredging with icing sugar.

An interesting effect can be obtained by placing across the sandwich before dredging a stick or piece of cardboard cut to a suitable width.

Readers will realise, of course, that if the goods are sold as 'Cream Sandwiches', then only pure dairy cream can be used in their manufacture. If using imitation cream, some other name, without the word 'cream', must be used and assistants should also be warned not to use the word 'cream'.

Gateau Bases

As stated previously, this mixing is quite satisfactory for this purpose, if the required colours and flavours are added into the batter immediately following the egg. For chocolate gateaux substitute 4 oz (110 g) cocoa for 4 oz (110 g) flour, using also chocolate colour and flavour.

Scaling weights will, of course, vary, but 8–12 oz (230–340 g) scaled into 1 lb (450 g) cottage pans will be found quite satisfactory. Baking temperature for this size should be 390°F (200°C).

Victoria Sandwiches

Whilst the general purpose mixing has its uses, a good quality victoria sandwich is very acceptable to the customer requiring something plain or simply finished by splitting and layering with raspberry jam, lemon cheese, imitation cream and raspberry jam or vanilla, custard, cold and well beaten. The following recipe will produce an excellent sandwich by the sugar-batter method.

1¾ lb (800 g) margarine	3¼ lb (1480 g) flour
12 oz (340 g) golden shortening	1¼ oz (43 g) baking powder
2 lb 6 oz (1080 g) castor sugar	egg colour
3 lb 2 oz or 2¼ pt (1420 g or 1·42 litres) egg	vanilla essence

Prepare the tins by cleaning thoroughly, then greasing and flouring, taking care to knock out all surplus flour. Scale at the required weights, an 8 in (20·3 cm) tin taking between 9 oz (255 g) and 12 oz (340 g) of batter, depending upon the desired selling price. Spread level with a palette knife or the back of the moistened hand, and bake at 400°F (205°C). Upon withdrawal from the oven, empty immediately on to clean cloths or sacks, and allow to cool thoroughly before packing or finishing.

Second-quality Sandwiches

The cost of this mixing is a few coppers per lb cheaper than the previous one, but in actual cost of units the difference is quite small. Rather than produce second-quality goods, I prefer to use the previous mixing and scale the sandwiches at slightly less, thus adjusting the selling price by differential weights.

Quality remains long in the memory after price is forgotten, but this cheaper quality recipe is included for the sake of completeness.

1 lb (450 g) margarine	2 oz (57 g) baking powder
14 oz (400 g) golden shortening	1 lb 14 oz or 1½ pt (850 g or 0·85 litres) milk
2 lb 10 oz (1190 g) castor sugar	2 oz (57 g) glycerine
2½ lb or 1 qt (1140 g or 1·14 litres) egg	egg colour
4 lb 2 oz (1420 g) flour	vanilla essence

Produced by the sugar-batter method, this mixing may also be used for the production of small buns.

Harlequin Cream Sandwich

Just a straightforward, good quality sugar batter sandwich, delightful to eat and always popular with the customers.

2½ lb (1140 g) castor sugar	2½ lb or 1 qt (1140 g or 1·14 litres) egg
4 oz (110 g) shortening	3 lb 2 oz (1420 g) weak flour
2¼ lb (1020 g) butter or margarine	1 oz (28 g) baking powder
3 oz (85 g) glycerine	egg colour

Scale into well-greased and lightly-floured sandwich tins using 8 oz (230 g) batter to 6 in (15 cm) tins. Other sizes *pro rata*.

Bake at 380°F (195°C) and allow to stand overnight before finishing.

For this, split the required number, masking the tops with boiled apricot purée.

On some, four different colours of fondant are used, but this can naturally be varied to the readers' own requirements. Divide the tops equally according to the required fondant colours and flavours, icing the individual tops in turn. Whilst the fondant is setting, cream the bases with fresh cream, building up in the centre.

Now, segment the tops, marking first with a torten divider before cutting with a hot, moist knife. Arrange the segments alternatively on the cream and complete with a whirl in the centre, topped by either a cherry or walnut half.

Queen Drops

Whether or not these small items should come under the category of cakes or biscuits is debatable, but produced by the sugar-batter method, I feel that they have a place in this chapter.

1¾ lb (800 g) margarine	2 lb (910 g) castor sugar
4 oz (110 g) shortening	2 lb (910 g) egg
2 oz (57 g) glycerine	3 lb 2 oz (1420 g) flour

Add the flour to the prepared batter and clear carefully, afterwards transferring a portion to a savoy bag fitted with an ½-in (1·3 cm) plain tube. Pipe out the batter in 1 in (2·6 cm) bulbs on to a sheet tin lined with cap or greaseproof paper.

To prevent dryness, these goods should be baked quickly at 440°F (225°C) and, when cold, are easily removed from the paper.

Currants, if desired, may be added for variety, and for the quantity above 2 lb (910 g) should be sufficient.

Cherry Whirls

1 lb (450 g) margarine
1 lb (450 g) shortening
1¼ lb (680 g) icing sugar
14 oz (400 g) egg

2 oz (57 g) glycerine
3 lb 2 oz (420 g) flour
vanilla essence

Produced by the sugar-batter method, the whirls are piped out with a savoy bag and star tube on to papered sheet tins and decorated with a small piece of cherry prior to baking at 440°F (225°C).

The important point to watch is the baking, for, if done in too cool an oven, the goods will lack bloom and eat dry. They are sold by weight.

Fruit Cakes

First Quality

1¼ lb (680 g) margarine
8 oz (230 g) golden shortening
2 lb (910 g) sugar
2 oz (57 g) glycerine
2¼ lb or 1 qt (1140 g or 1·14 litres) egg
3 lb 2 oz (1420 g) flour

2¼ lb (1140 g) currants
2 lb (910 g) sultanas
1 lb (450 g) peel
egg colour
vanilla, almond and rum essences

Produced by the sugar-batter method, scaling weights recommended are 1¼ lb (570 g) in 6 in (15 cm) or 2 lb 2 oz (970 g) in 8 in (20 cm) papered hoops. Spread level, decorate with split almonds as costings allow, and bake at 360°F (180°C) for the smaller sizes and 350°F (175°C) for the larger.

Second Quality

1 lb (450 g) margarine
1 lb (450 g) golden shortening
½-oz (14 g) salt
2½ lb (1140 g) sugar
2¼ lb or 1 qt (1140 g or 1·14 litres) egg
4 lb (1820 g) flour
1½ oz (42 g) baking powder

2lb (910 g) currants
1 lb (450 g) sultanas
8 oz (230 g) mixed peel
1 lb 14 oz or 1½ pt (850 g or 0·85 litres) milk
egg colour
vanilla essence

The method and scaling weights are similar to those given for the best quality mixing. Spread level, decorate with a sprinkle of flaked almonds and bake the smaller sizes at 370°F (185°C) and the larger at 360°F (180°C).

Sultana Loaf

This recipe will produce an excellent cake for the customer desiring one of good quality, yet lightly fruited.

1½ lb (680 g) margarine
8 oz (230 g) golden shortening
2 lb (910 g) sugar
2½ lb or 1 qt (1140 g or 1·14 litres) egg
3 lb (1360 g) flour

¼-oz (21 g) baking powder
2¼ lb (1020 g) sultanas
8 oz (230 g) peel
egg colour

Prepare sixteen 1 lb (450 g) bread tins by cleaning thoroughly, greasing, and dusting with flour, paying particular attention to the corners.

Prepare the batter by the sugar-batter method, scale off at 12 oz (340 g) for each cake. Spread level and bake at 360–370°F (180–185°C) for approximately 40–45 min.

Upon withdrawal from the oven, empty immediately from the tins and allow to cool thoroughly before packing for despatch and sale.

Cherry and Walnut Cake

For the customer requiring a cake that is different and prepared to pay a price commensurate with quality, this cake can be confidently recommended.

12 oz (340 g) margarine
4 oz (110 g) golden shortening
1 lb (450 g) castor sugar
1¼ lb or 1 pt (570 g or 0·57 litres) egg
1 lb 9 oz (710 g) flour

2 lb (910 g) cherries
1 lb (450 g) chopped walnuts
vanilla essence
egg colour

Prepare the cherries by washing and drying thoroughly. The walnuts should be of good sound quality and lightly broken, afterwards being shaken in a coarse sieve to remove any dust prior to adding to the flour.

The mixing is made by the sugar-batter method, adding the flour and partially clearing before adding the cherries, and then completing the clearing.

Scale at 1¼ lb (570 g) into 6 in (15 cm) hoops, spread level and decorate before baking with five half walnuts. Bake at 360°F (180°C).

Madeira Cakes

First Quality

Whilst a recipe was given earlier (page 223) for a first-quality madeira cake, a cheaper quality may be required, yet one that will have a reasonable shelf life. The following will be found to be satisfactory.

8 oz (230 g) golden shortening
2 lb (910 g) margarine
2½ lb (1140 g) castor sugar
3 oz (86 g) glycerine
3 lb (1360 g) egg

3¾ lb (1700 g) flour
¼-oz (21 g) baking powder
egg colour
vanilla essence

Produced by the sugar-batter method, the baking temperature will be 360–380°F (180–195°C), dependent upon scaling weight.

Cheaper quality madeira cakes

Third Quality

1¼ lb (570 g) golden shortening	5¼ lb (2390 g) flour
1¼ lb (570 g) margarine	2 oz (57 g) baking powder
3¼ lb (1480 g) sugar	1 lb 9 oz or 1¼ pt (710 g or 0·71 litres) milk
3 lb 2 oz or 2½ pt (1420 g or 1·42 litres) egg	egg colour
3 oz (85 g) glycerine	vanilla essence

Produced by the sugar-batter method, the batter should be cleared thoroughly after the flour and final portion of the milk have been added. Baking should be carried out at a slightly higher temperature than for the better quality mixing.

Almond Cakes

8 oz (230 g) golden shortening	2 lb 14 oz (1310 g) flour
12 oz (340 g) margarine	1¼ lb or 1 pt (570 g or 0·57 litres) milk
4 oz (114 g) marzipan	1¼ oz (35 g) baking powder
1½ lb (680 g) castor sugar	almond essence
1½ lb (680 g) egg	egg colour

Prepare seventeen straight-sided, 9 oz (255 g) malt-loaf tins by greasing and flouring, particular attention being paid to the corners. Produce by the normal sugar-batter method, beating in the marzipan with the fats and sugar. After all the egg has been added, break in half the milk, add the sieved flour and baking powder, partially mix, add the remainder of the milk, and clear. Scale at 8 oz (230 g).

Almond cakes

Spread level and, if costs permit, add a sprinkling of flaked almonds for top decoration. Bake at 370°F (190°C) for approximately 30 min, after which the cakes should be immediately emptied and allowed to cool thoroughly on a clean cloth or sack before despatch.

Picnic Cakes

8 oz (230 g) golden shortening
2 lb (910 g) margarine
2 lb (910 g) sugar
2¼ lb or 2 pt (1140 g or 1·14 litres) egg

½-oz (14 g) baking powder
3 lb (1360 g) flour
egg colour
vanilla essence

Prepare fourteen oval-shaped tins by greasing carefully and placing two thin slices of citron peel in the bottom of each.

Mix by the sugar-batter method and scale at 12 oz (340 g) each, levelling afterwards with the moistened back of the hand. Bake at 370°F (190°C) for approximately 35 min.

When baked, remove immediately from the tins and wash the citron peel with a gum arabic solution, sugar syrup or golden syrup whilst still hot to preserve an attractive appearance.

Allow to cool thoroughly and display this side up for sale.

Picnic cakes

Lemon Cakes

8 oz (230 g) shortening
12 oz (340 g) margarine
2 lb (910 g) sugar
1 lb 14 oz or 1½ pt (850 g or 0·85 litres) egg
4 lb (1820 g) flour

1¼ oz (42 g) baking powder
12 oz (340 g) milk
juice and zest of 4 lemons or 1½ oz (42 g)
    lemon paste
lemon yellow colour

Prepare seventeen oval, 1 lb (450 g) bread tins by greasing and flouring, afterwards producing the mixing by the flour-batter method. Scale at 9 oz (255 g) spread level, and bake at 360–370°F (180–185°C). When baked, remove from the tins and allow to cool thoroughly before brushing with boiled apricot and icing with lemon coloured and flavoured fondant, warmed and reduced to correct consistency by the addition of water or stock syrup. Complete by piping the word 'Lemon' in cool fondant.

If desired, the lemon may be replaced by orange zest and juice. The colour to be added to the mixing would then be ½-oz (14 g) orange colour and flavoured compound, with the fondant then being appropriately coloured and flavoured.

Lemon cakes

Caraway Seed Cake

12 oz (340 g) shortening
1¾ lb (800 g) margarine
2¼ lb (1140 g) sugar
4 oz (110 g) glycerine
2¼ lb or 2 pt (1140 g or 1·14 litres) egg
15 oz (430 g) milk

4½ lb (2040 g) flour
2 oz (57 g) caraway seeds
1½ oz (43 g) baking powder
lemon essence or lemon paste
egg colour

Whilst seed cakes are not popular in all localities, some confectioners do have a steady demand for them and the above recipe, made by the sugar-batter method, produces quite an acceptable article. The effect of the glycerine to prolong shelf life and to combat dryness is very evident in this mixing. Scale at 12 oz (340 g) into papered, 1 lb (450 g) bread tins, and bake at 370–380°F (190–195°C) taking care not to over bake. A further aid to prolonging shelf life is to wrap in transparent cellulose immediately the cakes are cold.

An alternative recipe is:

2 lb (910 g) castor sugar
1½ lb (680 g) butter
8 oz (230 g) shortening
½-oz (14 g) salt
2 oz (57 g) glycerine
3 oz (85 g) water

2 lb (910 g) egg
1 oz (28 g) lemon paste
1½ oz (42 g) caraway seeds
2 lb 2 oz (965 g) flour
egg colour

Place the caraway seeds and water into a small pan, heating gently until all the water is absorbed. Allow to go cold.

Produce by the sugar-batter method, adding the seeds/water solution after all the egg has been added. Clear gently but well, then scale into papered or greased and floured 1 lb (450 g) loaf tins at 12–14 oz (340–400 g). Spread level with a moistened hand or scraper, sugar if desired, and bake at 380°F (195°C).

Caraway seed cake

Lemon Cake

This is a simple, straightforward cake, the flavour being introduced from lemon cheese, which is perhaps the one unusual feature. Obviously, then, the quality of the lemon cheese used will have much bearing on the finished product and one of good quality should be used.

2 lb (910 g) castor sugar
2 oz (57 g) macaroon paste
1 lb (450 g) lemon cheese
4 oz (110 g) butter
12 oz (340 g) shortening

4 oz (110 g) glycerine
1¼ lb or 1 pt (570 g or 0·57 litres) egg
3¾ lb (1700 g) weak flour
2 oz (57 g) baking powder
1¼ lb or 1 pt (570 g or 0·57 litres) milk

Produce by the sugar-batter method, adding the lemon cheese to the batter and beating well in. Scale at 12–14 oz (340–400 g) into well-greased and floured oval tins, baking at 370–380°F (190–195°C).

When baked and cold, mask what was formerly the bottom with boiled apricot purée, followed by lemon-coloured and -flavoured fondant. The word 'lemon' simply piped on, with lemon jelly slice and cherry completes.

Lemon Split

Served from a deep freeze or refrigerated counter, this is an ideal line to complete the 'afternoon tea', especially during the summer months.

It is a clean-cutting cake and one that can be guaranteed to melt in the mouth.

4 lb (1820 g) castor sugar
1 lb 6 oz (620 g) shortening
3 oz (85 g) glycerine
¾-oz (21 g) salt
1 lb 14 oz or 1½ pt (850 g or 0·85 litres) egg

3 oz (85 g) lemon paste
3¾ lb (1700 g) high-ratio flour
1¼ oz (50 g) baking powder
2¾ lb (1250 g) milk
lemon yellow colour

Use the sugar-batter method and scale at 8 oz (230 g) into 6 in (15 cm) greased-and-floured sandwich tins, or 11 oz (310 g) into 7 in (18 cm) cottage pans. Spread level, bake at 350–360°F (175–180°C), tipping immediately on to clean cloths or sacks. Leave to become quite cold before finishing.

For this, a lemon filling is required, made in a similar manner to vanilla custard.

Lemon filling

4 lb (1820 g) milk
1 lb (450 g) sugar
2 oz (57 g) butter

6 oz (170 g) cornflour
14 egg yolks
4 oz (110 g) lemon paste

Place most of the milk, along with sugar and butter, into a suitable pan and bring to the boil, mixing eggs, cornflour and remainder of the milk together in a handbowl. When the liquid is near boiling, mix a little hot milk into the cornflour/egg solution and add to the boiling milk. Return to the heat and stir constantly until it thickens. Take off the gas, stir in the lemon paste, add colour as required and allow to go cold. Beat before use.

Types of finish

(a) Reverse the base, split, and pipe in a good layer of the filling. Replace the top, place a stick across and dredge with icing sugar.

(b) Split the base and sandwich with a good layer of lemon cheese. Pipe the lemon filling, spiral fashion, on the top, masking sides first with the filling, followed by roasted coconut.

This is obviously, without deep freeze, a line of limited shelf-life, so precautions should be taken not to finish off more than may reasonably be expected to be sold during a given period.

Honey Fruit Cake

This is another of those lines without pretension to finish, yet so good to eat that it can soon become a firm favourite.

2 lb (910 g) castor sugar	3 lb (1360 g) currants
2 lb (910 g) margarine	4 lb (1820 g) sultanas
8 oz (230 g) shortening	1 lb (450 g) mixed peel
2 lb (910 g) golden syrup	$9\frac{1}{2}$ lb (4410 g) medium flour
$1\frac{1}{2}$ lb (680 g) honey	$4\frac{1}{2}$ oz (130 g) bicarbonate of soda
2 lb (910 g) glycerine	6 oz (170 g) mixed spice
$2\frac{1}{2}$ lb or 1 qt (1140 g or 1·14 litres) egg	1 oz (28 g) ginger
$6\frac{1}{4}$ lb or 5 pt (2840 g or 2·84 litres) milk	

A line of quite good shelf-life under careful storage. Produce by the sugar-batter method, scaling at 12–14 oz (340–400 g) into well-greased cottage pans or 1 lb bread tins. Bake at 360–370°F (180–190°C).

Date Loaf

From the price angle, this is a relatively cheap line to produce, interesting to eat with the chocolate flavour supplied by the cocoa and with a reasonable shelf life.

$2\frac{1}{2}$ lb or 1 qt (1140 g or 1·14 litres) hot water	$\frac{3}{4}$-oz (21 g) bicarbonate of soda
$2\frac{1}{2}$ lb (1140 g) chopped dates	

Soak the above well together, meanwhile creaming thoroughly:

$1\frac{1}{4}$ lb (570 g) castor sugar	1 lb (450 g) margarine
$1\frac{1}{4}$ lb (570 g) brown sugar	$\frac{1}{2}$-oz (14 g) salt
4 oz (110 g) shortening	

Scrape down bowl and beater at intervals. Then add 1 lb 4 oz or 1 pt (570 g or 0·57 litres) egg in four or five lots.

Now sieve together:

1 lb 14 oz (850 g) strong flour $\frac{1}{4}$-oz (7 g) baking powder
4 oz (110 g) cocoa

Add these ingredients alternatively with the date solution, clearing well.

Scale at 12 oz (340 g) for greased and floured or papered 1 lb (450 g) bread tins, level off, and sprinkle on the top a mixture of flaked almonds, sugar nibs and grated chocolate, sieved to preclude any dust.

Bake at 370–380°F (190–195°C).

Sultana and Walnut Cake

8 oz (230 g) golden shortening
1 lb (450 g) margarine
1$\frac{1}{2}$ lb (680 g) sugar
1$\frac{1}{4}$ lb or 1 pt (570 g or 0·57 litres) egg
2 oz (57 g) glycerine
3$\frac{1}{2}$ lb (1530 g) flour

1$\frac{1}{4}$ oz (36 g) baking powder
12 oz (340 g) broken walnuts
1 lb (450 g) sultanas
1$\frac{1}{4}$ lb or 1 pt (570 g or 0·57 litres) milk
vanilla essence
egg colour

Rather cheaper than the cherry and walnut cake, this should, nevertheless, prove to be a good selling line. Produce by the sugar-batter method and scale at 12 oz (340 g) into lined, 1 lb (450 g) bread tins. Level with the moistened back of the hand, place two walnut halves as top decoration, and bake at 370°F (190°C).

If desired, the sultanas may be replaced by an equal amount of chopped dates.

Produced by the sugar-batter method, the baking temperature will be 360–380°F (180–195°C), dependent upon scaling weight.

Sultana and walnut cake

Currant Loaves

8 oz (230 g) shortening
1½ lb (680 g) margarine
2 lb (910 g) sugar
2½ lb or 2 pt (1140 g or 1·14 litres) egg
2 oz (57 g) glycerine

4 lb (1820 g) currants
3 lb (1360 g) flour
½-oz (14 g) baking powder
lemon and vanilla essences
egg colour

Produce by the sugar-batter method, afterwards scaling at 13 oz (370 g) into 1 lb (450 g) well-greased, bread tins. Bake at 360°F (180°C).

If desired, the fruit may be varied by substituting sultanas and peel for part of the currants.

Currant loaves, a very popular line

Coconut Cakes

No. 1

4 oz (110 g) golden shortening
12 oz (340 g) margarine
1½ lb (680 g) sugar
2¼ lb (1020 g) egg

1¼ lb (800 g) flour
½-oz (14 g) baking powder
8 oz (230 g) fine or medium coconut
lemon essence or paste

Prepare nine 6 in (15 cm) hoops or tins by papering in the usual manner. Produce the batter by the sugar-batter method, sieving the coconut through a coarse sieve before mixing with the previously sieved flour and baking powder.

Scale at 12 oz (340 g) into the lined tins, and spread level with the moistened back of the hand.

Two methods of finishing are apparent. The first is to sprinkle the tops of the cakes with medium coconut before baking at 360°F (180°C), thus giving that 'home-made' appearance.

The second method is to leave the tops plain, and, after baking, ice with white fondant, and then pipe the word 'Coconut', using cool, white fondant.

No. 2

Whilst the popularity of coconut cakes can never be doubted, they can, nevertheless, cause some discomfort to denture wearers. This second recipe carries coconut flour and, whilst the flavour of coconut is quite apparent, no annoyance is caused. The purchase of coconut flour may present a problem, for it is not stocked by all sundriesmen, but a small stock, specially obtained for this line, will be found well worth the trouble involved.

$1\frac{3}{4}$ lb (800 g) sugar
14 oz (400 g) margarine
15 oz or $\frac{3}{4}$-pt (430 g or 0·43 litres) egg
$1\frac{1}{4}$ lb (570 g) coconut flour

1 lb 6 oz (620 g) flour
$\frac{3}{4}$-oz (21 g) baking powder
10 oz or $\frac{1}{2}$-pt (280 g or 0·28 litres) milk

It will be noted that all the fat contained in this recipe is margarine, and that no essences or colours are added.

The tins used are, once again oval-shaped 1 lb (450 g) bread tins, well cleaned carefully greased and floured; twelve are required for this mixing.

Prepare by the sugar-batter method, the flour, baking powder and coconut flour being sieved together, and the mixing being thoroughly cleared before scaling at 9 oz (255 g).

Spread level and bake at 360°F (180°C). When baked, remove from the tins and allow to cool before icing with white or pink fondant, afterwards piping on the word 'Coconut', using the same coloured, cool fondant.

Rice Cakes

4 oz (110 g) shortening
12 oz (340 g) margarine
1 lb (450 g) sugar
$1\frac{3}{4}$ lb (800 g) egg

1 lb 9 oz (710 g) flour
3 oz (85 g) ground rice
1 oz (28 g) glycerine

Mixed by the sugar-batter method, the batter is scaled at $9\frac{1}{2}$ oz (270 g) into papered, straight-sided 9 oz (255 g) malt loaf tins, nine being required. Spread level and bake at 360°F (180°C) for approximately 35 min.

Cherry Cakes

Here is à line which always finds favour and the recipe given below will be found to give satisfaction to the customer, both from the point of view of quality and price.

2½ lb (1140 g) sugar
4 oz (110 g) golden shortening
1¾ lb (800 g) margarine
2½ lb or 1 qt (1140 g or 1·14 litres) egg
4 lb 2 oz (1870 g) flour

¼-oz (21 g) baking powder
13 oz (370 g) milk
3 lb (1360 g) cherries
vanilla essence
egg colour

One of the greatest drawbacks in this line is that quite often the cherries tend to sink. Two precautions should be taken to obviate this. First, wash the cherries thoroughly in lukewarm water, drain well and spread out on to a sheet tin covered with a clean cloth, and allow to dry out slowly at bakery temperature. Before use, place the required amount into a sieve, cover with flour and shake the sieve vigorously to remove any surplus.

The second precaution is to ensure that the batter is not beaten too lightly.

Prepare by the usual sugar-batter method. The scaling weight recommended is 14 oz (400 g) in 6 in (15 cm) hoops or tins, previously papered. Spread level, decorate with four or five half-cherries and then bake at 360°F (180°C).

Hoop Cakes

This is quite a popular line, which assists in keeping the 'crumb' problem within reasonable limits.

1¼ lb (570 g) sugar
1 lb (450 g) margarine
1 lb (450 g) egg
2½ lb (1140 g) flour
1¼ oz (36 g) baking powder
1 lb (450 g) sieved cake crumbs

1 lb (450 g) currants
8 oz (230 g) sultanas
4 oz (110 g) peel
1¼ lb or 1 pt (570 g or 0·57 litres) milk
lemon essence
egg colour

Produce by the sugar-batter method, mixing the sieved crumbs in with the flour. Scale at 11 oz (310 g) into 7 in (18 cm) greased sandwich tins, spread level, and bake at 370°F (190°C).

Honey Cake

A line with an unusual flavour.

12 oz (340 g) Barbados sugar
1½ lb (680 g) margarine
1¼ lb or 1 pt (570 g or 0·57 litres) egg
1¼ lb (570 g) honey

4 lb (1820 g) flour
1 oz (28 g) baking powder
¼-oz (21 g) cinnamon
10 oz or ½-pt (280 g or 0·28 litres) milk

Add the honey to the margarine and sugar and prepare by the sugar-batter method. Scale at 12 oz (340 g) into 1 lb (450 g) greased bread tins, spread level, add a sprinkling of flaked almonds as top decoration, if costs permit, and bake at 360°F (180°C).

Dundee Cakes

The high price that has, of necessity, to be charged for both this line and for genoa cakes has undoubtedly led directly to a lessening of demand. One way to reduce the price, whilst maintaining quality, is to scale the cakes smaller.

Scaling weight for both lines may be restricted to 1 lb (450 g) into 6 in (15 cm) hoops or tins, previously lined with paper.

Traditionally, both these lines are completed by a top decoration of split almonds, but no elaboration is required regarding the very high price of these and the labour costs required for placing them in position. Whilst tradition dies hard, a slight saving in costs, and consequent reduction in selling price, can be effected by substituting a sprinkling of fine flake almonds.

2 lb (910 g) Barbados sugar
2 lb (910 g) castor sugar
1 lb (450 g) golden shortening
3 lb (1360 g) margarine
4 oz (110 g) glycerine
5 lb or 2 qt (2270 g or 2·27 litres) egg
5 lb 14 oz (2670 g) flour

$\frac{1}{2}$-oz (14 g) baking powder
6$\frac{1}{2}$ lb (2950 g) sultanas
1$\frac{1}{2}$ lb (680 g) peel
rum, almond and vanilla essences
egg colour
2 oz (57 g) black jack

Baking temperature 360°F (180°C). Sugar-batter method.

Brazil Pound Cake

2$\frac{1}{2}$ lb (1140 g) castor sugar
1 lb (450 g) golden shortening
1 lb (450 g) butter
2 oz (57 g) glycerine
1 oz (28 g) salt
2$\frac{1}{2}$ lb or 1 qt (1140 g or 1·14 litres) egg

3 lb (1360 g) flaked brazil nuts
3 lb 10 oz (1650 g) flour
$\frac{1}{4}$-oz (7 g) baking powder
10 oz or $\frac{1}{2}$-pt (280 g or 0·28 litres) milk
3 lb (1360 g) raisins

Using washed, plumped raisins, this is a juicy cake, full of flavour, and one to be enjoyed.

Produce by the sugar-batter method, scale at 12 oz (340 g) into papered 1 lb (450 g) bread tins, damp down, sprinkle with flaked brazil nuts, and bake at 350–360°F (175–180°C), taking care not to overbake, thus preserving the moist eating characteristic.

Brazil pound cake

Louisa Cakes

This line is plain cake in its most simple form, but delicious to eat. It does not contain essences or flavours; it is a cake for the customer who can both appreciate and afford it, for it is certainly not cheap to make.

You need:

4 lb (1820 g) castor sugar
6 oz (170 g) golden shortening
2 lb 10 oz (1190 g) butter

$7\frac{1}{2}$ lb or 3 qt (3480 g or 3·48 litres) egg
$6\frac{1}{2}$ lb (2950 g) scone flour
egg colour

Produce by the sugar-batter method, scaling at 11 oz (310 g) into well-greased 1 lb (450 g) loaf tins, or as desired.

In order that the cake may be enjoyed at its nicest, small units are possibly the best to produce.

Baking temperatures: 360–380°F (180–195°C) according to scaling weight.

Lime Tarts

Here is another flavour only very rarely used, yet, using the fresh fruit paste, a wonderful taste is produced.

Line the required number of sandwich tins with sweet-paste in the normal way. Brush the bottom of the pastry with water and sprinkle with currants, sultanas, and peel.

Prepare the filling by the flour-batter method, using:

$1\frac{1}{2}$ lb (680 g) weak flour

12 oz (340 g) margarine

12 oz (340 g) shortening

1 lb 2 oz (510 g) castor sugar

$1\frac{1}{4}$ lb or 1 pt (570 g or 0·57 litres) egg

$1\frac{1}{4}$ lb or 1 pt (570 g or 0·57 litres) milk

$1\frac{1}{2}$ oz (43 g) lime paste

lemon yellow colour

2lb 2 oz (970 g) scone flour

For a 6 in (15 cm) sandwich tin, approximately 7 oz (200 g) filling will be required. This should be scaled, placed in the prepared tin and spread level.

A sprinkling of strip almonds may be added to some before baking at 370°F (190°C).

After baking, those almond decorated may be glazed with boiled apricot purée and water icing or thin, warm fondant.

Those not decorated may be masked with pale green fondant with the word 'lime' piped on in chocolate fondant.

Honey and Pineapple Topping

Quite often an ancillary can transform an otherwise ordinary line, and so with this topping. Although only two uses are given, the reader will readily find many more.

To provide the topping, mix well together:

2 lb (910 g) honey

1 lb 2 oz (510 g) melted butter

$\frac{1}{4}$-oz (7 g) salt

2 oz (57 g) lemon paste

Then add:

$3\frac{1}{4}$ lb (1480 g) crushed pineapple

12 oz (340 g) coconut

14 oz (400 g) cornflakes

Mix all well together, ensuring that the pineapple is well drained before use. Although, as mentioned, very many uses are possible, the first use is on a madeira type cake, produced from the general-purpose mixing and the same mixing used for the bakewell type tart, baked in a sponge sandwich tin, previously lined with sweetpaste.

After scaling the batter in the normal way, level, then scale the required amount of topping and sprinkle over the surface. Bake at 380–410°F (195–210°C), depending on the quality of the basic mix.

A light dredging of icing sugar provides a simple, quick and suitable finish.

Walnut Loaf

This walnut loaf falls into the limbo of being hardly cake, yet certainly not bread.

From the edible viewpoint, it appears to be a line to create either the greatest enthusiasm or deepest apathy, with no 'in betweens'.

A line that evokes either a love or hate response—walnut loaf

Whisk to full sponge:

1¼ lb or 1 pt (570 g or 0·57 litres) egg   12 oz (340 g) castor sugar

Add to the above:

1¼ lb or 1 pt (570 g or 0·57 litres) milk

Sieve together, add and partially clear:

4½ lb (2040 g) strong flour   3 oz (85 g) baking powder
1½ oz (42 g) salt

Add and clear:

1¾ lb (800 g) milk

Add and clear:

1¾ lb (800 g) walnuts

Scale at 1 lb 2 oz (510 g) into 1 lb (450 g), greased, bread or oval tins and bake at 380–400°F (195–205°C) for approximately 40 min.

Walnut Fruit Cakes

In these days of so very much high-ratio cake, it is good to have what may be termed 'old-fashioned' cake, as this is, yet different by virtue of the walnuts and fruit. A cake of good quality, the shelf life will be greatly enhanced by wrapping in moisture-proof film.

6 lb (2730 g) castor sugar   1 oz (28 g) lemon paste
5 lb (2270 g) butter   7½ lb (3380 g) weak flour
1 lb (450 g) shortening   6 lb (2730 g) sultanas
6 oz (170 g) glycerine   2 lb (910 g) glacé cherries
7½ lb or 6 pt (3380 g or 3·38 litres) egg   3 lb (1360 g) walnuts (lightly chopped)

Walnut fruit cake

Produce by the sugar batter method, scaling into papered hoops or tins at the desired weight; the cake illustrated was scaled at 1 lb 6 oz (620 g) into a $6\frac{1}{2}$ in (16·5 cm) hoop. Moisten the tops, when levelling, with water, baking at 360–370°F (180–190°C) depending on weight. As always, it is preferable to bake with a full oven, retaining the maximum humidity. It is an obvious advantage to decorate the tops of the cakes with walnuts before baking. Pecans, where obtainable, are superior to walnuts for this line.

Pineapple Cake

Obviously, the inclusion of pineapple is going to restrict the shelf life of this somewhat, but that can certainly be a very strong sales aid, for does not the vast majority of all confectionery taste that much better for eating really fresh?

2 lb (910 g) castor sugar	$\frac{1}{2}$-oz (14 g) salt
$1\frac{1}{2}$ lb (680 g) butter	$1\frac{1}{4}$ lb (570 g) chopped walnuts
8 oz (230 g) shortening	2 lb (910 g) small diced, drained pineapple
2 oz (57 g) glycerine	1 lb (450 g) glacé cherries
$2\frac{1}{2}$ lb or 2 pt (1140 g or 1·14 litres) egg	$\frac{1}{2}$-oz (14 g) lemon paste
$2\frac{1}{4}$ lb (1020 g) weak flour	$\frac{1}{2}$-oz (14 g) orange paste
8 oz (230 g) scone flour	

Produce by the sugar-batter method, clearing gently but well in the final stages. Scale at 14 oz (400 g) into papered 1 lb (450 g) bread tins, spread level with hands moistened with water, decorating top with pineapple rings and whole cherries in the centres of the rings. Some rings are rather too thick, so it is quite a sensible plan to split them midway, using a sharp knife—carefully—for the process. Bake at 360°F (180°C) and, as soon as the cakes are taken from the oven, wash the top decoration with a strong gum arabic solution. The enhanced appearance is well worth the slight extra trouble.

Rum Moulds

A deliciously light cake that does not rely upon finish in the true sense. A sugar-batter cake, scaled into greased fancy moulds, previously nutted with nibbed almonds, the flavour comes from an immersion in rum syrup.

$1\frac{3}{4}$ lb (800 g) butter or margarine	4 oz (110 g) shortening
$3\frac{1}{2}$ lb (1530 g) castor sugar	1 oz (28 g) orange paste
1 lb 6 oz (620 g) egg yolk	1 oz (28 g) lemon paste
1 lb 6 oz (620 g) whole egg	$1\frac{1}{2}$ lb (680 g) milk
3 lb (1360 g) cake flour	$1\frac{1}{2}$ oz (42 g) baking powder

Produce by the sugar-batter method, filling the prepared tins two-thirds full and baking at 370°F (190°C).

When baked, remove from the tins, allow to cool, then immerse in the following syrup as required:

3 lb (1360 g) cube sugar   1 lb 10 oz (740 g) water
1 lb (450 g) glucose

Bring to the boil, skim, allow to cool, then add 4 oz (110 g) liqueur rum.

Rum moulds

Many types of fancy tins may be used for this line, and here a variety of sizes, to appeal to families of all sizes, could very well be used.

Golden Moulds

Was the previous base too expensive? Well, here is a cheaper one but, nevertheless, an extremely nice cake if properly handled.

Cream very lightly:

2 lb (910 g) golden shortening   6 oz (170 g) milk powder
1 lb (450 g) butter or margarine   3 oz (85 g) glycerine
3 lb (1360 g) weak flour

Whisk 3 lb (1360 g) egg and 3 lb (1360 g) castor sugar to semi-sponge. Add to the above in five quantities.

Dissolve and add to the above in a steady stream on first speed:

2 lb (910 g) castor sugar   3 oz (85 g) salt
2¼ lb or 1 qt (1140 g or 1·14 litres) water   egg colour

Finally, sieve together, add and clear:

2¾ lb (1250 g) weak flour   1½ oz (43 g) baking powder

The reader will immediately have realised that the above is the flour-batter method and should, of course, be scraped down at intervals.

Scale into well-cleaned, greased and floured fluted moulds, weight according to mould size, and bake at 360–390°F (180–200°C), depending on size, tipping on to clean cloth or such as soon as baked.

To finish when cold, mask with boiled apricot purée, followed by pale yellow fondant. A seasonable finish is chicken motifs and chocolate piping, or, alternatively simply completed with half cherries and angelica.

This particular mixing is also suitable for gateau bases.

Cherry Banana Loaves

Rather heavy in character, this is another unusual line which, if given the opportunity, could prove to be a regular favourite.

The banana may be of the tinned variety, comparatively recently introduced here, or may be fresh, peeled and mashed. If the latter, an extra 50%

Cherry banana loaves

of requirements should be added and purchased to allow for loss in skin weight.

The recipe is:

10¼ oz (300 g) butter or margarine

10¼ oz (300 g) castor sugar

1 oz (28 g) glycerine

15 oz or ¾-pt (430 g or 0·43 litres) egg

2¼ lb (1020 g) weak flour

1¼ oz (36 g) baking powder

¾-oz (21 g) salt

egg colour

14 oz (400 g) chopped maraschino cherries

1 lb (450 g) chopped walnuts

2½ lb (1140 g) mashed banana

Produce by the sugar-batter method, adding the banana after all the egg has been added and well cleared, afterwards proceeding normally.

Scale at 12 oz (340 g) into 1 lb (450 g) bread tins, either well greased and floured or papered as desired. Spread level with the moistened hand, place three walnut halves on the top and bake at 370°F (190°C).

Angel Flan

Extremely tender, this line deserves to be displayed in a refrigerated counter. Preferably it should be boxed on completion, using window boxes, but could be ideal for serving in tea room or restaurant.

The base is of high-ratio cake which, when cold, is split, sandwiched with cold, beaten vanilla custard, and the top is patterned fruit set in table jelly.

First, the base:

5 lb (2270 g) high-ratio flour

6¼ lb (2930 g) castor sugar

1½ lb (680 g) high-ratio shortening

6 oz (170 g) baking powder

12 oz (340 g) milk powder

2½ oz (70 g) salt

3 lb (1360 g) water

With the exception of the water, place all in a machine bowl fitted with beater and mix together. Add all the water gradually over 1 min on slow speed, and mix for a further 3 min on slow speed. It will, of course, be necessary to scrape down the bowl and beater several times.

Mix together 2 lb (910 g) egg and 2 lb (910 g) water and add gradually to the mixing over 2 min, mixing for a further 4–5 min, scraping down bowl and beater as required.

Scale at 7 oz (200 g) into 6 in (15 cm) greased and floured sandwich tins, baking at 375–380°F (190–195°C).

To finish run a small amount of table jelly into a clean, rinsed 6 in (15 cm) sandwich tin and allow to set. Pattern with fruit to choice, quantity dependent on costings, top with jelly and refrigerate to set.

It is then comparatively quick to finish the flan, by splitting the sandwich and layering with vanilla custard.

Hold the jelly/fruit mould in hot water for approximately 7–8 secs and reverse on to the top of the sandwich, placing in position on the prepared base.

Angel flans

Date and Walnut Cakes

Here is a cheaper type of cake which, nevertheless, can be very popular, to be sold at a competitive price.

3 lb (1360 g) castor sugar	$2\frac{1}{2}$ oz (70 g) baking powder
2 lb (910 g) margarine	1 oz (28 g) orange paste
1 lb (450 g) shortening	$2\frac{1}{2}$ lb or 2 pt (1140 g or 1·14 litres) milk
4 oz (110 g) glycerine	egg colour
$2\frac{1}{2}$ lb or 1 qt (1140 g or 1·14 litres) egg	$1\frac{1}{4}$ lb (800 g) broken walnuts
7 lb (3150 g) weak flour	$2\frac{1}{4}$ lb (1020 g) chopped dates

Produce by the sugar-batter method, scaling into lined 1 lb (450 g) bread tins. Spread level with the moistened back of the hand, using as top decoration walnut halves placed carefully in position, the number used as many as costings will allow. Bake at 370°F (190°C). This line will obviously benefit by wrapping in film after thorough cooling.

Date and walnut cakes

Cherry and Walnut Cakes

1¼ lb (680 g) margarine
8 oz (230 g) shortening
2 lb (910 g) castor sugar
2 oz (57 g) glycerine
2¼ lb or 2 pt (1140 g or 1·14 litres) egg
½-oz (14 g) baking powder

3¼ lb (1480 g) weak flour
3½ lb (1530 g) cherries
2¼ lb (1020 g) chopped walnuts
vanilla essence
egg colour

Produce by the sugar-batter method, adding the washed and well dried cherries, together with the lightly broken walnuts, clearing well and carefully distributing the fruit and nuts.

Scale at the desired weight, spread level with the moistened hands and add a few carefully placed walnuts or pecans as top decoration before baking at 360°F (180°C).

Cherry and walnut cakes

Maraschino Banana Cakes

Delightful little cakes to eat, reasonable in cost, simple in production, low in labour costs. Could one ask for more? In short, well worth a trial.

4 lb (1820 g) castor sugar
2½ lb (1140 g) margarine
½ lb (680 g) shortening
1¼ lb or 1 pt (570 g or 0·57 litres) egg
2½ lb (1140 g) mashed bananas

¼-oz (7 g) salt
3 lb 6 oz (1530 g) weak flour
1½ oz (42 g) baking powder
12 oz (340 g) milk
14 oz (400 g) maraschino cherries

Maraschino banana cakes: shapes . . .

. . . and texture

Produce by the sugar-batter method, adding the banana after all the egg has been incorporated. Scale into well-greased and -floured fancy-shaped gateau tins and bake at 350°F (175°C).

Cherry Rings

This is quite a pleasant cake to eat, simple and without finish. The maraschino cherries should be well drained and lightly chopped, but not too small. The method of mixing is simple, if unusual, with the finished batter being quite 'thin' or 'wet'.

8 oz (230 g) shortening	$\frac{3}{4}$-oz (21 g) baking powder
1 lb 6 oz (620 g) medium flour	$\frac{1}{2}$-oz (14 g) salt
$\frac{1}{8}$-oz (3·5 g) mixed spice	$\frac{1}{4}$-oz (7 g) cinnamon
1$\frac{1}{4}$ lb (570 g) castor sugar	$\frac{1}{8}$-oz (3·5 g) nutmeg

Sieve the above dry ingredients together.

1$\frac{1}{4}$ lb or 1 pt (570 g or 0·57 litres) milk   10 oz or $\frac{1}{2}$-pt (280 g or 0·28 litres) egg
12 oz (340 g) chopped maraschino cherries

Cream the fat quite lightly, then add to it the dry, sieved ingredients. Mix in, add approximately half the milk, beat for 3 min, add the eggs in two lots, followed by the remaining milk and beat again for 2 min. The bowl and beater will, of course, have been well scraped down at intervals. Fold in the cherries and scale into greased and floured ring tins. Bake at 370–380°F (190–195°C).

Almond and Raisin Cake

With no pretensions whatever as regards finishing off, this is a down to earth cake of good eating quality. Once included on a production list regularly, it is certain to prove very popular.

3 lb (1360 g) castor sugar	$\frac{1}{4}$-oz (7 g) salt
2$\frac{3}{4}$ lb (1250 g) butter	$\frac{1}{2}$-oz (14 g) baking powder
4 oz (110 g) shortening	5 oz or $\frac{1}{4}$-pt (140 g or 0·14 litres) milk
3 oz (85 g) glycerine	3 lb (1360 g) roasted flaked or strip almonds
2$\frac{1}{4}$ lb (1020 g) egg	3 lb (1360 g) raisins
3$\frac{1}{4}$ lb (1480 g) flour	egg colour

Soak the raisins in hot water for approximately 20 min before use, draining and drying well before adding to the batter.

Produce the cake by the sugar-batter method, scaling at 12 oz (340 g) into either greased and floured or paper lined 1 lb (450 g) loaf tins. Sprinkle the tops with almonds as desired after damping down and levelling off.

Bake in a humid oven at 360–370°F (180–190°C).

Almond and raisin cake

Banana Loaf

Opinions vary on this particular line, popular in the USA, but opinion in Britain ranges from 'excellent' to 'stodgy'.

4 lb (1820 g) castor sugar   8 oz (230 g) golden shortening
3 lb (1360 g) butter

Cream the above lightly, then add gradually and cream well in:

3¼ lb (1480 g) egg

Now add:

8 lb (3600 g) mashed banana

Cream well in and add:

2 lb (910 g) buttermilk

When this is broken in, add and partially clear:

8½ lb (3830 g) flour of medium strength   3 oz (85 g) baking powder
2 oz (57 g) salt

Finally add and clear:

2 lb (910 g) strip almonds

For this recipe, it will obviously be more convenient to use tinned mashed banana and, quite probably, cheaper.

Banana loaf

Scale at 12–14 oz (340–400 g) into previously well greased or papered 1 lb (450 g) loaf tins. Moisten down, spreading level, and adding a sprinkle of strip almonds. Bake at 370°F (190°C).

SUET

Suet is the one type of fat rarely seen in the bakery. Yet, it has any number of uses, in addition to the very popular one of mincemeat. By 'suet', of course, is meant the prepared type, which arrives ready for use in the packet—not that obtainable from the butcher.

Possibly some of the nicest chou paste seen by the writer was produced using suet instead of the normal butter or margarine, etc. To the reader desiring to try this, just substitute suet for the usual fat, keeping recipe and method of all other ingredients as usual.

Hallowe'en Cake

4 lb (1820 g) flour	2 oz (57 g) ginger
1 lb (450 g) prepared suet	3 oz (85 g) bicarbonate of soda
1 lb (450 g) soft brown sugar	1 oz (28 g) mixed spice
$3\frac{1}{2}$ lb (1530 g) treacle or part golden syrup	1 lb 14 oz or $1\frac{1}{2}$ pt (850 g or 0·85 litres) milk
$3\frac{1}{2}$ lb (1530 g) cake crumbs	

Place all the dry ingredients into the machine bowl fitted with the hook, and start the machine on first speed. Add the treacle, followed by the milk, to produce a clear dough.

If desired this may lie overnight before scaling at 1 lb (450 g). Mould, place into well-greased 1 lb (450 g) loaf tins, wash with milk and place split almonds in position.

Bake at 340°F (170°C), washing the tops of the cakes with a gum arabic solution on withdrawal from the oven.

Country Cake

Despite the unorthodox method of mixing, this is a really tasty, old-fashioned type of cake to eat.

The method of mixing is extremely simple, and one that an unskilled person should be able to manage without difficulty.

1 lb (450 g) suet	1 lb 14 oz or $1\frac{1}{2}$ pt (850 g or 0·85 litres) milk

Place together in a suitable pan and, stirring constantly, bring to the boil and allow to cool.

Beat 12 oz (400 g) egg well to break the grain, add to the above and beat well in.

Sieve together and add:

1 oz (28 g) white pepper	2 lb (910 g) brown sugar
2 oz (56 g) cinnamon	3 lb (1360 g) weak flour
$\frac{3}{4}$-oz (21 g) bicarbonate of soda	

Partially clear, then add:

4 oz (110 g) roasted flaked almonds	1 lb currants (450 g)
8 oz (230 g) cut peel	1 lb (450 g) raisins or sultanas

and clear well.

Scale at 12 oz (340 g) into 1 lb (450 g) greased and floured bread tins, spread level, sprinkle with flaked almonds, and bake at 370°F (190°C).

Here, again, is another cake that requires a week to mature.

Christmas Puddings

Whilst one could debate whether these constitute a line rightfully demanding a place in this chapter, they are, along with many other lines, reverting back to the smaller producer, customers being ready to pay for the quality article which they are unable to obtain elsewhere.

What quantity are we to produce? For the reader with a catering outlet, the problem is relatively simple, but for the reader producing these for the first time, perhaps a reasonably small batch is to be advised, but any remaining unsold can, if properly stored, be sold next year. Hence, there is no wastage problem.

Basins

Are we to use the traditional pot, or glazed earthenware, basin?

Advantages here are that they are traditional and useful to the customer afterwards. Being traditional, they do have that 'old-fashioned' appeal of their own, give a greater stamp of individuality on the product and look different to the mass produced article.

Disadvantages are that they are easily chipped and broken, with attendant dangers to the product, and are rather expensive. They require pudding cloths, which may be of the linen type, in which case, after use, they may be boiled for further use; an alternative could be the thin muslin type which, depending on quality, could be either disposable or may be laundered.

Foil basins

Complete with lids, these are light and convenient to handle. They are specially treated with a mould inhibitor but silicone liners should be used. Also they are considerably cheaper than the pot basin. Once the pudding batter has been scaled into the basin, the lids are secured by a special 'lip' and here, perhaps, is one of the drawbacks in that it is not usual to open them to examine the contents, which is possible with the pot basin. This can also be an advantage immediately after cooking, for there is no pudding cloth to remove.

Perhaps the greatest drawback in using these is that they are used in such large quantities by the factory producer that the customer might be lead to believe that the puddings were not home made.

Plastic containers

Most probably, these are the answer to the problem, for they are light, durable and practically unbreakable, whilst, from the point of view of price, they compare quite favourably with the traditional 'pot' basin. Naturally, the price will depend upon size and quantity purchased, but speaking of size, why not produce some of the puddings in small sizes, say sufficient for two people?

These plastic containers require no greasing or other preparation, save to ensure that they are clean and dry. If a steamer is being used, no pudding cloths will be necessary as each will be covered with a greaseproof paper disc, and each wire tray can be covered by a sheet of greaseproof paper laid lightly on the top to prevent the ingress of water.

For boiling, the pudding cloths would be required as for the china basins, and should the reader query how the string may be tied, a lip is provided on the containers for this purpose.

Method

Now for the recipe:

1 lb 2 oz (510 g) weak flour
3 lb (1360 g) Tates fourths sugar
3 lb (1360 g) breadcrumbs
3 lb (1360 g) prepared suet
2 lb (910 g) mixed peel
3½ lb (1530 g) currants
3½ lb (1530 g) sultanas
3½ lb (1530 g) raisins
1¼ oz (36 g) baking powder
12 oz (340 g) grated carrots
2½ oz (70 g) mixed spice

1¼ oz (36 g) nutmeg
1½ oz (43 g) salt
3 oz (85 g) lemon paste (or zest and juice of fresh lemons)
2 oz (57 g) orange paste (or zest and juice of fresh oranges)
5 oz or ¼-pt (140 g or 0·14 litres) rum
15 oz or ¾-pt (430 g or 0·43 litres) beer, stout or old ale
1 lb 14 oz or 1½ pt (852 g or 8·5 litres) egg
2 oz (57 g) caramel colour

The puddings will be no better than the ingredients that they are made from, so, especially from the point of view of the fruit, buy the best that is obtainable. Wizened and dried up fruits will not impart the luscious flavour required.

Good bold currants, fleshy sultanas of good colour and last, but not least, the beautiful large seedless raisins are the types of fruit required. All should be well washed in lukewarm water, drained, and allowed to dry on sheet tins or boards previously covered with clean cloths or sacks. Immediately before use, pick over very carefully to remove all stones, stalks and other foreign bodies, together with inedible individual fruits.

This washing will ensure that, during cooking, the fruits will 'plump up' and make for moist eating. It is of the utmost folly to neglect this preparation, for use of dirty fruit is betrayed by gritty eating of the article, together with the ever present danger of more serious trouble—that of deleterious matter in foodstuffs.

The prepared suet is as purchased and, I am sure, preferable and cheaper in the long run to buying what we may term the 'raw' suet from the butcher. It may be purchased to order in larger packs than that normally seen exposed for retail sale.

The day previous to mixing the puddings, scale and pick over the washed fruit, mix all well together, place in a suitable bowl, add the rum, covering over with a clean damp cloth. Added this way, the flavour will not disperse during cooking, but be retained in the fruit and, during storage and maturity, will percolate through the pudding. The amount of rum shown is the minimum and could, if costs permit be increased to double with advantage to the finished flavour.

Mixing

If using the machine, place all the dry ingredients together, sieving where practicable. Add the liquids, previously mixed together and to which the caramel colour or 'black jack' has been added. Mix all well together on slow speed, using the dough hook or pastry attachment, scraping well down as necessary. After thorough mixing add the fruit and clear gently so as not to tear it and discolour the crumb.

Should the reader prefer to mix by hand, sieve all the dry ingredients together where practicable, make a large bay, distributing the mixed fruit round the edges. Add the liquids to the bay and mix all well toglether.

Scaling

When this stage has been reached, scale off the batter at the required weights, ball up in the hands and drop into the chosen basins. Pot or china basins should be well greased with fresh, creamed compound fat, but the foil or plastic basins will not require any treatment save to check that they are clean and dry.

Quantities in relation to basin size should be carefully ascertained, for too much can, during expansion in cooking, force off the cloths or, in the case of the foil basins, force off the foil lid, whilst too little could permit the entry of water into the basin. As a rough guide, after the batter has been put into the basins, the distance between the top of the pudding and the top of the basin should be no greater than one $\frac{1}{2}$-in (1·3 cm).

In the case of pot or plastic basins, place two discs of greaseproof paper on the top of the puddings and tie up with a clean cloth. To do this, place the square of cloth over the top of the basin with the corners overhanging. Take a length of string twice round the basin and under the rim, knotting tightly. Bring opposite corners of cloth to the top of the basin and tie with a reef knot, left over right and under, right over left and under, repeating the process with the other two corners.

Using the foil basins, slip the lid into the recess made for the purpose, thumbing the edges well down to retain the lid in position.

Cooking the puddings

Boiling or steaming will depend upon the number being produced and the facilities available.

Small quantities may be boiled in a large saucepan or other container, or a copper boiler will be found quite satisfactory.

Have the water boiling vigourously and drop in the puddings carefully, ensuring that all are completely immersed in the water during the whole of the cooking time. Foil basins should be lowered in with a basket or net, otherwise difficulty could be experienced in taking them from the water. The water *must* be kept boiling during the whole of the cooking time, and if, as will be required, more water must be added, then it *must* be boiling water. To keep loss down to a minimum and preserve flavour in the pudding, keep the lid in position during boiling.

As a guide, a $1\frac{1}{2}$ lb (680 g) pudding will require a minimum of 4 h cooking and maximum of 6 h, with other sizes in proportion.

Alternatively, and if available, the puddings may be cooked in a commercial steamer at $\frac{1}{2}$-lb (230 g) pressure.

At the end of the cooking period, if being boiled, the water must be kept constantly boiling as the puddings are being removed. If a basket has been employed, lift it out of the water, otherwise remove them one by one, using a piece of new broom stail or similar wood to which a large pot hook has been firmly screwed in at the end. Whilst this work is proceeding, assistants should be employed removing the cloths immediately—a relatively simple (though warm) job, if, as suggested, reef knots have been used to tie the cloths. The greaseproof paper discs may be left in position undisturbed, but the cloths should be thoroughly boiled, dried, and carefully stored for re-use. Allow the puddings to cool off thoroughly in a dry store room until quite cold, generally overnight.

The next day, clean round the basins thoroughly, place a clean disc of greaseproof paper on the top and prepare for display and sale. This can involve the use of greaseproof paper, muslin, seasonally motified transparent cellulose, red ribbon, holly piquets etc., and not forgetting that most important item to comply with the law, a label stating the ingredients used in the manufacture of the puddings. It is, also, a good plan to include a note informing the customer that the puddings should be boiled for two hours prior to serving.

Referring again to the foil basin, after removal from the steamer do *not* remove the lid, but allow to cool naturally. Well clean the outside of the foil and dress for display and sale.

In conclusion, perhaps we may consider some of the causes of the puddings going mouldy, for fear of this could well deter a reader from 'having a go'.

The root cause of mouldiness here is undoubtedly moisture. A variety of reasons exist, the most frequent ones being too soft a mixture, scaling insufficient into the basins, thus leaving space for water to enter during cooking; allowing the water to go off the boil is so fatally easy, as is trying to rush the cooking, thus leaving an uncooked core. The temptation to leave the cloths on when the puddings have been removed from the water is very great, especially if any number are being produced, for it is certainly a hot job, but one where discipline will repay. Adequate cooling in a dry atmosphere is a 'must' as is dry storage.

To produce or not to produce? Whilst the choice must be made by the reader, it has always been my experience that seasonal goods of top quality bring in new 'all the year round' customers, and Christmas Puddings are a particularly good line for they may be made *now,* well in advance, and if the few simple rules are followed there is no waste. Nothing but good can come of the exercise properly carried out.

Genoa Cakes

4 lb (1820 g) castor sugar	5 lb (2270 g) currants
1 lb (450 g) golden shortening	4 lb (1820 g) sultanas.
3 lb (1360 g) margarine	3½ lb (1530 g) cherries
4 oz (110 g) glycerine	2 lb (910 g) peel
5 lb or 2 qt (2270 g or 2·27 litres) egg	rum. almond and vanilla essences
6¼ lb (2840 g) flour	egg colour
¾-oz (21 g) baking powder	

Baking temperature 350–360°F (175–180°C). Sugar-batter method.

Simnel Cakes

Whilst it is the author's opinion that the wisest policy in the matter of festive seasonal fare is to produce the finest quality, this rather cheaper fruit cake base is included for the sake of completeness, and to cater for the reader to whom this recipe, quite good in its way, appeals.

The alternative is to adapt the wedding cake slab, described later in this chapter, to this traditional mid-Lent cake.

2 lb (910 g) Barbados sugar	2¼ lb (1140 g) sultanas
8 oz (230 g) golden shortening	1 lb (450 g) mixed peel
1½ lb (680 g) margarine	½-oz (14 g) mixed spice
2½ lb or 1 qt (1140 g or 1·14 litres) egg	½-oz (14 g) nutmeg
2 lb 14 oz (1310 g) flour	black jack
½-oz (14 g) salt	egg colour
2½ lb (1140 g) currants	lemon and almond essences
2 oz (57 g) glycerine	

These specialities normally have an inside layer of almond paste which, it may be found in these days of high costs and prices, may price the cakes beyond the range of the customer's purse. Should this be the case, it could be omitted and, together with scaling smaller units, should be sufficient to keep this line within the purchasing power of the customer.

I feel that this is a course to avoid if at all possible, it being preferable to produce the traditional article, charging a price commensurate.

For the confectioner wishing to produce the traditional cake containing the centre layer of almond paste, the following recipe will be found quite satisfactory:

3¾ lb (1700 g) castor sugar	egg colour
2½ lb (1140 g) ground almonds	
10 oz or ½-pt (280 g or 0·28 litres) egg	

This should be prepared before the cake mixing, made by the sugar-batter process, is ready for scaling.

Mix the almonds and sugar, make a bay, add the egg, colour and produce a stiff paste, afterwards scaling at the required weight, moulding round and rolling to a size slightly smaller than the hoop or tin.

Scaling weights will, of course, vary with the size of hoops or tins used but recommended weights for 6 in (15 cm) tins are 7 oz (200 g) batter top and bottom with 6 oz (170 g) almond paste, whilst 7 in (18 cm) tins require 12 oz (340 g) batter top and bottom with an 11 oz (310 g) layer of almond paste.

It is advisable to scale the bottom layers of a full tray, spread level, and then, with the aid of an assistant, add the almond paste layer, afterwards completing scaling of the batter. Level normally, adding no top decoration, and bake at 350–360°F (175–180°C) with other sizes in proportion.

After baking, allow the cakes to become cold before proceeding with the top decoration.

For the weights of the cakes indicated, 6 oz (170 g) and 11 oz (310 g) respectively of almond paste will be required for each cake. This is produced by mixing equal quantities of ground almonds and castor sugar, with sufficient egg and egg colour to give a paste of good modelling consistency: $3\frac{3}{4}$ lb (1700 g) sugar and $3\frac{3}{4}$ lb (1700 g) ground almonds require approximately $\frac{1}{2}$- pt (280 g or 0·28 litres) egg, together with egg colour.

Remove the cakes from the tins or hoops, strip off the papers and replace with a double thickness of greaseproof paper standing approximately 1 in (2·6 cm) above the top level of the cake, using a spot of egg, as necessary, to hold the paper in position.

Afterwards brush the tops of the cakes with boiled apricot purée before replacing close together on a paper-lined sheet tin.

The required amount of almond paste should now be applied, and this may take the form of a ring, afterwards forked to give a roughened appearance or an attractive design 'pinched', using marzipan nippers. Again the paste can be divided into balls of equal size, moulded round, or pear shaped and placed in position.

For the confectioner requiring a more speedy finish, an almond paste may be produced from one-third each of castor sugar, icing sugar and ground almonds, mixed to a fairly stiff consistency with whole eggs, and sufficient egg colour to give an attractive tint. This is then piped on to the outer edge, using a savoy bag and large star tube.

Whichever method is adopted, the paste should now be carefully egg-washed and the cakes placed on wires or upturned sheet tin in an oven of 480°F (250°C) to toast the paste to a nice, golden brown. Immediately on withdrawal from the oven, brush with a gum arabic solution, stock syrup, or boiled apricot purée. Of all three methods, I would strongly recommend the former for having the quality of a 'non-sticky' finish.

When the cakes have again been allowed to cool, remove the paper bands. The decoration can now be continued by flooding the centre of the cake with fondant warmed and reduced to the correct consistency, coloured as desired to lend attractiveness to the window display. The word 'Simnel' is now piped on, using cool chocolate fondant, and the cake completed with small marzipan fruits, woolly chickens, or simply one or two small piped sugar flowers with a small spray of maidenhair fern.

The sides of the cakes can now be finished by the application of a double thickness of greaseproof paper, tied in position with a narrow ribbon of colour to match the fondant, a double thickness of transparent cellulose, again tied with matching ribbon, and with the top edges of the paper snipped to give a 'frilly' finish. Alternatively, use a silver or gold cake band.

Bury Simnels

Very much a local speciality, there is, however, no reason why these should not become popular in any locality.

12 oz (340 g) Barbados sugar
12 oz (340 g) margarine
½-oz (14 g) black jack
4 oz (110 g) egg
7½ oz (210 g) milk
1½ lb (680 g) flour
½-oz (14 g) yeast

¼-oz (7 g) spice
⅛-oz (3·5 g) ginger
½-oz (14 g) baking powder
12 oz (340 g) currants
6 oz (170 g) sultanas
3 oz (85 g) peel

Bury simnels, a typically English local speciality

Sieve the flour and powders together on to the bench, and make a bay. Cream together the sugar, margarine and black jack, afterwards adding the egg in two quantities, taking care not to get the batter too light. Break down yeast in the milk afterwards adding a small portion at a time in order not to break down the batter, afterwards transferring the whole to the bay. Now mix in the flour to produce a dough of rather soft scone consistency, finally adding the fruit and clearing thoroughly. In this final stage, a small amount of dusting flour will be found necessary to assist in handling.

The mixing as given will produce seven Bury simnels scaled at 12 oz (340 g).

Mould round and place in position on a cleaned, greased sheet tin, allowing sufficient room to flow during baking, afterwards flattening with the hand to a diameter of 6 in (15·2 cm).

Wash with milk, dredge with castor sugar, and form a cross in the centre with split almonds, completing the decoration with two thin slices of citron peel at each side of the cross, and bake on wires or an upturned sheet tin at 380°F (195°C) for approximately 30–35 min.

On withdrawal from the oven, lightly wash the almonds and peel with a gum arabic, stock syrup solution or boiled apricot purée.

Simnel Slices

Though the name may suggest a seasonal line, this is not the case, and these slices will find favour in an assortment of fancies all the year round.

A firm favourite in any season, simnel slices

9 oz (255 g) margarine
9 oz (255 g) golden shortening
1 lb 2 oz (510 g) Barbados sugar
1¼ lb or 1 pt (570 g or 0·57 litres) egg
5 oz (140 g) milk
1½ lb (680 g) flour
¼-oz (7 g) baking powder

¼-oz (7 g) spice
8 oz (230 g) peel
8 oz (230 g) sultanas
8 oz (230 g) chopped cherries
½-oz (14 g) black jack
egg colour

Clean and grease thoroughly a 30 × 18 in (76 × 46 cm) sheet tin, placing a stick at the end, unless a four-sided sheet is available.

Produce the mixing by the sugar-batter method, divide into two and spread one half quite thinly on to the prepared sheet tin.

Roll sufficient almond paste, prepared from the recipe given for the centre paste of the simnel cakes, quite thinly and to a size slightly larger than the sheet tin. Roll round a long rolling-pin, transfer to the edge of the sheet and unroll carefully, afterwards trimming off the edges and pressing level. Add the second portion of the mixing, spread level and now roll out sufficient almond paste prepared from the recipe given for the top of the simnel cakes, once again to a size slightly larger than the sheet tin. Roll out with the fancy basket roller and, once again, roll round the larger rolling-pin and transfer on to the mixing, pressing down lightly as necessary, and placing a stick on the end to prevent flowing.

Egg-wash, bake at 380°F (195°C) for approximately 35–40 min and immediately on withdrawal from the oven wash with one of the solutions previously mentioned. When cold, cut into slices of a size predetermined by costings, using a stick or seven-wheel cutter to ensure uniformity.

Christmas and Birthday Cakes

The fashion in children's birthday cakes has veered—and sensibly so, to my mind—to the butter sponge and genoese type base, but the heavily-fruited cake still has much appeal for the older celebrant. I believe strongly that for cakes in this category quality should be predominant, and I am convinced that a first-quality Christmas cake brings back custom later in the year in the form of birthday and wedding cakes.

Here is a first-quality recipe:

4 lb (1820 g) butter	$5\frac{1}{4}$ lb (2610 g) flour
4 oz (110 g) glycerine	$6\frac{1}{2}$ lb (2930 g) currants
2 oz (57 g) black jack	$4\frac{1}{2}$ lb (2040 g) sultanas
2 lb (910 g) Barbados sugar	$1\frac{1}{2}$ lb (680 g) mixed peel
2 lb (910 g) castor sugar	egg colour
6 lb (2730 g) egg	vanilla and rum essences
8 oz (230 g) roasted ground almonds	orange and lemon pastes

Whilst it may be traditional to include spice in these cakes, it is my proved and firm conviction that this is not welcomed by all customers, hence its exclusion here. Where, however, this is demanded by local taste, up to $\frac{1}{2}$-oz (14 g) may be included in the recipe given.

WEDDING CAKES

The wedding cake is perhaps the most important cake that a confectioner can ever be called upon to make. It is seen, scrutinised, criticised and tasted by more people than any other cake he makes, and is sufficient to make—or break—any confectioner's reputation. I have talked with confectioners who stoutly aver that they are not profitable to make, so consequently neglect this most important side of the business. To put this argument into its correct perspective, one has only to know the capabilities of the confectioner concerned to realise that, in all probability, the production of the cake is, perhaps, rather beyond him.

The cake should be of the highest possible quality, with no necessary expense being spared. Similarly, the price charged should be commensurate with the finished article.

I have known prospective customers, after enquiring the price, remark that 'Mr. Blank only charges so much'. My reply would be to tell the customer courteously that, if that is the quality required, it would be far better to give Mr. Blank the order.

Heavily fruited wedding cake, produced as a large slab from which a variety of sizes and shapes can be produced

A confectioner should make only the highest quality and, for the sake of an order, should not on any account reduce either his price or quality. It should be remembered that the guests at a wedding criticise only the cake and confectioner and do not apportion the blame to where it rightfully belongs—to the person who ordered it to be made down to a price.

Again, it should be remembered that a number of the guests at the wedding may, in all probability, be engaged couples who, in their turn, will also want to order a wedding cake in due course. Thus can the repercussions of a good job have endless possibilities.

Fashions have changed over the years. Whereas wedding cakes were, almost entirely, round, with only the odd customer requesting a square cake, the pattern is completely reversed. Orders come in for heart, double heart, horse shoe shape and so on. What is the confectioner to do about this? My advice is that the cake should be baked as a large slab, using a 30 × 18 in (76 × 46 cm) wooden frame on a sheet tin—an old wooden confectioners board with bottom removed is ideal. Paper lined, this will hold 40 lb (18·2 kg) batter, the oven can be filled and the cake baked at 330–340°F (165–170°C), taking approximately $3\frac{1}{2}$ h to bake. Store in a cool situation, and it is a simple matter to cut from this slab the size and shape required.

Gone is the irksome task of lining up myriads of tins, of scaling the batter to different weights, of differing baking times, of wrapping individual cakes, of buying expensive 'shape' tins to be used once in a while and thereafter to collect dust and go rusty in some out of the way corner of cellar or attic. Gone is the drying of the larger cakes through the opening and closing of oven doors, whilst testing and removing smaller sizes. Regularity can be the keynote, with cakes cut from the slab by size or by template, this latter being produced from long lasting materials.

These are my firm convictions and I am, therefore, giving only one recipe for this cake, and that is of the highest qulity. Waste? Very little, for 'off cuts' are easily absorbed in any variety of fancies.

Rich Fruit Slab

The heading here could just as easily read 'Wedding Cake', for this mixing is very acceptable in any context.

$16\frac{1}{2}$ lb (7500 g) butter	$13\frac{1}{2}$ lb (6130 g) strong flour
$13\frac{1}{2}$ lb (6130 g) Barbados sugar	$\frac{1}{2}$-oz (14 g) nutmeg
9 oz (255 g) glycerine	$\frac{1}{2}$-oz (14 g) mixed spice
3 oz (85 g) black jack	5 lb (2270 g) mixed peel
18 lb (8180 g) egg	40 lb (18 300 g) currants
2 oz (57 g) lemon paste	25 lb (11 400 g) sultanas
2 oz (57 g) orange paste	10 oz (280 g) rum

Scaling weight between 40 lb (18·3 kg) and 43 lb (19·6 kg), the above will make three, 30 × 18 in (76 × 46 cm) slabs.

Butter is the only fat used, not only for flavour, but also to ensure that the batter is not allowed to incorporate too much air, or a crumbly cake could very well result.

Produced by the sugar-batter method, the fruit should be well washed and dried, mixed together with the liqueur poured over the previous day with a damp cloth placed over. That way, most of the flavour is retained and, during storage and maturing, the flavour is released into the crumb.

A mixing with a very high egg content, it is one of moist eating and excellent keeping quality. The type of fruit may be altered as desired.

After taking from the machine, scale as previously detailed, wet well down and bake at 330°F (165°C) for about 3¼ h in a humid oven.

A popular line using wedding cake slab. Split the cake through the centre, joining the pieces together with almond paste. Almond paste the top, mask with chocolate, allow to set, re-mask and comb, setting walnuts or pecan nuts on top. Cut into convenient sized pieces and wrap in transparent cellulose

This slab may be used for wedding or Christmas cake, cut to size for the customer to decorate her own cake, or cut into convenient sized pieces, wrapped in moisture proof transparent cellulose and sold by weight.

As a change, the slab may be split and sandwiched with a good layer of almond paste, with a further layer placed on the top, using boiled apricot purée as the adhesive. The top is then masked with chocolate which, after allowing to set, is re-masked and combed with a comb scraper, finally being decorated with walnuts or, for personal preference, pecans. This decoration of the slab can be further enlarged using white fondant and ginger, or merely icing with a coat of royal icing.

It has been the author's experience that a better cake has been produced by allowing the cake to stand after scaling, for 24 h before baking. This appears to give improved flavour and more plump fruit.

It is, nevertheless, useful to have knowledge of sizes/constituents for wedding cakes, and so the table is given below, scaling weight being batter weight.

SIZES/CONSTITUENT WEIGHTS TABLE FOR WEDDING CAKES
(Imperial units)

	Bottom (lb)	Size (in)	Centre (lb)	Size (in)	Top (lb)	Size (in)	Almond Paste (lb)	Royal Icing (lb)	Approx. Finished Weight (lb)
Two-tier	5	8	–	–	2	$5\frac{1}{2}$	3	4	$13\frac{1}{4}$
Do.	8	$9\frac{1}{2}$	–	–	2	$5\frac{1}{2}$	$4\frac{1}{4}$	5	$18\frac{1}{2}$
Do.	10	11	–	–	$2\frac{1}{4}$	$5\frac{1}{2}$	$5\frac{1}{4}$	$5\frac{1}{4}$	22
Do.	13	12	–	–	$2\frac{1}{4}$	6	$6\frac{1}{4}$	6	28
Three-tier	9	10	$4\frac{1}{4}$	8	2	6	7	$6\frac{1}{2}$	$28\frac{1}{4}$
Do.	12	11	$5\frac{1}{2}$	9	$2\frac{3}{4}$	7	10	$7\frac{1}{2}$	$34\frac{1}{2}$
Do.	14	12	6	9	$2\frac{1}{4}$	6	11	9	38

SIZES/CONSTITUENT WEIGHT TABLE FOR WEDDING CAKES
(Metric units)

	Bottom (g)	Size (cm)	Centre (g)	Size (cm)	Top (g)	Size (cm)	Almond Paste (g)	Royal Icing (g)	Approx. Finished Weight (g)
Two-tier	2270	20·3	–	–	910	14	1360	1820	6000
Do.	3600	24·1	–	–	910	14	2040	2270	8400
Do.	4540	28	–	–	1020	15·2	2500	2500	10 000
Do.	5910	30·5	–	–	1020	15·2	3070	2730	12 800
Three-tier	4180	25·4	1930	20·3	910	15·2	3250	2950	13 020
Do.	5450	28	2500	22·8	1250	17·7	4540	3480	15 700
Do.	6360	30·5	2730	22·8	1020	15·2	5000	4180	17 200

The tables may prove to be of value, and it will be noted that very little variation is shown in either size or scaling weight of top-tier cakes for two- or three-tier cakes.

The cake weights as shown are scaling weights, whilst the approximate finished weight has taken into consideration a baking loss of somewhere in the region of 10%.

Icing and Almond Paste

The weight of royal icing may prove a debatable point to many readers. There are those who maintain that three or four coats are essential, but with this I emphatically disagree. Where the sides and top of a cake are covered with almond paste, this is not necessary, and two coats, properly applied, should be sufficient. Extra coats entail more labour, whilst these only serve to build up a hard, flinty wall between the customer and the cake, and what wedding guest has not heartily sympathised with a bride trying to hack her way through the mass.

Again, wedding cakes are normally sold by weight, and the customer does not anticipate being called upon to pay for an inedible mass.

Almond paste may be prepared from equal quantities of ground almonds, icing sugar and castor sugar, with approximately $1\frac{1}{2}$ oz (43 g) whole egg being required to each 1 lb (450 g) dry ingredients. This, with sufficient egg colour to give a rich tint, is mixed to a stiff paste—essential when two- or three-tier cakes are to be produced.

Often a customer comes to order a cake with but the vaguest notion of what is required, and leaves the confectioner to suggest what size it should be. An allowance of $1\frac{1}{2}$ oz (43 g) per guest should be made, and it should always be remembered that a certain amount will be required to be despatched in cake boxes. Here, again, is another chance for further business, for the confectioner can supply these, which are obtainable from any sundriesman.

It is not my intention here to give details for the decoration of wedding cakes, for this is being admirably dealt with within the pages of other books.

For the enthusiastic confectioner wishing to specialise in this field, no better advice could be given than he should purchase that mine of information, *Cake Design and Decoration,* by L. J. Hanneman and G. I. Marshall, wherein full details of all types of cake decoration are given. Copiously illustrated and clearly explained, the art of cake decorating is taken from the most elementary stage until the enthusiast, with practice, can successfully tackle an exhibition cake.

Suffice it for me to say here that, on the happiest day in the life of any couple, the cake should be a personal thing to the two people concerned, possibly incorporating *motifs* denoting hobbies or occupation, but, whatever style is employed, it should be a work of art and beauty as befits its important place on this most memorable day.

Miniature Cakes

The saying that 'there is nothing new under the sun' may be trite, but, in the case of miniature cakes, is perfectly true, for these were commonplace before the war. It may be merely due to the fact that these have been forgotten over the years, but the novelty of them commands a ready sale and, for this reason, also commands an extremely good price, hence making them quite profitable to produce.

Miniature cakes, a novelty of great popularity

Three-inch (7·6 cm) diameter cake tins are lined with a single paper liner, with a paper circle placed in the bottom of the tin. Any of the good-quality mixings of birthday or wedding cakes may be used, with a batter scaling weight of 3 oz (85 g). Press level in the tins and bake at 360°F (180°C), taking care not to over-bake, and thus dry, the cakes.

When baked and quite cool, remove from the tins, strip off the papers and roll out sufficient almond paste to a thickness of slightly less than $\frac{1}{4}$-in (6 mm), afterwards cutting out the required number of discs with a 3 in (7·6 cm) cutter. Reverse the cakes, brushing the original bottom of each with boiled apricot purée. Upon each affix one of the almond paste discs. When all are so completed, apply a thin layer of the apricot purée to the sides of the cakes and stand on draining wires.

Cover in fondant

Now prepare sufficient fondant in the usual manner, either left white or coloured to a pastel shade of pink, lemon or very pale green, and apply either by enrobing or fork or finger dipping, whichever method is preferred. Stand on the draining wire until the fondant is quite dry. When this stage is reached, pass a palette knife, dipped repeatedly into hot water, beneath each cake and transfer to a 4 in (10·2 cm) diameter silver strawboard.

Prepare royal icing in the usual manner and, using a star tube, pipe a shell border to hide the joint between board and cake, afterwards piping a similar border along the top edge of the cake to complete.

Pipe on the top a suitable inscription and this, generally, can be 'Best Wishes', it being appropriate for any occasion. Add a small piped sugar flower and spray of maidenhair fern, and finish by fixing on a gaily coloured ribbon, complete with a bow of a colour to match the fondant.

During the Christmas season, of course, the piped sugar flower and fern can be replaced by a holly piquet, whilst in Lent miniature simnel cakes can be reproduced exactly as for the larger units.

SLAB CAKES

The majority of the slab cake trade now seems to have been captured by the factory bakeries and the reason is not difficult to see, for this is a line which lends itself admirably to mass-production methods. Thus, uniformity, attractive presentation and, most important, a reasonably good quality product at a popular price, all combine to make for stiff competition.

One has only to walk round the popular chain stores to see all varieties displayed ready cut in convenient weights, each piece individually and hygienically wrapped in attractive transparent cellulose to see that methods of presentation have been studied as carefully as methods of production.

Thus the smaller confectioner is faced with stiff competition and yet, with a cake of good quality, carefully baked, he can hold his own. The price to be charged is naturally a matter of choice, but in computing costs it should be borne in mind that labour production costs are, or should be, low, and this, coupled with the fact that, generally speaking, no finish is required, should enable the slabs to be sold at a competitive price.

The tins to be used are worthy of some thought and I favour the long, narrow tin, with approximate measurements of 18 × 5 in (46 × 13 cm) for the top, bottom 16 × 4 in (41 × 10 cm) and a depth of 4 in (10 cm). This shape of tin avoids getting the crusty corner pieces that are not favoured by the customer and the cake can, after thinly trimming both ends, be cut into uniform pieces. Individual pieces can then be wrapped in transparent cellulose, thus giving a longer shelf life. Alternatively, wooden frames measuring 30 × 4 in (76 × 10 cm) or 30 × 5 in (76 × 13 cm) are ideal and simply made.

Alternatively, there are, of course, the normal slab tins, of square or oblong shape, and wooden frames. The latter, however, have the disadvantage of being poor conductors of heat, giving white, unattractive, crustless sides, being awkward to store when not in use and having only a relatively short life as compared with tins.

The baking of slabs is quite often the point where production goes wrong and yet, with a balanced recipe, this should not be so, provided that the idiosyncrasies of the particular ovens used are carefully studied. The temperature should be correct when the oven is loaded and the time of day for the baking judged in the case of the solid fuel oven so that the heat is gently falling during the baking period. So far as is practicable the oven should be fully loaded and, for a peel oven, loaded in reverse baking order in the case of a mixed batch. This means that heavily fruited varieties, taking a longer baking time, will remain undisturbed at the back of the oven, whilst plain and madeira slabs will be at the front of the oven in the most accessible place.

In addition, one or two tins of water should be placed inside to give the humid atmosphere necessary for correct baking.

All tins should be lined with a double thickness of paper—white cap paper next to the tin and greaseproof next to the cake—to facilitate easy stripping without damage to the crust after baking and when cold. For protection against bottom heat several thicknesses of brown paper or newspaper can be placed upon the sheet tin. The amount of protection required will naturally depend upon the amount of bottom heat generated by the particular oven used.

The aim should be to produce all slabs, whether plain or fruited, of uniform height, or depth, and it is recommended that this should be in the region of 3–4 in (7·5–10 cm). As the reader will be well aware, the trend of the customer today is 'value for money' and as a larger circumference apparently satisfies that demand, it is recommended that the depth veer towards the lower limit.

All the recipes given here will produce good commercial slab cake. Scaling weights have been purposely omitted, for this will depend upon the size of tin.

The question of shelf-life is one of great importance, especially in the case of plain slabs, and so I strongly urge the use of glycerine.

Remember, also, that the bowl should be scraped down regularly, both during mixing and scaling, otherwise, when scaling, the last slab of the mixing is likely to consist of cores, and, with fruited slabs, a very sparsely fruited cake, which can only lose custom. Again, as far as possible, scaling should be carried out in one operation with the mixing transferred to the prepared tin in a manner to prevent trapping air in the batter and causing unsightly holes.

Any scrapings from the scale end should be placed carefully into the corners, thus preventing 'streaks'.

Madeira Slab Cake

5 lb (2270 g) castor sugar
1 lb (450 g) golden shortening
4 lb (1820 g) margarine
6 oz (170 g) glycerine
6 lb (2730 g) egg

6¼ lb (2950 g) flour
½-oz (14 g) baking powder
egg colour
vanilla essence

Use sugar-batter method. Scale into the prepared tins, spread level and bake at 350°F (175°C).

Attractive madeira slab cake

Caraway Seed Slab Cake

This may be produced from the above recipe with the addition of 3 oz (85 g) caraway seeds to the quantities given, mixed in with the flour.

After scaling and spreading level, add a sprinkling of seeds to the top of the slab. Bake at 350°F (175°C).

Coconut-flavoured Slab Cake

As mentioned earlier in page 245, the use of coconut can cause discomfort to wearers of dentures, to whom the flavour of coconut is still attractive. However, the use of a good essence can obviate this discomfort, but it is strongly urged that, in use, it is accurately measured. To the mixing given ½-oz (14 g) will be found quite sufficient, using this in place of vanilla essence, otherwise mixing and baking are as for madeira slab.

To prevent confusion to sales staff the coconut-flavoured slab should be iced with white fondant, and, if desired, decoration can be completed in the case of cut, wrapped pieces by using neatly cut—not broken—half-cherries and angelica.

Buttercream Slab Cake

4 lb 10 oz (2100 g) castor sugar
1¼ lb (570 g) shortening
2½ lb (1140 g) margarine
4 oz (110 g) glycerine
1 oz (28 g) salt
3 lb 2 oz or 2½ pt (1420 g or 1·42 litres) egg

5 lb 14 oz (2700 g) flour
1 oz (28 g) baking powder
1 lb 7 oz (650 g) milk
egg colour
vanilla essence

Produce by either the sugar- or flour-batter methods, scale and spread level, afterwards baking at 360°F (180°C).

When baked and cold, strip off the papers, split twice and layer with white vanilla flavoured buttercream or with one layer of cream and one of jam.

Cherry Slab Cake

2½ lb (1140 g) castor sugar
8 oz (230 g) golden shortening
2 lb (910 g) margarine
3 oz (85 g) glycerine
2½ lb or 2 pt (1140 g or 1·14 litres) egg

3¼ lb (1480 g) flour
¼-oz (7 g) baking powder
5 lb (2270 g) cherries
egg colour
vanilla essence

Wash the cherries thoroughly in luke-warm water to remove the syrup, well dry and coat with flour, sieving to remove the surplus.

Mix by the sugar-batter method, scale, spread level and, if desired, place a few washed and dried cherries in position as top decoration. Bake at 350°F (175°C).

Cherry slab cake, using the modern trend of shallow, rather than deep, cake

Genoa Slab Cake

4 lb 14 oz (2200 g) castor sugar
1½ lb (680 g) golden shortening
2¾ lb (1250 g) margarine
4 oz (110 g) glycerine
4 lb 6 oz or 3½ pt (1990 g or 1·99 litres) egg
½-oz (14 g) salt
5 lb (2270 g) flour

¼-oz (7 g) baking powder
4 lb (1820 g) currants
3½ lb (1530 g) sultanas
1½ lb (680 g) cherries
1 lb (450 g) mixed peel
egg colour
almond and vanilla essences

Genoa slab and cakes, the latter prepared for Christmas sale.

Use sugar-batter process. After scaling, spread level, and decorate with split almonds as costings allow. Bake at 350°F (175°C).

Sultana Slab Cake

4½ lb (2040 g) castor sugar
1 lb (450 g) golden shortening
3 lb (1360 g) margarine
½-oz (14 g) salt
4 oz (110 g) glycerine
5 lb or 4 pt (2270 g or 2·27 litres) egg

5 lb 10 oz (2560 g) flour
6 oz (170 g) scone flour
10 lb (4500 g) sultanas
egg colour
lemon and vanilla essences

Prepare by the sugar-batter method. The batter should then be scaled at the required weights into the prepared tins, spread level, and a sprinkling of flaked almonds added. Bake at 350°F (175°C).

Dundee Slab Cake

3 lb (1360 g) Barbados sugar
8 oz (230 g) golden shortening
2½ lb (1140 g) margarine
3 oz (85 g) glycerine
2 oz (57 g) black treacle
3¾ lb or 3 pt (1700 g or 1·7 litres) egg

4¼ lb (1930 g) flour
11 lb (5000 g) sultanas
zest and juice of 2 oranges
egg colour
vanilla, almond and rum essences

Use sugar-batter method. Scale, spread level, and place split almonds neatly in position as top decoration. Bake at 350°F (175°C)

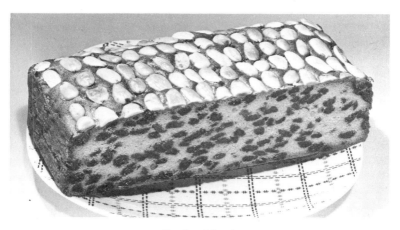

Dundee slab cake

Currant Slab Cake

4½ lb (2040 g) castor sugar
1 lb (450 g) golden shortening
3 lb (1360 g) margarine
¼-oz (14 g) salt
4 oz (110 g) glycerine
5 lb or 4 pt (2270 g or 2·27 litres) egg

5¼ lb (2390 g) flour
4 oz (110 g) scone flour
12 lb (5450 g) currants
egg colour
lemon and vanilla essences

Use sugar-batter process. Scale, spread level and, if desired, a top decoration of nib or strip almonds may be added. Bake at 350°F (175°C)

High-ratio Slabs

The recipes and methods given constitute the normal range of slab cake productions, although high-ratio slabs, enjoying fair popularity, may be used to give further variety, many recipes for these being in existence.

These recipes are quite easily obtained on request from millers of speciality cake flours and manufacturers of high-ratio fats.

Pineapple Slab Cake

Here is a further and unusual cake of traditional variety.

4 lb (1820 g) castor sugar
1 lb (450 g) golden shortening
3 lb (1360 g) cake margarine
5 lb or 4 pt (2270 g or 2·27 litres) egg
5¼ lb (2390 g) flour

4 oz (110 g) scone flour
9 lb (4180 g) glacé pineapple
egg colour
pineapple paste

The pineapple should be well drained, chopped into reasonably sized pieces, placed in a sieve, and coated with flour, the surplus being removed by shaking the sieve.

Produce the slabs by the sugar-batter method. Spread level and bake at 350°F (175°C).

After baking and when cold, strip off the papers and ice with white fondant, placing neat slices of glacé pineapple immediately in position before completing by dredging with castor sugar.

If desired, preserved ginger, treated in a similar manner, may be substituted for pineapple, thus producing slab cake; of course, the pineapple essence would not be used.

Combining two slabs

Further variety can be introduced by combining two slabs in a manner similar to simnel cakes, e.g. a layer of dundee slab, a layer of almond paste, and a further layer, this time of cherry slab. This, when cut, has a very attractive appearance and proves to be very popular.

Variation of Dundee Slab

Again, the dundee slab, after baking and when cold, may be covered with a thin layer of almond paste masked with chocolate fondant, and the decoration completed with good quality half-walnuts.

GENOESE

Two distinct types of genoese can be produced, light and heavy, the names being indicative of the nature of the baked product. Whilst the former is generally produced as a butter sponge, the latter is in the character of a madeira cake. In this part of the book therefore, I shall deal solely with the heavy type, which has the advantage of being suitable for the production of afternoon tea fancies, fondant dipping, and of various types of layer cake.

All the recipes given being of good quality, sufficient for a week's supply may be produced, more if using the deep freeze, usually during the early and quieter part of the week. But however it is made, genoese should be allowed at least 24 h to mature before use.

The more widespread use of deep freeze has enabled the confectioner to produce less frequently and in far greater batches at one time.

It is also of advantage for the baked genoese to be 'stacked' about three high. This gives a genoese of closer texture and thus easier to handle.

Batter scaling weights will, of course, vary with the size of sheet tin used, but the popular size of 30 × 18 in (76 × 46 cm) will require between 8 and 10 lb (3·7 and 4·5 kg) of batter. Hence a slight reduction in scaling weights can give, when using the genoese for fancies, a greater yield, therefore using slightly less decorative material, thus enabling the yield to vary as regards costs without interference with the selling price of the finished product.

No. 1

2 lb (910 g) castor sugar	2½ lb or 1 qt (1140 g or 1·14 litres) egg
1¾ lb (800 g) margarine	2¾ lb (1250 g) flour
4 oz (110 g) golden shortening	egg colour
2 oz (57 g) glycerine	vanilla essence

No. 2

2½ lb (1140 g) castor sugar	3 lb (1360 g) flour
2 lb (910 g) margarine	½-oz (14 g) baking powder
8 oz (230 g) golden shortening	egg colour
2 oz (57 g) glycerine	vanilla essence
2½ lb or 1 qt (1140 g or 1·14 litres) egg	

No. 3

2¼ lb (1140 g) sugar	½-oz (14 g) baking powder
2 lb (910 g) margarine	5 oz or ¼-pt (140 g or 0·14 litres) milk
2 oz (57 g) glycerine	egg colour
2¼ lb (1020 g) egg	vanilla essence
3 lb (1360 g) flour	

All these recipes are produced by the sugar-batter method, scaled off at the required weight and spread level on a sheet tin previously papered and fitted with a stick to prevent flowing. Baking temperatures 360–370°F (180–190°C).

Other Flavours

Colours and flavours, e.g. raspberry, strawberry, orange, etc., may be added, in which case, the egg colour and vanilla essence will be deducted.

For chocolate genoese, delete in any of the recipes given 8 oz (230 g) flour and replace with 8 oz (230 g) cocoa powder, chocolate colour and flavour, and a spot of pink colour to give a truer chocolate colour.

'Cross-bow' Cutter

One of the difficulties in the production of fancies comprising genoese bases is undoubtedly the varying thickness of the genoese. The more usual causes are bad spreading, buckling sheet tins, and varied scaling weights, but whatever the cause it inevitably leads to considerable waste if the craftsman is to turn out goods of regular size and depth. Again, for good results the genoese must be skinned, and unless this is done very carefully it can lead to further waste.

To confine waste to a very thin skin, it would be a good idea to use a tool which may be referred to as a 'cross-bow'. The handyman may easily produce it himself, or have it made for a few shillings.

A length of tubular or other suitable metal is bent to a U shape, the width of this being about 2 in (5 cm) wider than the sheet tins used. A hole at each end is drilled through the metal, and a length of thin steel wire threaded through either hole and fastened tightly across. Should steel wire be difficult to procure, a banjo 'G' string will be found satisfactory.

With a good knife make a slight incision in one end of the genoese level with the top of the tin. Place the wire of the cross-bow in the incision and, keeping the wire at each end of the bow in contact with the top of the sheet tin, draw steadily along to the opposite end. Pick up the sheet tin, jerk slightly, and the genoese top may be slid off the base straight on to the bench, leaving the genoese absolutely level, skinned and ready for use. This is an excellent

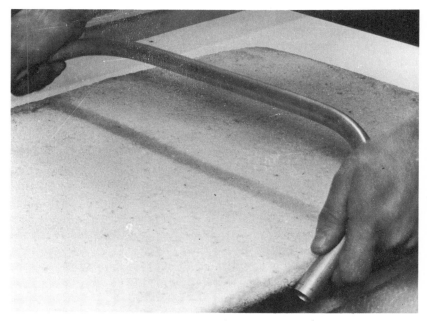

The 'cross-bow' in use to level a sheet of genoese

method for achieving the accuracy required to produce battenburg, layer cakes, and so on.

The tops are used to make the rainbow cake mentioned below.

Rainbow cake

When preparing genoese as detailed above, try to arrange that differently coloured and flavoured genoese are prepared in rotation. Thus, the first may be white, vanilla flavoured. As the top is slid on to the bench, spread with vanilla-flavoured buttercream. The next genoese may be pink, raspberry-flavoured genoese. Slide the top of this on to the prepared vanilla base, spread with raspberry jam, and repeat the process introducing differently coloured and flavoured genoese as available. Continue the process until the required height has been reached, which should be somewhere in the region of 3 in (7·5 cm).

Cut into bare 3 in (7·5 cm) widths, which will give 10 to the 30 × 18 in (76 × 46 cm) size sheet, and enrobe with a good-quality baker's chocolate, preferably milk or blended. Decorate with walnut halves and cut into convenient-sized blocks ready for sale by weight.

This is a line of such popularity that it may often be necessary to produce it from the genoese itself.

A simple gadget for cutting a number of sheets of genoese quickly and accurately. The 'box' has 2 drop sides, hinged, with all four sides slit at equidistant spaces, to give the pre-determined number of pieces per sheet

Uniformity in size of genoese intended for afternoon tea fancies must be of great priority, and if the reader concedes that these shapes can be squares, oblongs and diamonds, then this problem can be solved without spending a great deal of money in buying a genoese cutting machine and still not have the efficiency of the simple arrangement here illustrated. This can be produced quite easily by the reader handy with simple tools or, alternatively, a joiner should be able to produce it quite reasonably.

The base of the box should be of stout timber of a variety that will not warp, and should be a minimum of 1 in (2·6 cm) thick. The size will depend upon the size of the reader's genoese sheets, but the inside measurement should allow for a sheet of genoese to fit exactly on the base, with no play or overlap.

The ends and sides of the box should be of five- or seven-ply so that, after use, the box may be washed without fear of warping. One end and one side of the box will be fixed, whilst the other end and side are hinged to allow ease of access. Small 'hook and eye' fasteners will be necessary to hold the drop members in position when the box is closed.

Before assembly, the reader will have decided the size of the individual genoese pieces. If, for instance, these are to be 2 × 1 in (5·1 × 2·6 cm) then it will be necessary to make saw cuts in both sides of the box at 2 in (5·1 cm) intervals. These cuts must be absolutely perpendicular, and should be taken to a point slightly below the top level of the base. This will ensure that the sheet of genoese at the bottom is cut right through.

In a similar manner, 1 in (2·6 cm) cuts will be made at either end of the box whilst saw cuts should 'groove' the base-board to the size required.

The only other item of equipment required will be another 'cross-bow' similar to the one described previously. Made exactly as described, it must be long enough to fit from end to end of the box, with about 6 in (15 cm) over. The depth required will again be that of the box, plus 2–3 in (5–8 cm).

The genoese placed in the box ready for cutting

For use, remove the tops of the genoese as described previously and produce from these tops 'rainbow cake'. The use of the cross-bow should then have given a perfectly level genoese, the first requirement for uniformity.

Now tip the first sheet of genoese into the box, lift the sheet tin clear, peel off the paper and, using both hands flat in a light, circular motion, remove the crust from what was previously the bottom of the genoese. Sweep away the crumb and repeat the process until the required number of genoese are in the box. Here it should be said that it is possible to cut eight sheets of genoese, exactly uniform, all at the same time. When all are assembled, close the box, fastening the small 'hook and eye' fasteners.

Cutting the genoese

Place the wire of the cross-bow into the first cuts at either side of the box and, employing a slightly sawing motion, cut through the genoese. Continue

The genoese being cut by a larger version of the 'cross-bow'. The end would normally be closed, but was left open for photographic purposes

until the whole length of the box has been traversed, carefully ascertaining that the wire enters each corresponding saw cut on the other side. Now turn the box end-on, and repeat the process. When finished, all the pieces of genoese should be absolutely uniform, and yet all together as a sheet.

With the box still closed, mask the top genoese with apricot purée; then release the 'hook and eye' catches, open the box and set the prepared pieces of genoese on draining wires, reasonably close yet not touching. Any topping required may now be added. Thus, with one stroke, we have disposed of the first two points, which were uniformity and speed of production.

The few shillings required for the production of the box and cross-bow will very soon be returned with interest.

Now cut, the pieces of genoese are placed on wires ready for enrobing

Genoese Fruit Slice

June may be the month of roses, but any time is fruit time for the confectioner, for this, we find, is always popular. The greatest difficulty about this line is that very careful handling is required, but, nevertheless, it is well worth the effort.

White, or yellow, vanilla-flavoured genoese is required, and should be cut into $2\frac{1}{2}$ in (6·4 cm) widths. Spread the top with apricot purée, and along the sides place a $\frac{1}{2}$-in (1·3 cm) strip of similar genoese, thus producing a trough.

Into this trough, and upon the apricot jam, set fruit, nicely patterned and to choice, in position. Mask well with quick-set jelly, decorate the sides with either roasted coconut or almonds after masking with apricot purée, and finally, using a star tube, pipe fresh whipped and sweetened cream along the sides to complete.

Genoese fruit slice, ideally presented on a log card

Chocolate Boxes

This is a line that scarcely needs introduction, such a firm favourite has it become, but unfortunately, all too often the finish leaves much to be desired, whilst any colour of genoese seems to be used.

Using chocolate coloured and flavoured genoese, remove the tops as previously detailed, tip from the sheet tin, strip off the paper and skin, afterwards cutting the genoese into squares of the required size. This may be done by marking with the seven-wheeled cutter to a size pre-determined by the size of the chocolate squares to be used. These latter may be purchased already produced or, alternatively, may be produced by spreading greaseproof or wax paper thinly with tempered couverture or bakers' chocolate, holding the opposite corners of the paper and tapping gently to ensure that the chocolate is spread evenly over the surface. Just as setting point is reached cut to the desired size with the seven-wheel cutter.

To make up the genoese pick up two of the cut squares, one on top of the other, and mask the four sides with apricot jam. Separate and place a chocolate square on each side to completely enclose the genoese.

In the hollow between the top of the genoese and the top of the chocolate, pipe in a whirl of whipped and sweetened fresh cream, and complete by placing one chocolate square at an angle to represent the 'lid'.

AFTERNOON TEA FANCIES

Many and varied are the types that can be produced in this range, but care should be exercised that all, despite the variation in actual shape, are of approximately the same size. To avoid wastage of genoese, circles should be avoided at all costs, and it will be found in practice that squares, oblongs, triangles and diamonds will be sufficient to give all the variety necessary.

One very important point to watch is the size, for far too often today is one confronted by a confectioner's shop window displaying goods so large that they hardly come under the category of 'fancies'. Indeed, the size, coupled with the low price, makes one wonder how the proprietors of the business make these lines pay. Maximum weight of any fancy should not exceed $1\frac{1}{4}$ oz (50 g).

Afternoon tea fancies are generally understood to comprise genoese finished with decorative materials other than fondant, and one of the predominant materials in this category is buttercream. It is, perhaps, ideal if two types be produced, one for spreading and sandwiching, the other for piping, but in general commercial practice one type is used, being suitable for either purpose. In this respect the recipes given hereafter will be found quite satisfactory.

Nothing can, of course, compete with butter in this field and I have heard many times the 'pros and cons' argued for the use of unsalted, as against salted, butter, but that, of course, is a matter of taste.

Buttercream

It is well known that human beings are creatures of habit, confectioners finding habits formed as easily as other members of the community.

Among these is the usual production of buttercream, for we tend to stick to the same recipe over the years. It is thought-provoking to contemplate how many sales may possibly be lost by the habit of using a buttercream which may be below par or otherwise unsuitable for its particular purpose.

The habit of making a particular buttercream because it is quick and easy to make or the staff are 'always busy' is far too easy to develop. That, of course, is the whole point.

Are we to produce a buttercream because it is quick and easy to make, or are we to produce a type best suited to a specific purpose?

At this point it will doubtless assist readers to consider various recipes and methods of production. It is hoped that they will, by comparing these with their own, be helped to the right conclusion, and thus to an increase in quality and sales.

Firstly, what is buttercream? The definition given by 'The Bakers' Dictionary' is 'A lightly beaten mixture of butter and sugar, with or without other additions, including colours and essences'. It would be next to impossible to improve upon that, but first a word regarding the butter.

Many and furious are the arguments whether this should be salted or unsalted. That, of course, must depend upon the taste of the individual, but it should be borne in mind that, as butter is the basic ingredient, the importance of correct choice cannot be overrated. In none of the recipes has essence been included; this, again, being entirely up to the individual.

WITH ICING SUGAR

Equal weights of butter and icing sugar + colour and flavouring. Cream butter until smooth, add the icing sugar and remainder of ingredients, beat until very light.

WITH FONDANT

Equal weights of butter and fondant (stock fondant) + colour and flavouring.

Fondant slightly warmed, if necessary: no reducing syrup needed. Add the fondant a little at a time to the butter, beating until smooth and light.

WITH MARSHMALLOW

The marshmallow can be used whipped or unwhipped.

A. Piping Cream

$1\frac{1}{2}$ lb (680 g) butter
1 lb (450 g) stock marshmallow
1 lb (450 g) sieved icing sugar

$\frac{1}{2}$-lb (230 g) evaporated milk
colour and flavour
Beat together adding in order

B. Spreading Cream

$1\frac{1}{4}$ lb (570 g) butter
$\frac{1}{4}$-lb (110 g) stock marshmallow
$\frac{1}{4}$-lb (110 g) stock fondant
$\frac{1}{4}$-lb (110 g) sieved icing sugar

$\frac{1}{4}$-lb (110 g) warmed commercial glucose
$\frac{1}{4}$-lb (110 g) evaporated milk
colour and flavour

Continental Fillings

BOILED 'BUTTERCREAM'

4 lb (1720 g) sugar
1 pt (570 ml) water

pinch cream of tartar

Boil to 240°F (120°C) and pour slowly into a stiff sponge made with:

1 pt (570 g) egg   1 lb (450 g) castor sugar

Continue whipping 5 min then leave to cool. When the above mixture is cool, blend the following into it:

1½ lb (680 g) butter   1½ lb (680 g) sieved icing sugar

Cream lightly. Colour and flavour added as desired.

BOILED MERINGUE 'BUTTERCREAM'

4 lb (1720 g) sugar   pinch cream of tartar
1 pt (570 g) water

Boil to 245°F (120°C). Pour this slowly into a stiff snow or foam prepared from:

12½ oz (360 g) egg white   pinch cream of tartar

Continue whipping whilst pouring in the sugar and for some time afterwards. Leave to cool.

Meantime, beat 3 lb (1360 g) butter until light and then beat in the cool meringue. Add colour and flavour as desired.

SPONGE 'BUTTERCREAM'

¾-pt (430 g) egg   1 lb (450 g) castor sugar

Beat to stiff sponge:

2 lb (910 g) butter   1 lb (450 g) sieved icing sugar

Beat until light. Add the sponge to the batter in small portions, beating well between each addition. Colour and flavour as required.

LEMON 'BUTTERCREAM'

2 lb (910 g) stock fondant   8 oz (230 g) lemon curd
1 lb (450 g) butter

Beat together until light. Best used for sandwiching.

1 lb (450 g) sieved icing sugar   8 oz (230 g) sieved milk powder

beaten in to the above, produces a stiffer filling.

CUSTARD CREAM

1½ lb (680 g) butter   12 oz (340 g) sieved icing sugar

Beat until light. Then add:

1½ lb (680 g) cold boiled vanilla custard

Blend thoroughly into the cream.

CHOCOLATE 'BUTTERCREAM'

Sufficient melted unsweetened block chocolate beaten into a 'buttercream' produces best results.

Alternatively, a chocolate paste made from unsweetened couverture and glucose may be used to replace unsweetened block chocolate.

American Buttercream

Cream, but not too lightly:

2¼ lb (1140 g) butter	3½ lb (1530 g) icing sugar
12 oz (340 g) high-ratio fat	

Add on slow speed:

2 lb (910 g) whipping cream	1 lb (450 g) evaporated milk

Fold in:

1¼ lb (570 g) whipped marshmallow

Ganache

Ganache is the name given to variously compounded blends of chocolate and boiling cream. The standard mixing is:

2½ lb (1140 g) grated couverture over which is poured	1 pt (570 g) boiling dairy cream

The two are mixed together and stirred occasionally until cool. Plain or milk couvertures or cake coatings may be used. The cream can be replaced with imitation cream, milk or even with stock syrup to produce a range of ganache pastes of varying quality.

If it is desired to flavour ganache with such items as rum, kirsch, coffee, etc., it is advisable to use milk chocolate, as plain chocolate has a predominant chocolate flavour, thus masking the added flavour detrimentally.

Before use the ganache mixture is treated in the same way as buttercream, i.e. beating until light in a machine bowl, warming slightly if necessary.

Some Varieties of Afternoon Tea Fancy

No. 1

Cut vanilla-flavoured genoese strips 2½ in (6·5 cm) wide, split and layer with apricot jam. Cover with marzipan rolled out very thinly, using boiled apricot purée as the adhesive medium, afterwards coating with baker's chocolate. Cut into 1 in (2·5 cm) fingers and complete by piping chocolate buttercream, using a star tube, into rosettes on the top of each.

No. 2

Split 2½ in (6·5 cm) widths of genoese and sandwich with apricot jam. Mask the top and sides with praline flavoured buttercream, afterwards masking the sides with fine roasted flake almonds and the top with chopped walnuts. Pipe a whorl of coffee coloured and flavoured buttercream in the centre of each, dredge lightly with icing sugar, and complete with a sprinkle of green nibs on the piped whorl.

No. 3

A strip of genoese is split and layered with lemon cheese, afterwards masking the sides with buttercream flavoured with lemon cheese. Press roasted coconut along each side and pipe four ropes of vanilla-flavoured buttercream, using a star tube, along the length of the strip. Fill in with lemon cheese and, as previously, cut into 1 in (2·5 cm) fingers.

When cutting the fingers, use a sharp knife dipped constantly into hot water to give a clear cut.

No. 4

Strips of genoese are split and sandwiched with apricot jam, and the sides are masked thinly with buttercream and the top heavily with either buttercream or stock marshmallow whipped with the addition of 1 pt (570 g) albumen or egg whites until stiff.

Pin out sufficient marzipan very thinly, and enclose each strip of genoese by laying the edge of this along the edge of the marzipan and gently rolling over. Trim the marzipan to shape, stand the strip upright and smooth with the palm of the hand. Brush the sides with baker's chocolate.

It is of considerable assistance in cutting if the strips can be placed in a refrigerator beforehand. Use a sharp knife dipped constantly into hot water.

No. 5

A variation of No. 4; here the marzipan is brushed over the whole of the surface with a sprinkling of green almond nibs to complete.

No. 6

The top of a strip of genoese is masked with raspberry-flavoured piping jelly, and a rope of pink marzipan placed down the centre. The sides are masked with white, vanilla-flavoured buttercream and roasted coconut; the buttercream top is finished in pyramid fashion. Allow a short time in the refrigerator for the buttercream to set before dressing heavily with icing sugar and cutting into fingers.

Very many more varieties are possible, of course, than the six detailed, but these are samples of quick finish, attractive appearance and popularity with the customers.

Each confectioner, however, should strive to produce a variety, both in finish and taste, which is individual. Again, so vast a range of materials are at our disposal that constant variety may be introduced rather than keeping to the same lines every week.

Uniform Slices

A leading figure in the trade once remarked that the most difficult problem we have to face is the maintenance of quality. A new line is easy to produce, but to maintain that quality day in and day out, month in, month out, year in, year out, is extremely difficult, as the practical reader understanding the fluctuating

The cutting trough, a simple gadget to ensure . . .

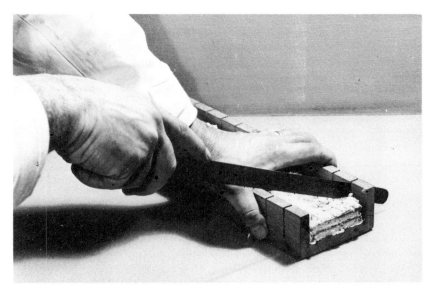

. . . accurate cutting. The troughs, simply made, can be of a size suitable for any particular business

demands upon, sometimes, changing staff, will readily agree. Therefore, the introduction of any small gadget, no matter how simple, that will help to standardise sizes and lines is welcome.

The photographs of the trough will be more or less self-explanatory. The length of this is the same as the width of the sheet tins used, comprising $\frac{1}{2}$-in (1·3 cm) timber for base and sides. These latter are securely screwed to the base, with cuts made in the side at 1 in (2·6 cm) intervals to permit the reasonably easy access of a cutting knife, the cuts going down to the base. A length of continental slice, genoese or other similar material to be sliced is placed in the trough. Use the knife with a backward motion to keep the slice pressing against the side of the trough nearest the body, thus preventing the layers sliding and ensuring a clean cut. Inside measurement width of three inches should be ample.

Genoese Fruits

Apples

Using a $1\frac{1}{2}$ in (3·8 cm) plain, round cutter, cut out circles from a white, vanilla-flavoured genoese and mask the sides, two at once, with good-quality lemon cheese. Now, with a savoy bag and ½-in (1·3 cm) plain tube, pipe a good bulb of pale green, pistachio-flavoured buttercream on the top of each.

Pin out marzipan or almond paste quite thinly. Dust castor sugar as required, cut out with a 3 in (7·6 cm) plain cutter, place centrally over the buttercream bulb and wrap, ensuring that the marzipan adheres to the lemon cheese and is brought to the base of the genoese.

Cake or real fruits? Peaches and apples, which may be produced from genoese or crumb paste

Make an indentation with a marzipan modelling tool in the top centre and insert a clean currant, pressing down well to represent the core. If an aerograph is available, spray one side apple green and blush the other side with red. If an aerograph is not available, a similar effect can be obtained by brushing on the colour, with the absolute minimum of colour on the brush.

Peaches

The make-up here is very similar to that detailed for the apples. Apricot jam is used in place of lemon cheese, and flavouring of the cream in this instance is done with syrup produced from crystallising tinned peaches. The cream is suitably coloured.

Mark in the 'crack' of the peach and blush each side with orange yellow colour. If desired extra finish may be given by placing in position a pear calyx.

It is appreciated that the production of these lines necessarily creates cuttings of genoese which, unless carefully watched, can cause waste.

Sacher Slices

Cut coffee-coloured and -flavoured genoese into strips $2\frac{1}{2}$ in (6·4 cm) wide. Split through the centre and mask the tops with coffee-flavoured baker's chocolate, afterwards cutting into 1 in (2·6 cm) fingers using a good knife dipped constantly into hot water. On each finger pipe the word 'Sacher' in piping chocolate.

On the base spread a thick layer of whipped and sweetened fresh cream. Place the tops in position and cut through carefully, wiping the knife constantly to prevent cream smears appearing on the top. The keeping quality of this line will depend very much upon the type of cream used in the filling.

Lemon Slices

Strips of lemon-coloured and -flavoured genoese are cut $2\frac{1}{2}$ in (6·4 cm) wide split, and sandwiched with cream cheese.

Lemon slices

Pin out the amount of marzipan or almond paste required to approximately $\frac{1}{8}$-in (3 mm) thick and roll with the basket roller, dusting with castor sugar to prevent sticking. Reverse the marzipan carefully so as not to disturb the marking and wrap two sides and the top in the prepared marzipan, using lemon cheese as the adhesive medium.

The strips thus prepared will keep some time, depending upon storage, and the type of genoese used. Finally, cut into 1 in (2·6 cm) slices.

Afternoon Tea Fancies

Cut white, vanilla-flavoured, genoese into easily handled blocks. Spread with white, vanilla-flavoured buttercream and place in the refrigerator to harden.

Dip a knife constantly into hot water and cut into square of the required size. Using a two-pronged fork, dip into couverture or baker's chocolate, removing the surplus to prevent the formation of 'feet'.

Pipe a whirl of white, vanilla-flavoured buttercream in the top centre of each to cover the fork marks, and surmount with a small chocolate curl, lightly dredging with icing sugar to complete.

Cauliflowers

From a sheet of vanilla genoese cut out the required number of circles, using a $1\frac{1}{2}$ in (3·8 cm) plain cutter. Mask the sides with apricot purée or, if the flavour is preferred, lemon cheese. Around the sides place four discs of green marzipan, cut with the $1\frac{1}{2}$ in (3·8 cm) plain cutter and pressed into the cup of the hand to form leaf shape. Complete by piping on to the top the representation of the 'flower'.

Pineapple Genoese

Prepare the pineapple-coloured and -flavoured genoese by removing the top with the 'cross-bow' as previously detailed, and cutting into $1\frac{1}{2}$ in (3·8 cm) squares.

Place each piece on to a dipping fork and immerse sides and base in chocolate, making certain that base and sides are dipped properly, with surplus removed so as not to show 'feet'.

Blanch pineapple pieces in sugar syrup boiled to the thread degree (225°F (110°C)), drain, and mix the fruit into boiling apricot purée. Place carefully in position on the top of the genoese, taking care that the chocolate sides are kept 'clean'.

Petits Fours Glacés

We, in Britain, understand these as cut genoese in a variety of shapes dipped into fondant and finished in various ways, whilst our continental friends take the meaning to be 'small filled fancies, fondant dipped' and include a large assortment of bases in their variety. Here, however, I am dealing solely with our interpretation.

Unless a system is adopted and strictly adhered to, this job is one that can very soon turn a tidy confectionery room into chaos, with consequent deterioration in the finished goods, thereby greatly detracting from the attractive appearance that should characterise these goods. A few golden rules, if strictly observed, will assist considerably.

If a cutting box is not available genoese should be tipped out on to the marble slab, the paper removed and any soft crumb scraped off and swept up. Now cut into convenient sized pieces, which can be reversed without danger of breakage. The top skin should be removed with a thin bladed knife, afterwards sweeping up all loose crumbs and placing into a hand-bowl for later use.

Any fillings can be added after the genoese has been split and these may take the form of various jams (excluding the seeded varieties such as raspberry), piping jelly, lemon cheese, and various coloured and flavoured buttercreams, etc. Replace the top and spread very thinly with well-boiled apricot purée, afterwards cutting into the required shapes with a sharp knife, wiped constantly to prevent drag.

Any cutters used should be rotated slightly to prevent dragging and consequent crumbling. The remarks made previously regarding size and shape also apply here and sticks of correct widths will assist considerably in standardising the sizes.

Topping

Next add to the cut pieces of genoese any toppings required. These may take the form of crumb paste (made from sieved genoese crumbs, apricot jam and a few spots of rum mixed to a smooth paste), marzipan, buttercream, or marshmallow, but it must be stressed that all toppings should be of soft-eating materials—hardness should be avoided. Those with buttercream tops should be placed in a refrigerator to harden before dipping, whilst marshmallow tops should be dipped as soon as possible after this has been added.

The shapes should now be placed on wires or trays in the order of the colour required, so that all those to be dipped in white fondant, for instance, are together, all pinks, and so on; this will save much time during actual dipping.

Preparing the fondant

Whilst this work has been proceeding, it is, of course, an advantage, if a bain marie is available, to render the fondant to a workable condition. Failing this, sufficient pans may be filled with fondant and stood in a large hand-bowl, containing hot water, over a very low gas jet, allowing this gentle heat to warm and soften the fondant. When ready for use, the fondant should be at about 105°F (40°C), sufficiently thinned with water or stock syrup, just to coat the spatula when this is removed from the pan. Whilst conditioning the fondant, the spatula should be employed with a stirring, not beating, motion, otherwise air will be incorporated, leaving bubbles in the coated genoese.

One of the major faults in this work is to get the fondant too thick, thus making the finished fancies sickly to eat and wasteful in material. The aim should be to get the covering thick enough to hide the genoese, yet thin enough to make for a pleasant eating quality.

Colours

Colours should, of course, be kept to a pastel shade, apart from chocolate which should be definite and contain a proportion of melted, unsweetened chocolate; hideous pinks and violent orange colours are to be avoided.

Dipping the fancies

The genoese, now ready for dipping, should be placed on the left-hand side of the bench, cleaned and free from crumbs, with the prepared pan of fondant immediately to the right hand, and to the right of this a draining wire placed to receive the dipped fancies.

After dipping, start placing them at the extreme right-hand side of the wire, so that subsequent fancies, when dipped and dripping, do not have to be carried over those completed.

Three methods of dipping are possible: firstly, the fork method, where the piece of genoese is placed on a fork, sometimes an old table fork with two prongs bent to prevent them going right through the genoese. Using this method, the piece of genoese is placed on the prongs, reversed and immersed in the fondant and withdrawn in a circular motion, surplus fondant being removed with a small palette knife.

The second method is to take the genoese with the left hand, transfer to thumb and forefinger of the right hand, immerse and remove from the fondant in a manner similar to the first method, placing immediately on the draining board wire to enable surplus fondant to drain off.

In the third method, hold the cut genoese in the left hand and, using the right hand immersed in the fondant, lay this over the genoese, afterwards placing immediately on the wire to drain.

Each method has its own advantages and disadvantages, but the operative soon finds a natural aptitude for one particular method.

Any fondant required for piping should be taken from the pan before dipping commences. After a particular colour has been used, the draining wire should be removed and all scrapings replaced in the pan, which should be scraped and wiped down and a little cold water poured on top of the fondant to prevent crusting. All colours should be kept separately, for it is wrong to place scrapings of all colours and varieties into one pan and hope to produce a good chocolate fondant from them.

Fondant Dipped Fancies

For the smaller producer, much time can be wasted in producing these together with too thick a covering being applied and corresponding escaltation of costs.

Problems easily overcome

To the plant baker, this is easily overcome by the use of an enrober, and although there are models designed for the smaller man, the expense of purchase is not warranted if the use is only to be an hour or two per week. This, however, can quite easily be overcome.

The quantity of genoese dipped weekly varies but very little, so the finishing-room staff should have a good idea of the amount of fondant required.

Before commencing to prepare the genoese, as previously described, the amount of fondant should be cut up and, piece by piece, dropped into a suitable machine bowl fitted with the dough hook. If the machine is started on slow speed, with a very small flame on a gas-ring placed beneath, then, by the time the genoese is prepared, the fondant is ready. No time is wasted standing over the stove with small pan and spatula.

Any fondant needing colouring may be taken from the bulk and the remainder transferred to a suitable wide pan or bowl and placed in another, slightly larger, receptacle, containing warm water. A mobile gas-ring under this will, with very little trouble, keep the fondant in condition for enrobing.

Enrobe with ladle

Actual enrobing can be carried out by using a large soup ladle and holding the wire over the bowl. The fondant must be at the correct temperature—approximately 105°F (40°C) or this is not possible.

In the writer's experience, two good operatives, working together as a team, can get through far more dipping in the manner described than by the more conventional manner of individual dipping. Furthermore, and of great importance, the work done in the manner described is generally of far higher standard.

No. 1 Vanilla Fondant

A diamond shape of vanilla-flavoured genoese is enrobed with white fondant, with the simple motif piped on, freehand, in chocolate piping fondant. Complete with a silver dragée at the joining points of the piped motif.

Vanilla fondant, shamrock and coffee fondant

No. 2 Shamrock

A square of lemon-coloured and -flavoured genoese is enrobed with lemon-coloured and -flavoured fondant. A piped-chocolate-fondant St. Andrew's cross divides the top and a similar medium outlines the shamrock, the centre of which is filled with lime piping jelly.

No. 3 Coffee Fondant

A coffee-genoese oblong is enrobed with coffee fondant. A straight line in chocolate piping fondant divides the fancy lengthwise, with two 'C' scrolls backing on to it. A coffee bean either in moulded chocolate or modelled coffee marzipan, placed in the centre, completes the effect.

No. 4 Cherries

Two small pieces of marzipan are moulded round and placed in one corner of an oblong-shaped piece of vanilla genoese. Each 'cherry' is touched with pink colour and, when dry, enrobed with pale yellow fondant. Complete by piping in the stalks in chocolate fondant, hiding the joint of the stalk with a 'leaf' piped in green buttercream.

No. 5 Pears

A variation of the previous variety, a pear-shaped piece of marzipan is placed corner to corner on a square piece of vanilla-flavoured genoese. Again touch with pink colour and enrobe with yellow fondant. Complete by piping on stalk and eye with chocolate fondant, and leaf in green buttercream.

No. 6 Chocolate Truffle

Enrobe a square of chocolate genoese with chocolate fondant, and on the top pipe a spiral of chocolate fondant. Complete with a truffle ball produced from ganaché or marzipan, rolled in liquid chocolate and immediately in chocolate vernicelli. Lightly dredge with icing sugar.

No. 7

A diamond-shaped genoese, with lemon cheese filling, is dipped in lemon coloured and flavoured fondant; a whirl of buttercream, flavoured with lemon cheese, with a half chocolate disc, produced from baker's chocolate or chocolate couverture, stood upright, completes.

No. 8

A square genoese with orange piping jelly filling is dipped in orange coloured and flavoured fondant; a segment of orange jelly slice, with two orange fondant bulbs, is used as a finish. This could be varied by using lemon fondant and slices.

No. 9

Raspberry-flavoured genoese, of triangular shape, with a vanilla buttercream filling containing chopped cherries, is dipped in pink, raspberry-flavoured fondant; the shape is outlined with the same coloured piping fondant, and a simple finish of a piece of cherry and three green piped buttercream leaves is employed.

No. 10

Oblong chocolate genoese, with vanilla buttercream filling, is topped with crumb paste, and dipped in chocolate fondant; a split almond completes.

No. 11

Oblong white genoese, with apricot jam filling, is dipped in white fondant and completed with half a cherry, chocolate fondant stalk and pale green piped buttercream leaves.

No. 12

Dominoes—the children's favourite. White genoese, with vanilla buttercream filling, is dipped in white fondant, with chocolate fondant piping in the 'spots'.

No. 13

Easter chicken—diamond-shaped genoese, with buttercream flavoured with some lemon cheese as filling, is dipped in white fondant, then a chicken outline is piped in white piping fondant and filled in with top quality lemon cheese; pipe in beak and eye with chocolate fondant.

No. 14

Vanilla genoese, with lemon cheese filling, is dipped in white fondant and then immediately diagonally into coconut. Overpipe the fondant-coconut joint with white piping fondant and complete with a piece of walnut placed on the fondant.

No. 15

A vanilla genoese square, with apricot jam filling and a vanilla buttercream pyramid top, is dipped in white fondant: add a spiral of the same colour in piping fondant, and complete with a silver dragee.

No. 16

Take genoese squares, with vanilla buttercream filling; a small piece of marzipan is moulded round and cut into two, one piece being placed on each square. Dip in pale yellow fondant and complete with a spot öf chocolate fondant and a piece of angelica.

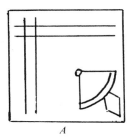 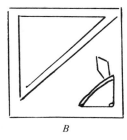 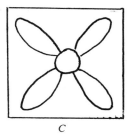

| A | B | C |

A Lemon: *Enrobing and linework in lemon coloured and flavoured fondant, placing a lemon jelly segment in one corner, completing with angelica diamond and spot of raspberry piping jelly*

B Orange: *Enrobe and pipe with orange coloured and flavoured fondant, finishing with a segment of orange jelly slice, angelica diamond and spot of raspberry piping jelly*

C Chocolate: *Enrobing with and piping with chocolate fondant, complete with chocolate truffle as top decoration*

 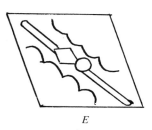

| D | E |

D Pineapple: *enrobing and outer lines with pineapple fondant, inner line with chocolate fondant, completing with segment of crystallised pineapple, cherry and angelica*

E Maraschino: *enrobe and pipe centre line with fondant coloured pink, flavoured with maraschino. Pipe outer lines with chocolate fondant, complete with portion of maraschino cherry and angelica*

No. 17

A genoese triangle, with a praline buttercream filling, is dipped into coffee fondant and quickly completed with small chocolate squares produced from coffee flavoured baker's chocolate.

No. 18

Chocolate genoese, oblong shape, with chocolate buttercream filling, is dipped into chocolate fondant, and completed by piping three lines on each side of a half-circle of chocolate couverture, or baker's chocolate, placed on top.

No. 19

A variation of No. 1, using walnuts as an alternative to the chocolate, and having the three lines piped diagonally across the top.

These varieties are merely a few of the quick, commercial types that may be produced. So great are the possibilities that one can merely scratch the surface. It will be noticed those illustrated are cut from the genoese with a minimum of waste, for the use of cutters has been purposely avoided to illustrate that variety can be introduced with no waste.

Preparing for Sale

After drying, the fancies should be removed from the wires by means of a palette knife dipped constantly into hot water, and placed into paper cases ready for sale. Rather than rely on variegated colours of cases, which quite often clash with the colours of fondant, it is a good idea to adopt a basic colour and to stick to it, with the firm's name printed on the inside base of the case. These, then, give a certain uniformity to the window display and allow the fancy to appeal to the customer rather than the case. It is also a form of advertising to customers out of your own district and they can be a source of increased trade, especially after orders have been completed for parties and dances, etc., outside the normal trading area.

For cocktail parties

Quite often, a cocktail party order includes a number of fancies. A percentage of these should include petits fours glacés, but, especially for these orders, the genoese should be cut approximately one-half to two-thirds the normal size.

Remember, a cocktail party is not a meal, but a snack, and the fancies should be in keeping with the size of the savouries.

If these orders are regular, then it is worth while ordering a stock of small paper cases specially for these.

For an isolated order it is possible to purchase small chocolate coloured paper cases, which are quite satisfactory.

Battenberg

A line that has proved popular over the years and which, admirably lending itself to pre-packing in transparent wrappers, has a good shelf-life is the battenberg.

Battenberg, with the Christmas motif of holly piquet

Using equal proportions of pink raspberry-flavoured genoese and white vanilla-flavoured genoese, remove the top and bottom skins and spread with white vanilla-flavoured buttercream or raspberry piping jelly, afterwards placing one squarely upon the other. Should it be intended to wrap the battenberg after completion, it is advisable to use buttercream or apricot purée for the adhesive medium, as piping jelly, after being enclosed for a short time, is apt, I have found, to render the marzipan sticky.

Preferably using a stick of the correct width as a guide, cut the prepared genoese in widths the same as the thickness of one single genoese. Turn the first strip on to its side, spread with buttercream or piping jelly, and place the second strip on to the first, pink genoese to white, continuing until all the strips have been so treated.

Pin out sufficient marzipan quite thinly and, if the first method is adopted, roll first with the ribbed marzipan roller. Now roll the marzipan round a long rolling-pin and reverse on to the slab. Taking the first piece of prepared genoese, spread one side with the buttercream or apricot purée and place in position on the marzipan, trimming the latter neatly along the side and edges. Next spread the second side with the adhesive medium and roll over, continuing until the genoese is totally enclosed, afterwards cutting the marzipan off neatly at the joint.

Spreading the genoese with the cream or purée, does, I find, obviate any marzipan cuttings having to be wasted through contact with these mediums.

If the second method of finish is adopted, then, of course, the ribbed roller is dispensed with and, after wrapping in marzipan, the edges of the strip pinched with marzipan nippers. After the strips have been completed, all that remains is for the ends to be neatly trimmed and for the strips to be cut into convenient lengths.

Chocolate Battenberg

It is indisputable that the ordinary four-square battenberg is a very firm favourite and the chocolate battenberg becomes a firm rival wherever it is introduced.

Produce as for the normal four-square battenberg, adding to this another two squares. If desired, of course, another colour of genoese could be introduced, but the raspberry and vanilla, or chocolate and vanilla genoese, as traditionally used, should be sufficient. Any additional flavour of genoese would, naturally, only increase the cost, and it is doubtful if this would be of any advantage.

Wrap two sides and the top only in thinly-rolled marzipan, using apricot jam, piping jelly or buttercream as the adhesive medium.

Enrobe the top and two sides with chocolate, quite thinly, removing the surplus and decorating the top with good-quality walnut halves. Allow to set on a piece of greaseproof or wax paper, before cutting into pre-determined-sized pieces. Wrapping and sealing in transparent cellulose make this an ideal line to prepare for the busy season, especially if high-ratio genoese is used.

Motifs can be used to denote season, so that, at Christmas time, holly

Chocolate battenberg, suitable for a festive occasion if given a seasonal motif

piquets could be used in place of walnuts, and at Easter one can cut out marzipan or sugar-paste rabbits or chicks could be utilised.

Many Variations

The battenberg described is, of course, the basic simple type, but many variations may be made, using differently coloured and flavoured genoese bases, with coloured marzipan, and finished by cutting a centre channel from the top marzipan and flooding this with fondant, completing the decoration with cherries, angelica, walnuts, etc.

Lemon or Orange Layer Cake

Using two strips of the appropriately coloured and flavoured genoese, remove the top and bottom skins and split, sandwiching with the appropriately coloured and flavoured buttercream, afterwards joining together with the same medium.

Wrap three sides in a very thin layer of marzipan before covering with fondant. Complete the decoration very simply with segments of orange or lemon jelly slices, piping three fine lines of fondant along each side.

If desired fine coconut may be applied along the side of the cake to give extra finish.

Raspberry Layer Cake

Sandwich alternately two bars of white vanilla-flavoured genoese and two of pink raspberry-flavoured genoese with raspberry piping jelly and vanilla buttercream.

Enclose three sides in pink marzipan, cover with pink fondant, and complete with piped fondant bulbs and, inside these, two parallel lines piped with the same medium.

Complete with half cherries and angelica diamonds.

Chocolate Walnut Layer Cake

Layer alternate slices of white and chocolate genoese with vanilla buttercream to which chopped walnuts have been added. Cover two sides and the top of the genoese with a thin layer of marzipan before masking with baker's chocolate.

Just before the setting point of the chocolate is reached, mark off into diamond shapes with a palette knife and complete with half walnuts.

An alternative finish would be to apply a second masking of baker's chocolate after the first has dried and, just before setting point is reached, to comb with a comb scraper, completing with a pinch of green nib almonds or, alternatively, walnuts.

Pyramid Layer Cake

Using white vanilla-flavoured buttercream, sandwich one thickness of white genoese between two thicknesses of chocolate genoese. Place the prepared genoese parallel to the edge of the bench and, using a good cutting knife, split diagonally from the lower corner at the nearest point and place the two pieces back to back to form a pyramid shape.

Wrap on the three sides with marzipan and brush two-thirds along each side with couverture or baker's chocolate.

As a cheaper alternative to wrapping three sides with marzipan, sweet paste, previously rolled, docked and cut to the correct width before baking, may be utilised for the base.

Both this and the previous line may, of course, be produced smaller, cut into slices, and placed in paper cases to provide two further varieties of fancies.

Coffee-chocolate Layer Cake

Sandwich alternatively two layers of coffee and two of chocolate genoese, in this instance cut square, with coffee-coloured and flavoured buttercream. Mask the sides with coffee-flavoured baker's chocolate and, using a star tube, decorate the top simply with the coffee buttercream.

Complete by placing in position half circles of coffee-flavoured baker's chocolate, prepared by spreading a thin layer of the chocolate on to grease-proof paper, and cutting with a fluted cutter of suitable size just before setting point is reached.

To halve the circles, use a sharp knife dipped constantly into hot water.

Coffee-vanilla Layer Cake

Alternative layers of coffee and white vanilla-flavoured genoese are sandwiched with apricot purée. Mask the sides with coffee-flavoured baker's chocolate and, using a star tube, pipe five parallel lines of coffee-coloured and flavoured buttercream, filling the spaces between with the coffee-flavoured baker's chocolate. When set, trim the ends with a sharp knife dipped into hot water before cutting into lengths of the required size.

Cherry Layer Cake

The basis for this layer cake is two bars of white vanilla-flavoured genoese and two bars of pale pink, flavoured with kirsch. The buttercream is similarly coloured and flavoured and that for sandwiching contains a proportion of chopped cherries.

After masking the assembled genoese, comb the top and mask the sides with fine, roasted, flake almonds, afterwards framing with a star tube and piping corner pieces to hide the joints. Complete by using half and quarter cherries to form a flower centre-pattern, with half cherries and diamond pieces of angelica at each end.

Chocolate Logs

Two bars of white vanilla-flavoured genoese and two of chocolate genoese are sandwiched, alternatively, with white vanilla-flavoured buttercream. Cut the strips into the required length and mask all over with chocolate ganache, previously warmed and well beaten to a good spreading consistency. Allow a short period for this to set before masking with couverture or baker's chocolate and completing simply with three walnut halves.

Torte-type Gateau

This is an ideal line for milk- or snack-bar trade, and gateaux produced in this manner may be kept on one side whilst more perishable goods are sold, thus ensuring that the proprietor always has a stock of confectionary on hand ready for any unexpected rush of trade.

One illustration will be sufficient to give the general idea, for these gateaux may be carried out in various colours and flavours.

White vanilla-flavoured genoese is scaled at $1\frac{1}{4}$ lb (570 g) in 10 in (25·5 cm) hoops. When baked and cold, split and sandwich with a good quality lemon cheese. Mask top and sides with buttercream flavoured and coloured by the addition of lemon cheese, afterwards masking the sides with fine, roasted, flake almonds.

Mark with torten divider or palette knife to divide the top into sixteen portions and, using a star tube and lemon buttercream, pipe a design on each segment, with a simple centre rosette. Complete by piping a spot of lemon cheese on the design of each segment.

Lemon-Coconut Gateau

A plain gateau base produced from the general purpose mix is scaled at $7\frac{1}{2}$ oz (215 g) into 1 lb (450 g) cottage pans.

After baking and when cold, split and sandwich with lemon cheese, afterwards masking with lemon buttercream, using lightly roasted, fine, desiccated coconut for the sides. The top design is piped in lemon buttercream, and good quality lemon cheese used to complete.

Coffee Gateau

A $7\frac{1}{2}$ oz (210 g) coffee-flavoured gateau, produced from the general purpose mix, is sandwiched with white vanilla-flavoured buttercream. Mask with boiled apricot purée applied thinly, followed by coffee fondant, running a thin masking of roasted flake almonds round the base.

The top design is piped in coffee-coloured and flavoured fondant, and the 'coffee beans' are produced in a plastic mould, using coffee-flavoured baker's chocolate to complete the decoration. Should such a mould not be available, the coffee beans can be produced from coffee-flavoured marzipan, moulded to shape and with the 'split' made with the back of a knife or marzipan modelling tool.

Fondant Chocolate-coffee Layer Cake

A marked similarity will be noticed here to the coffee gateau, but for this layer cake four bars of chocolate genoese are layered with vanilla buttercream.

Enclose the top and two sides with a thin layer of marzipan, and cover with coffee fondant, again using flake almonds along the base.

Complete the decoration with coffee beans, outlining each twice with cool, coffee, piping fondant.

Coffee, mushroom, almond and praline gateaux

Mushroom Gateau

Using as the base a $7\frac{1}{2}$ oz (210 g) plain gateau made from the general purpose mix, scaled into 1 lb (450 g) cottage pans, split and sandwich with apricot purée, afterwards masking with the same medium.

Completely wrap the top and sides with white marzipan, reversing to show the base uppermost.

Using chocolate buttercream and a star tube, pipe in the representation of the underside of a natural mushroom, working from the outside to the centre, afterwards dredging with a mixture comprising equal quantities of cocoa and icing sugar.

Roll out under the hands a rope of white marzipan to a diameter of 1 in ($2 \cdot 6$ cm) afterwards cutting into $1\frac{1}{2}$ in ($3 \cdot 8$ cm) lengths. Place one length in the centre of each gateau at a slight angle, making an indentation with the thumb to represent the 'picked' stalk.

Almond Gateau

The base is from the general purpose mix, almond flavoured, and scaled at $7\frac{1}{2}$ oz (210 g) into 1 lb (450 g) cottage pans.

Lemon, chocolate and orange gateaux

After baking, split, and sandwich and mask all over with almond-flavoured buttercream. Before masking the sides with roasted flake almonds, dredge the top heavily with icing sugar and mark into squares, using the edge of a palette knife. Complete with small whorls of chocolate buttercream, into the centre of which are placed half circles of chocolate.

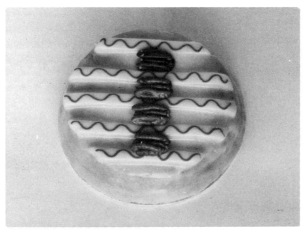

A simple lemon coloured and flavoured gateau base, with strips of marzipan across, enrobed with lemon fondant and wavy chocolate lines on the marzipan. Decor completed with pecans or walnuts

Plain Gateau

A plain gateau base from the general purpose mix, scaled at 8 oz (230 g) into 9 in (23 cm) sandwich tins, is split and sandwiched with apricot purée and vanilla buttercream. Mask the top with apricot purée, followed by white fondant, placing in the centre a disc of white sugar paste before the fondant has set. Mask the sides with white buttercream and lightly roasted coconut.

Pipe a continuous crinkled rop of white vanilla buttercream round the edge, using the same tube and medium at the joint between sugar paste and fondant. Complete with half a cherry in the centre and buttercream piped from a leaf tube to form a flower.

Rose Gateau

A raspberry-flavoured pink-coloured gateau base of similar size to the previous one is split and sandwiched with pink raspberry-flavoured buttercream. Mask the top with apricot purée, followed by pink fondant, and the sides with pink raspberry-flavoured buttercream and roasted flake almonds.

Complete by piping ever-widening circles of the basic-coloured fondant, placing in the centre two roses, two rosebuds, modelled in pink marzipan or sugar paste, and a very small spray of maidenhair fern.

Lemon Gateau

A lemon coloured and flavoured gateau base is split and sandwiched with lemon buttercream. Mask with apricot purée and pale yellow fondant, running a thin line of roasted coconut round the base.

Complete, with piping, the design in cool fondant of the basic colour, and a whorl of lemon buttercream in the centre surmounted by a half cherry, with small leaves piped in piping chocolate.

A simple buttercream finish, using cut chocolate pieces to accentuate the design

Orange Gateau

Using an orange-flavoured base, sandwiched with orange buttercream flavoured by the zest and juice of fresh oranges, the finish is of appropriately coloured fondant with the word 'Orange' piped in a similar medium.

The representation of an orange is modelled in marzipan, before being rolled in castor sugar and offset on the gateau by two pieces of angelica cut in a diamond shape.

Chocolate Gateau

No. 1

A $7\frac{1}{2}$ oz (210 g) chocolate gateau from the general purpose mix is sandwiched with vanilla buttercream and masked with apricot purée, followed by chocolate fondant with a thin mask of roasted flake almonds at the base.

Just prior to setting point, place a disc of baker's chocolate or couverture, prepared previously and cut with a fluted cutter, in the centre of the gateau, afterwards piping in the design with cool, chocolate fondant. Complete by piping in the centre of the chocolate disc another disc of white fondant, with a quarter walnut on each.

Chocolate gateaux with autumnal seasonal motif

No. 2

A very simple line, of quick finish, which admirably lends itself to those bakeries equipped with an enrober, and which, in spite of its simplicity, is popular with the public.

A $7\frac{1}{2}$ oz (210 g) gateau, chocolate flavoured, is split and sandwiched with apricot jam and vanilla buttercream. Mask with ganache; allow sufficient time for this to set, and mask with chocolate couverture or baker's chocolate, with a pinch of green almond nibs to complete.

Whilst chocolate couverture is of better flavour, it splinters on confectionery, making the goods untidy when cut. A baker's chocolate of good flavour is to be preferred.

These, then, are some of the more usual types of gateaux, but other varieties are possible, using genoese bases in conjunction with meringue and jap bases.

Buttercream Gateau

Split and sandwich with an appropriately flavoured jam, curd or cream, then mask the top with the basic-flavoured buttercream. Thus would an orange gateau require orange buttercream, and so on.

The parallel lines of buttercream are piped with a coarsely-cut star tube, leaving approximately the width of the tube between each line. The space thus caused is filled with a piping jelly or curd compatible with the basic flavour, the original masking of the base now reflecting through the jelly, giving a clean, bright appearance.

Buttercream gateau

Sprinkle the top with chocolate; mask the sides of the gateau with the buttercream, followed by jap crumbs, roasted coconut, almond nibs or any one of the ancillaries to match the gateau.

Orange or Lemon Gateau

An appropriately coloured and flavoured base is split, sandwiched with buttercream, masked with apricot purée, followed by fondant of the colour and flavour desired, with a narrow masking of roasted coconut round the base.

The gateau is then divided simply into four by neat fondant piping, and a segment of lemon or orange jelly slice placed in each quarter.

Hawaiian Gateau

Pineapple appears to be a fruit of which the public never tire. Using this particular mixing, method and idea, we can produce one line that is most unusual in character and, in addition, use the same mixing to provide excellent gateau bases. Sandwich tins are utilised, size optional, and these must be very carefully prepared. *Careless preparation will ruin the entire effect.*

Multiple ring Hawaiian gateau . . .

First, grease well in the normal manner, then cream together 1 lb 14 oz (850 g) brown sugar and 1 lb 2 oz (510 g) shortening. When light, stop the machine, add and beat in 9 oz (255 g) honey.

Re-grease with the above mixture, using a liberal quantity, then pattern the tin with pineapple rings taken straight from a tin, with the syrup only dried off.

The number of rings used will, of course, depend upon the diameter of the sandwich pan. Whole glacé cherries should be used for the centre of the rings, for this will add colour.

. . . single ring for reduced costs

Now for the mixing.

1 lb 3 oz (540 g) shortening	1¼ oz (50 g) salt
5 oz (140 g) milk powder	2¼ oz (64 g) baking powder
3¼ lb (1480 g) weak flour	

Cream the above together until light, approximately 7 or 8 min.

3¼ lb (1700 g) castor sugar   2 lb (910 g) water

Warm to dissolve the sugar, allow to go cold, then add to the above ingredients in four quantities.

1 lb 14 oz or 1½ pt (850 g or 0·85 litres) egg   10 oz (280 g) unsweetened pineapple juice

Add the final stage, again in four or five quantities, ensuring that bowl and beater are well scraped down at intervals.

Scale into the prepared tins and, as a guide, a 6 in (15 cm) sandwich tin will require approximately 7 oz (200 g) batter with other sizes *pro rata*.

Bake at 340–350°F (170–177°C) for approximately 40 min, and empty on to a clean cloth or sack immediately, leaving undisturbed until cool. The cake is then, of course, ready for immediate sale, with no finish required.

Pineapple Gateau

As can be seen from the illustration, the mixing also produces a first-class base, 10 oz (280 g) being scaled into a 7 in (18 cm) cottage pan, this having been previously greased and floured in the normal way. The cake produced is bold, light, tender eating and of good keeping quality.

Hawaiian gateau base

Type No. 1

Split the gateau base and sandwich with buttercream, well flavoured by the addition of the syrup from crystallised pineapple. If a quick sale is assured, a little chopped, tinned pineapple may be added, but it should be remembered that this could quite quickly cause deterioration, so care should be exercised.

Mask the base thinly with boiled apricot purée, enrobe with fondant, coloured and *flavoured* pineapple, completing with the design illustrated. Piping here is carried out with chocolate fondant. Segments or crystallised pineapple, half cherries and angelica diamonds provide the finishing touch.

Type No. 2

Is split and sandwiched with pineapple jam and again masked with boiled apricot purée, followed by pineapple-coloured and *-flavoured* fondant.

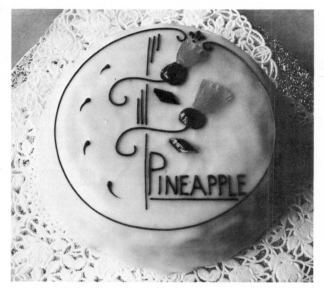

Pineapple gateau No. 1 . . .

. . . and No. 2

The design, again utilising chocolate fondant, crystallised pineapple, half cherries and angelica diamonds, is a much simpler version of No. 1. Indeed, speaking from a commercial viewpoint, the writer is loath to use very much piping on gateaux for, all too soon, can it become slip-shod and 'rough', thus lowering the whole tone of the window display. Far better a minimum of piping, used effectively, and kept neat, than an attempt to overelaborate.

This is especially noticeable at Christmas and other busy times, when tiredness and 'rush' creep in, with inevitable results.

Banana Sponge

We find the banana sponge to be a line tender in character, unusual in flavour and unique in that mashed banana can replace, either wholly or in part, the egg content of a mixing. This particular recipe does, indeed, require no egg, yet is of excellent keeping quality, tender eating and delicious.

Perhaps one of the drawbacks of using bananas is the cost, for, if using fresh banana, twice the required amount must be bought to compensate for the weight of skins.

However, tinned mashed banana is now obtainable here, very reasonably priced, and if one costs the following recipe, it is obvious that the banana cost

Banana layer cake, produced from . . .

. . . banana sponge

is no more expensive than if egg were included. Considered this way, it is therefore possible to provide the line that is 'different' at no extra cost or increase in selling price.

You need:

2½ lb (1140 g) high-ratio flour	2¼ oz (64 g) baking powder
3 lb (1360 g) castor sugar	¾-oz (21 g) salt
3 oz (85 g) milk powder	

Sieve the above together then add:

1 lb 2 oz (510 g) high-ratio shortening   1 lb 3 oz (540 g) mashed bananas

Mix all together on slow speed until clear for approximately 5 min, then add 1 lb 12 oz (795 g) water in several portions, scraping well down to clear well.

This may be scaled into papered sheet tins as for genoese, baking at 350–360°F (175–180°C). When cold, press and leave for 24 h before using.

Very many uses for this will spring readily to mind, with the simple finish of banana layer cake to provide a starting point.

Banana Layer Cake

For this, cut strips of the sponge 2½ in (6·4 cm) wide and layer two together, sandwiching with apricot jam.

Mask the top thinly with banana-coloured and -flavoured buttercream and place in a refrigerator to harden.

Re-mask, comb with comb scraper, mask the sides with a similar buttercream, followed by roasted flaked almonds. The length will, of course, depend on costings.

An alternative to genoese is to scale the batter as for swiss roll. Spread generously with fresh whipped cream before rolling, dredge with icing sugar afterwards and sell from a deep freeze or refrigerated counter. Thus is produced a really tasty, tender-eating line that can prove a firm favourite and ready winner.

Banana Gateau

Another line making use of mashed banana to give the real fruity flavour. Although fresh bananas may be used, it will obviously be more economical to use the tinned variety.

Banana gateau bases

Banana gateaux

Mix to a smooth paste:

3½ lb (1530 g) brown sugar	5 lb (2270 g) mashed bananas
3 lb (1360 g) castor sugar	2½ oz (70 g) baking powder
2 lb 6 oz (1080 g) high-ratio fat	1¼ oz (36 g) bicarbonate of soda
5 lb (2270 g) high-ratio flour	3 oz (85 g) salt

Then add 2 lb (910 g) milk and colour, as required.

Continue mixing on first speed to a smooth batter, taking approximately 5–7 min. Then add 3 lb 4 oz (1480 g) eggs and 12 oz (340 g) milk, blending into the above in three or four parts, scraping well down at intervals. Scale at 10 oz (280 g) into greased and floured cottage pans, baking off at 370°F (190°C). As the illustration shows, the base is of good volume.

Whilst numerous finishes will readily come to mind, two simple ones are illustrated, using fondant appropriately coloured and to which a little tinned mashed banana has been added. This was used to enrobe the bases, with marzipan modelled bananas painted and added as the motif.

The simple piping is carried out in chocolate fondant, keeping this as neat as possible.

Easter Gateau

A Festive season calls for something different, and these bases have always been well received.

4 lb (1820 g) castor sugar	2 oz (57 g) lemon paste
8 oz (230 g) shortening	4 lb (1820 g) egg
3½ lb (1530 g) butter or margarine	3 lb 6 oz (1530 g) weak flour
2 lb (910 g) marzipan (60/40)	1 lb 2 oz (510 g) cornflour
4 oz (110 g) glycerine	egg colour

Produce by the sugar batter method, creaming the marzipan with the fats and sugar. A nice, light batter should be produced, warming as necessary, and it should be well, but gently, cleared in the final stage.

Scale at 12 oz (340 g) into greased and floured cottage pans, but this can very easily be adjusted by the reader to suit his particular circumstances. Bake at 360°F (180°C), emptying as soon as baked, allowing to mature until next day before finishing.

Finish No. 1

Split the gateaux, layering with lemon buttercream or lemon cheese, mask with boiled apricot purée, followed by lemon coloured and flavoured fondant. Pipe the word 'Easter' in chocolate fondant, completing with Easter motifs such as chickens and rabbits, produced from a marzipan or sugar paste, and readily available from the sundries supplier. Alternatively, piped sugar flowers and a small sprig of fern, asparagus or maidenhair, lend the necessary seasonal touch.

Finish No. 2 (Egg Gateau)

Utilising the previous base, a disc of sweetpaste is required for each gateau. This should be rolled to something like ⅜-in (9 mm) thick and, after being cut to the diameter required, transferred very gently to a greaseproof papered sheet tin. It could be that the diameter could be cut after the paste has been transferred to the sheet. Now, using an oval cutter, cut out four shapes, one in each quarter of the paste, after a short rest baking at 410°F (210°C).

To finish the gateau, split and layer as desired, mask the top with boiled apricot purée and place the baked, cold, sweetpaste disc in position. Mask the sides with buttercream, lemon flavour being suggested, followed by roasted flaked almonds.

Now prepare two bags of fondant, each warmed and adjusted to the usual consistency, one of white, the other a definite egg yellow. Starting with the first of the egg shaped cut-outs, pipe white fondant round the outer edge of the perimeter, filling the centre immediately with yellow fondant, to give the appearence of a sliced, hard boiled egg. Continue until all are completed.

Finish the gateau by piping in the centre a fairly small chocolate 'button', standing in this one of those delightful small, fluffy chicks, or other Easter motifs that really enhance the gateaux.

Almond gateaux with a 'something different' finish

Hazelnut Chocolate Gateau

A medium-quality, reasonably-priced cake is the base for this line, which produces one of good volume, flavour and shelf-life.

Produced by the sugar-batter process, the following ingredients will be required:

2½ lb (1140 g) castor sugar	1½ lb (680 g) milk
1 lb (450 g) golden shortening	3 lb 2 oz (1420 g) weak flour
1 lb (450 g) butter or margarine	1¼ oz (43 g) baking powder
2 oz (57 g) glycerine	5 oz (140 g) cocoa
½-oz (14 g) salt	8 oz (230 g) roasted ground hazelnuts
1¼ lb (680 g) egg	

Scale at 11 oz (310 g) into greased and floured cottage pans, baking at 380°F (195°C) and allowing to stand overnight before finishing.

To do this, split, and layer with apricot jam.

Finishes are, of course, many and varied and illustrated are four variations, all similar, yet all different.

Hazelnut chocolate gateau base

No. 1

Mask top and sides with praline buttercream, combing the top by placing the base on to a turntable, holding comb scraper in position and spinning the table round. Dredge lightly with a mixture of equal quantities of icing sugar and cocoa, mask sides with roasted flaked hazelnuts, and complete with four roasted, dehusked whole hazelnuts.

No. 2

Mask top and sides with praline buttercream, finishing the top with the tip of the palette knife in a paddling motion. Turn the gateau round, so that the 'scribbled' chocolate effect falls across the ridges, and place three roasted, dehusked hazelnuts across the gateau. Mask the sides with roasted flaked hazelnuts.

No. 3

Using chocolate buttercream, mask top and sides of the gateau, followed by grated coffee-flavoured chocolate. Dredge lightly with icing sugar, pipe three

Hazelnut chocolate gateaux 1, 2 . . .

. . . 3 and 4

whirls of chocolate buttercream on the top of the gateau, and place on the top a roasted whole hazelnut.

No. 4

Once again utilising chocolate buttercream, mask the top and sides of the gateau. Comb in a rather haphazard way to give the illustrated effect, placing a pinch of mauve décor in the centre. Mask the sides with roasted flaked hazelnuts.

Mixed Nut Cake

Customers with a weakness for nuts will find this cake a real delight and, for the confectioner, it is a pleasure to produce, for, despite a rather unorthodox method of mixing, the cake is quite stable and bold.

No essence or other other flavour is employed, for, obviously, the type of nut used will provide this influence.

Cream thoroughly together. Scrape down at intervals:

2½ lb (1140 g) castor sugar	3 oz (85 g) weak flour
1 lb (450 g) butter	1¼ oz (36 g) salt
10 oz (280 g) shortening	

Add slowly, scraping down at intervals:

1 lb 10 oz (740 g) egg	egg colour

Add and mix well by hand:

2¼ lb (1020 g) flour	1¼ lb (570 g) mixed nuts
¾-oz (21 g) baking powder	

Whisk to full peak and fold into the above:

1 lb 14 oz or 1½ pt (850 g or 0·85 litres) egg white	15 oz (430 g) castor sugar

Add and well clear:

5 oz or ¼-pt (140 g or 0·14 litres) milk

Scale into previously greased and nutted cottage pans or bread tins. Damp down, sprinkle with mixed nuts and bake at 360–370°F (180–190°C).

When baked, dredge with icing sugar to complete.

Scaling weight will, of course, be determined by costings, but 12 oz (340 g) in either cottage or bread tins should produce a cake of optimum size and price.

Mixed nut cake

Spice Gateau

Even though the quantity of raisins used is quite small, they help to produce a gateau base so different from our usual plain ones.

Cream together:

2½ lb (1140 g) castor sugar	1½ oz (43 g) bicarbonate of soda
1¼ lb (570 g) high ratio shortening	1½ oz (43 g) salt

Add in five quantities, scraping down bowl and beater as required:

2½ lb or 2 pt (1140 g or 1·14 litres) egg

Then break in:

1 lb 14 oz or 1½ pt (850 g or 0·85 litres) milk

Add and partially clear:

3 lb (1360 g) high ratio flour   ⅛-oz (3·5 g) nutmeg, ensuring that these have
¼-oz (7 g) cream powder   been well sieved together
¼-oz (7 g) cinnamon

Finally add and clear:

1 lb 14 oz or 1½ pt (850 g or 0·85 litres) milk

Scale at 11 oz (310 g) into greased and floured cottage pans, baking at 370–380°F (190–195°C). Allow to mature overnight before finishing.

To do this, mask with the raisin icing, followed by roasted flaked almonds. Dredge lightly with icing sugar, completing with a whirl of coffee buttercream and piece of crystallised violet.

Spice gateau

Raisin Icing

Mix together, using beater:

3 lb 2 oz (1420 g) icing sugar $\frac{1}{4}$-oz (7 g) salt
10 oz (280 g) high-ratio shortening   3 oz (85 g) milk powder

Then add 6 oz (170 g) warm water. Beat up quite lightly, then add 10 oz (280 g) raisin jam* and 6 oz (170 g) almond nibs (roasted) and clear well.

*Raisin Jam

Stand 8 oz (230 g) hot water and 8 oz (230 g) raisins for 10 min, then boil to thicken:

8 oz (230 g) sugar
1 oz (28 g) glucose $\frac{1}{4}$-oz (7 g) salt

Border Gateau

Oats are but rarely seen in the bakery, yet here is a line that utilises them and is really 'different'.

12 oz (340 g) boiling water	1½ lb (680 g) evaporated milk
6 oz (170 g) quick-cooking oats	

Pour the boiling water over the oats, stir in the milk, add the above and cook for 1 min.

1¾ lb (800 g) brown sugar	12 oz (340 g) compound
7 oz (200 g) castor sugar	

Cream well together. Scrape down bowl and beater. Add and cream in:

15 oz or ¾-pt (420 g or 0·43 litres) egg	½-oz (14 g) salt
1 lb 2 oz (510 g) weak flour	⅛-oz (3·5 g) cinnamon
¼oz (7 g) bicarbonate of soda	

Sieve together and add alternately with the rolled oat mixing. Mix well after each addition. Add and clear:

9 oz (255 g) soaked, drained raisins	8 oz (230 g) roasted strip almonds

Scale at 9 oz (255 g) into greased and floured sponge sandwich tins, baking at 380–390°F (193–200°C). When baked, leave until the following day to finish, producing, for this, the frosting.

Frosting

Cream well together:

8 oz (230 g) butter	5 oz (140 g) evaporated milk (unsweetened)
12 oz (340 g) high-ratio fat	¼-oz (7 g) proprietary coffee preparation
5 lb (2270 g) icing sugar	

Add:

8 oz (230 g) evaporated milk	⅜-oz (10·5 g) salt

beating in to the required consistency.

Mask the top and sides with the frosting, following on the sides with roasted almonds or jap crumbs. 'Paddle' the top with palette knife tip, then place in position three coffee beans, either modelled by hand from coffee-coloured and -flavoured marzipan, or moulded from coffee-flavoured baker's chocolate, using the plastic coffee-bean moulds.

Border gateau

Brazil Nut Cake

Here we have another 'nut' cake, sold without finish, good to eat and yet reasonably priced.

Prepare the required number of cottage pans by greasing thoroughly and 'nutting' with flaked brazil nuts—another commodity seen all too infrequently in bakeries these days.

Produce the mixing by the sugar-batter process. For this you require:

12 oz (340 g) golden shortening
12 oz (340 g) butter
2 oz (56 g) glycerine
3 lb (1360 g) castor sugar
1½ lb (680 g) egg yolk
3 lb 2 oz (1420 g) weak flour

1¼ oz (43 g) baking powder
½-oz (14 g) salt
2½ lb or 1 qt (1140 g or 1·14 litres) milk
egg colour
vanilla essence

Scale at 11 oz (310 g) into the prepared tins, baking at 360–370°F (180–185°C).

Honey Raisin Gateau

This particular base is of great interest, as the entire sugar content takes the form of honey. Quite nicely flavoured, the base is bold.

Before use, the raisins should be treated to ensure clean cutting and soft eating, either of two ways being suitable:

1—Cover the raisins with cold water, bring to the boil and allow to stand 5 min. before draining.

2—Soak for 20 min. in warm (*not boiling*) water, and well drain.

For the base, blend together 5 lb (2270 g) honey and 1 lb 12 oz (800 g) shortening.

Sieve together three times, add approximately one quarter to the above and beat well in:

5 lb (2270 g) weak flour	1 oz (28 g) salt
3½ oz (100 g) baking powder	1½ oz (43 g) cinnamon
¾-oz (21 g) bicarbonate of soda	1¼ oz (36 g) nutmeg

Now add 2 lb 8 oz or 1 qt (1140 g or 1·14 litres) egg in four or five portions, scraping bowl and beater well at intervals. Add the remaining dry ingredients, partially mix in, then add 2 lb 12 oz (1250 g) milk.

Finally, add and clear:

2¼ lb (1140 g) chopped raisins	1¼ lb (570 g) lightly-roasted almond nibs

Scale at 12 oz (340 g) into 7 in (18 cm) cottage pans, greased and floured, and bake at 360°F (180°C).

Allow to cool, then ice with honey icing.

To make this, boil 2 lb 8 oz (1140 g) honey and ⅛-oz (3·5 g) salt to 240°F (115°C), then add to 5 egg whites previously whipped to wet peak. Add the honey in a steady stream and whip to the desired consistency.

Mask top and sides quickly with the hot icing—which greatly resembles marshmallow, but only in appearance—and mask the sides with croquant, crushed to suitable size.

Butterscotch Gateau

This cake is one where the flavour has very great appeal. The actual cake is very light and sweet, but perhaps the greatest drawback is that the shelf life of the filling is limited. So a quick sale is advisable.

Beat well, scraping down bowl and beater at intervals:

2½ lb (1140 g) high-ratio flour	1 lb 6 oz (620 g) shortening

Mix well together and add to the above over 4 min:

3½ lb (1530 g) castor sugar	½-oz (14 g) cream powder
1½ oz (43 g) salt	14 oz (400 g) water
2½ oz (70 g) baking powder	4 oz (114 g) milk powder

Mix well together and add gradually over 5 min to ensure a smooth batter:

1 lb 14 oz or $1\frac{1}{2}$ pt (850 g or 0·85 litres) egg white	1 lb 2 oz (510 g) milk
	$\frac{1}{2}$-oz (14 g) lemon paste

Scale at 7 oz (200 g) into greased and floured sandwich tins, baking at 380°F (195°C).

Filling

For this, bring to the boil:

$1\frac{1}{4}$ lb (570 g) brown sugar	$\frac{1}{2}$-oz (14 g) salt
1 lb 2 oz (510 g) castor sugar	8 oz (230 g) glucose
2 lb (910 g) water	

Skim as necessary, then add 8 oz (230 g) cornflour dissolved in $\frac{1}{2}$-pt or 10 oz (280 g) water, cook to thicken and clear, then remove from the heat, finally adding 2 oz (57 g) burnt butter and vanilla essence.

To produce the burnt butter—which, incidentally, produces the wonderful flavour—place in a pan or tin on the gas, bring to the boil and allow to cook until discoloration takes place, then add and stir well into the 'gel'.

Caramel Icing

Boil to 242°F (116°C):

$1\frac{1}{4}$ lb (800 g) brown sugar	$\frac{1}{4}$-oz (7 g) cream of tartar
4 oz (110 g) butter	8 oz (230 g) water
$\frac{1}{2}$-oz (14 g) salt	

Cream well together, add the hot syrup and mix for 3 min:

5 lb (2270 g) icing sugar	6 oz (170 g) milk
1 lb 2 oz (510 g) shortening	vanilla essence
8 oz (230 g) butter	

Finally, add 4 oz (110 g) burnt butter.

To finish the gateau, split, fill with a good, generous amount of the filling, replace the top and ice with caramel icing. Lightly 'spattle' the top and mask the sides with roasted nib almonds.

Chocmalt Milk Gateau

Malt as a flavour is rarely found in confectionery, yet the following line is extremely pleasant to eat, relatively easy to produce, and reasonable in price.

Mix for 5 min. on second speed:

1 lb 14 oz (850 g) high-ratio flour
1¼ lb (570 g) high-ratio shortening

8 oz (230 g) melted bitter chocolate

Dissolve together, add to the above over 5 min, (scrape down bowl and beater at intervals to produce smooth batter):

2½ lb (1140 g) castor sugar
10 oz (280 g) high-ratio flour
1½ oz (43 g) salt
⅜-oz (10·5 g) bicarbonate of soda

2½ oz (70 g) baking powder
¼-oz (7 g) mace
1½ lb (680 g) malted milk*

Add the following to the above in slow stream with machine on first speed and mix until clear:

1 lb 6 oz (620 g) egg
3 lb (1360 g) malted milk*

vanilla essence

Scale at 10 oz (28 g) into greased and floured cottage pans, baking at 375°F (190°C). Leave until next day to finish. These bases, if properly made, are extremely tender.

Prior to finishing, split and sandwich with apricot jam.

All are finished with malted milk icing, made from:

1½ lb (680 g) shortening
¾-oz (21 g) salt
5 oz (140 g) milk powder
6 oz (170 g) malted milk powder

12 oz (340 g) melted bitter chocolate
1½ lb (680 g) water
5 oz (140 g) icing sugar
vanilla essence

Cream up the shortening along with salt and milk powders. When light, add the melted bitter chocolate, beating in well. Add the icing sugar, beat in, then add the water steadily; in cold weather, the water could be tepid. Cream all well together, adding finally the essence.

All are firstly masked with the icing.

No. 1. Completely covered with grated chocolate, then lightly dusted with icing sugar.

No. 2. The sides are masked with chopped chocolate, top 'spattled' with the tip of a palette knife and chocolate 'scribbled' at right angles to the masking.

Nos. 3, 4 and 6 are variations on 'marbling' using piping chocolate, whilst No. 5 employs 'scribble' on a combed background.

*Malted Milk

Whisk well together:

10 oz (280 g) malt flour
10 oz (280 g) milk powder

3 lb 6oz (1540 g) water

Chocolate Coconut Gateau

As is obvious from the title, this cake is the result of marrying together two popular flavours—chocolate and coconut.

5 lb (2270 g) castor sugar	3 lb (1360 g) weak flour
3 lb (1360 g) shortening	1¾ oz (50 g) baking powder
6½ lb (2950 g) egg	1¼ lb (570 g) cocoa powder
½-oz (14 g) salt	4½ lb (2040 g) fine coconut
2 oz (57 g) lemon paste	

Produce by the sugar-batter method, scaling at 10 oz (280 g) into greased and floured cottage pans, before baking at 350°F (175°C). Allow to stand overnight before finishing.

Split and sandwich the bases with lemon curd of good quality. Produce a nicely flavoured lemon cream, masking top and sides with this. Follow with a mixture of roasted coconut and chopped chocolate, pressing well down to ensure adherence to the buttercream.

One is completed simply by placing a stick across the gateau and dredging with icing sugar.

The second utilises cut chocolate shapes on to which is piped a whirl of lemon buttercream. These discs are affixed to the gateau by another, and smaller, whirl of buttercream.

Caramel Cake

This produces quite a tasty cake, one which could, quite easily, be consumed in large quantities before the customer was really aware of it. Quite straightforward to produce, the reader may be surprised that the batter, when completed, is rather 'thin' to handle.

Sieve together:

2½ lb (1140 g) high-ratio flour	1¼ oz (35 g) salt
3 lb (1360 g) Barbados sugar	2½ oz (70 g) baking powder
4 oz (114 g) milk powder	

Add to the above:

1 lb 2 oz (510 g) high-ratio shortening

Place in a machine bowl, fit on the beater and mix smooth. Then add in several portions:

1¼ lb (680 g) water	vanilla essence

Scraping down bowl and beater at intervals. This stage should take about 4 min. Mix together:

1¼ lb or 1 pt (570 g or 0·57 litres) egg white   1 lb (450 g) water
8 oz (230 g) whole egg

Adding to the above over 5 min.

Scale to 10 oz (280 g) into greased and floured 7 in (18 cm) cottage pans. Bake at 360°F (180°C), empty from the pans and allow to go quite cold before icing with boiled icing. For this, boil together:

3 lb (1360 g) cube sugar   1 lb (450 g) water
8 oz (230 g) glucose   pinch of cream of tartar

to 242°F (116°C), adding the cream of tartar moistened with water at 225°F (107°C).

Meanwhile whisk to a peak on the machine:

1 lb (450 g) egg whites   vanilla essence
¼-oz (7 g) salt

Add this to the boiling syrup, continuing to whisk to full peak.

Mask top and sides immediately with the icing, slightly roughing the top and masking the sides with roasted almonds or jap crumbs as desired.

Peppermint Gateau

Peppermint is a popular flavour in sugar confectionery, yet only very rarely does one come across it in flour confectionery. The following has proved popular when introduced.

2¼ lb (1020 g) castor sugar   ¾-oz (21 g) salt
2 oz (57 g) shortening   2 oz (57 g) glycerine
1 lb (450 g) margarine

Cream the above lightly, then add:

1 lb 2 oz (510 g) milk   pale green colour

Add and partially clear:

2 lb 10 oz (1190 g) weak flour   1¾ oz (50 g) baking powder

Then add and clear:

1 lb 2 oz (510 g) milk

Finally add to the batter:

1¾ lb (800 g) egg white   12 oz (340 g) castor sugar

Previously whisked to a firm meringue, and gently clear.

The pale green colour may be unusual but, provided that it is pale green, and a yellow-green rather than a blue-green, it will be found quite attractive.

As the recipe does not contain any egg yolks, the colour should be quite easy to obtain.

Scale at 11 oz (310 g) into greased and floured cottage pans, baking at 350–360°F (175–180°C).

Peppermint gateau texture

The cake, when baked, will be found to be quite tender, so it is advisable to leave overnight before finishing. For this chocolate mint cream is required. The recipe is:

1 lb (450 g) butter or margarine	8 oz (230 g) evaporated milk
1 lb (450 g) stock marshmallow	½-oz (14 g) salt
oil of peppermint to flavour	8 oz (230 g) melted chocolate
4 lb (1820 g) icing sugar	

Place the ingredients in the order named into a suitable machine bowl fitted with beater, beating well until a fairly light, smooth cream results, warming and scraping down the bowl as required.

To finish the gateaux, mask top and sides with the cream, masking the sides with chocolate coralettes. Place a neat line of chocolate mint curls down the widest part of the gateau, place a stick across and dredge with icing sugar.

Before spreading the chocolate—either couverture or baker's—on the slab to produce the curls, add and stir well in a few drops of peppermint oil, then produce the curls in the usual way, trimming off the edges with a hot knife to keep them uniform.

Peppermint gateau finish

Honey Gateau

Despite the rather unorthodox method of mixing, the cake produced is extremely tasty. Not expensive to produce, a quantity of cake crumbs are also incorporated in the mix. The raisins are preferably of the small variety, well washed and moist so that, during baking, they will 'plump up' and thus give a better eating and cutting cake.

3¼ lb (1530 g) honey	5 lb (2270 g) milk
1 lb 10 oz (740 g) cake crumbs	14 oz (400 g)
4 oz (110 g) roasted nib almonds	

Soak the above well together until crumbs are soft.

Group 2 comprises:

2 lb 2 oz (970 g) castor sugar	12 oz (340 g) egg
1¼ lb (680 g) shortening	5 oz (140 g) baking powder
5 lb (2270 g) weak flour	1½ oz (43 g) salt
½-oz (14 g) cinnamon	

Place the items of Group 2 into a suitable machine bowl fitted with whisk, start the machine and incorporate all well together for approximately 1 min. Add the soaked items, change to top speed and whisk until quite light and fluffy, the whole mixing taking only 6 or 7 min.

Scale into greased and floured cottage pans at 10 oz (280 g) before baking at 370°F (190°C) for approximately 25 min. When cold, split and layer with ginger jam, or, alternatively, apricot jam to which a little well-chopped ginger has been added.

Mask with beaten marshmallow, masking the sides with jap crumbs, and completing the top with a simple abstract design, piped in marshmallow, silver dragées and discs of crystallised ginger.

Fig and Ginger Cakes

Just a straightforward cake made by the sugar-batter method. If, when cold, it is wrapped in moisture-proof, transparent film, its shelf-life should be good.

1 lb (450 g) butter	1 lb (450 g) chopped ginger
3 lb (1360 g) castor sugar	2 lb (910 g) chopped figs
10 oz (280 g) shortening	$\frac{1}{2}$-oz (14 g) cinnamon
2 oz (57 g) glycerine	$1\frac{1}{2}$ oz (42 g) baking powder
1 lb – 9 oz or $1\frac{1}{4}$ pt (710 g or 0·71 litres) egg	2 lb (910 g) milk
3 lb 14 oz (1760 g) weak flour	egg colour

Scale at 14 oz (400 g) into long malt-loaf tins and bake at 370–380°F (190–195°C). If desired, a top decoration of two or three walnut halves before baking may be employed.

Mocha Chocolate Gateau

In common with other high-ratio cakes, this is extremely tender but, properly stored, has an exceedingly good shelf-life.

$2\frac{1}{2}$ lb (1140 g) high-ratio flour	3 lb 14 oz (1760 g) castor sugar
$1\frac{1}{4}$ lb (570 g) high-ratio shortening	$\frac{3}{4}$-oz (21 g) bicarbonate of soda
$\frac{1}{4}$-oz (7 g) coffee concentrate	1 oz (28 g) salt
10 oz (280 g) cocoa	$1\frac{1}{2}$ oz (42 g) baking powder
8 oz (230 g) milk powder	

Mix the above on slow speed to blend. Scrape down bowl and beater at least twice.

Add 2 lb 4 oz (1020 g) water slowly, clear and scrape well down. Then mix together:

$1\frac{1}{4}$ lb (800 g) egg	$1\frac{1}{2}$ lb (680 g) water

add slowly and clear, scraping well down.

All ingredients should be at room temperature to give a batter of approximately 70°F (20°C). Scale at 10 oz (280 g) into greased cottage pans, and into the bottom of which a greaseproof-paper circle has been placed. Bake at 360–370°F (180–185°C).

When cold, mask with the coffee icing given below, masking the sides with roasted flaked hazelnuts, and complete with three coffee beans, either moulded from coffee-flavoured baker's chocolate, or from coffee-coloured and -flavoured marzipan.

To make the coffee icing cream lightly:

1½ lb (680 g) high-ratio shortening	1½ lb (680 g) butter
½-oz (14 g) coffee concentrate	2½ lb (1140 g) icing sugar

Then add in portions 5 lb (2270 g) fondant, beating until quite light.

Next add 8 oz (230 g) egg white. Stock syrup should then be added to adjust to required spreading consistency. Any of the icing remaining after use may be warmed and re-beaten.

Croquants

The base for this line is one using a fair amount of crumbs, cheap to produce, yet of good keeping property. Two finishes are suggested, the first something unusual, which should command a good price, and the second a quick finish to enable it to be sold as a fairly cheap line.

1 lb (450 g) castor sugar	2½ oz (70 g) bicarbonate of soda
1 lb (450 g) Barbados sugar	5 lb (2270 g) weak flour
2 lb (910 g) shortening	½-oz (14 g) salt
1 lb 14 oz or 1½ pt (850 g or 0·85 litres) egg	½-oz (14 g) cinnamon
2 lb (910 g) glucose	¾-oz (21 g) ginger
3 lb (1360 g) cake crumbs	½-oz (14 g) mixed spice
3¾ lb or 3 pt (1700 g or 1·7 litres) milk	

Produce by the sugar-batter method, adding the glucose after all the egg has been incorporated. Add the crumbs, break in the milk into which the bicarbonate of soda has been dissolved and, finally, add the flour, previously sieved with the various spices.

Pipe out into greased custard tins, or into tins previously papered with greaseproof baking cases. Approximately 1¼ oz (36 g) should be sufficient. Bake at 390–400°F (200–205°C). To finish this line, crushed nougat is utilised.

To make this, weigh equal quantities of castor sugar and lightly roasted nib almonds, slightly warmed.

Place the sugar in a copper pan on the gas and warm gently, stirring constantly. Add a little lemon juice and continue heating until the sugar reaches a pale straw colour. Remove from the gas, add the nuts and stir well in, transferring immediately to an oiled slab. Level with an oiled rolling-pin and, when cold, crush to 'nib' size.

For the buns baked in greased tins, mask the sides with buttercream well flavoured with stem-ginger syrup and roll in the crushed nougat. Pipe a whirl of the same cream on to the top of the cake—previously the bottom—and top with a decorative, thin slice of dried stem ginger.

The 'bun' type is simply finished by masking with coffee buttercream then rolling into the crushed nougat.

Honey Fudge Slice

Line a sheet tin 30 × 18 in (76 × 46 cm) with sweetpaste. Fit a stick at the end to prevent flowing and produce the topping by the sugar-batter method:

2 lb (910 g) castor sugar	1 lb 2 oz (510 g) egg
11 oz (310 g) butter or margarine	1 lb 2 oz (510 g) weak flour
9 oz (255 g) glucose	12 oz (340 g) roasted mixed nuts
9 oz (255 g) honey	

Spread on to the prepared, pasted sheet—no jam is required—and spread level. Bake at 360–370°F (180–185°C) and, when baked and cool, mask the top with fudge followed by a sprinkling of fine, roasted flaked almonds. Complete by cutting into 2½ × 1 in (6·5 × 2·5 cm) fingers.

Walnut and Coconut Wafers

It is always interesting to reflect on how a finish can change a line completely and, providing that the base is fairly 'neutral' in taste, the type of finish will, with the flavour added, give something totally different, both in appearance and taste. So it is with this line.

2 lb (910 g) sugar	3 lb (1360 g) weak flour
1¾ lb (795 g) butter	1 oz (28 g) baking powder
1½ lb (680 g) egg	vanilla essence
10 oz or ½-pt (280 g or 0·28 litres) milk	

Produce by the sugar-batter method, using the round, rubber stencil mat for the walnut wafers and the oval stencils for the coconut, sprinkling these latter with desiccated coconut before baking at 400°F (205°C). The sheet tins should be covered with greaseproof paper prior to stencilling.

To finish the walnut wafers, join three together, open fashion, with praline or coffee buttercream. Immerse the top one in chocolate, allow to set, re-mask and comb, completing with a good walnut half.

For the coconut wafers, join three together, 'jap' fashion, with lemon-coloured and -flavoured buttercream. Mask top and sides with the same medium, followed by roasted coconut and complete with a small 'button' of lemon cake coating.

Coconut wafers

Walnut wafers

Coconut Drops

No. 1

Mix together on the machine and using beater:

2½ lb (1140 g) castor sugar   ¼-oz (7 g) salt
1½ lb (680 g) egg

Add to the above:

9 oz (255 g) milk   1½ lb (680 g) fine coconut
4 oz (110 g) melted butter

Sieve together, add and clear well:

2½ lb (1140 g) weak flour   2 oz (57 g) baking powder

Pipe out the mixing on to greased and floured sheet tins, keeping the size rather small, as a considerable flow takes place during baking at 370°F (185°C).

When baked, trim with cutter to assist in a neat finish. Join together with lemon-coloured and flavoured buttercream, tops together, and mask the sides and tops with the same buttercream before rolling into roasted coconut. Complete with a neat button of lemon-coloured and flavoured fondant.

No. 2

1¼ lb (570 g) castor sugar   8 oz (230 g) coconut flour
1 lb (450 g) margarine   ½-oz (14 g) baking powder
15 oz or ¼-pt (430 g or 0·43 litres) egg   egg colour
2 lb (910 g) weak flour

Produce the above by sugar-batter method, making certain of a really good, light, free batter.

Using a savoy bag and ½-in (1·3 cm) plain tube, pipe out about 1½ in (3·8 cm) diameter on to greaseproof or silicone paper placed on sheet tins upside down in a manner similar to producing savoy biscuits. Bake at 390–400°F (200–205°C) and, when cold, lift easily from the paper, no moistening required. Store in an airtight situation until required.

No. 1. FINISH

Join together in pairs with lemon buttercream, half dipping in bakers chocolate, ensuring a clean neat finish. Chocolatey finger marks and spots are to be deprecated. Complete with a pinch of green decor whilst the chocolate is still in a soft condition.

No. 2. FINISH

A very attractive alternative is to join together in pairs with the lemon butter-cream, (this flavour being best to bring out the coconut) and half dipping into lemon cake coating. Complete by scribbling with chocolate at right angles.

Coconut drops, using two finishes

Pineapple Orange Slices

Cream well together:

6 oz (170 g) castor sugar
8 oz (230 g) shortening
¾-oz (21 g) salt

½-oz (14 g) bicarbonate of soda
¼-oz (7 g) cinnamon
2 lb (910 g) pineapple jam

Add and beat in:

6 eggs

Add and break in:

10 oz or ½-pt (280 g or 0·28 litres) milk   1 oz (28 g) orange paste

Add and well clear:

1 lb 10 oz (740 g) flour   4 oz (110 g) nib almonds

Place on to a greased and floured sheet tin, area 18 × 26 in (46 × 66 cm), and spread level, placing a stick at the end to prevent flowing. Bake at 360–370°F (180–185°C).

To finish, sandwich with pineapple jam, mask the top with orange-coloured and -flavoured buttercream and scatter liberally with roasted almonds—strip, flaked or nib, as desired. Allow a short period in the refrigerator to harden before cutting into the desired shapes.

Coconut Cookies

This line is another of U.S. origin and which, to our methods of mixing, may seem very peculiar. Nevertheless, it produces an interesting base and a very nice fancy.

Place in a machine bowl fitted with beater and mix until smooth:

12 oz (340 g) coconut	8 oz (230 g) egg
8 oz (230 g) shortening	1¼ lb (680 g) milk
1¼ oz (36 g) bicarbonate of soda	vanilla essence
½-oz (14 g) salt	

Add and clear:

3¼ lb (1480 g) weak flour	1¾ lb (800 g) castor sugar

Pipe out on to greased and floured sheet tins, using a savoy bag and plain tube. Sprinkle with sugar nibs and bake at 380°F (195°C) on wires or up-turned sheet tins.

Round Cookies

Join together two round cookies with marshmallow, whisking 4 lb (1820 g) stock marshmallow to 1 pt (0·75 litres) egg white or albumen solution. Pipe a button of white cake coating or fondant on the tops, completing with a small piece of cherry.

Coconut cookies (round)

Fingers

Join together in pairs with lemon buttercream, finishing by 'scribbling' with bakers chocolate.

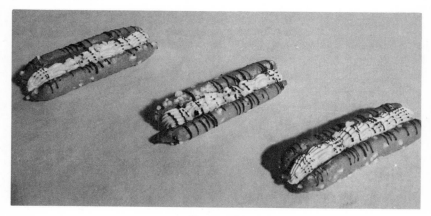

Finger cookies

Coconut Croquants

This is another line using a different ancillary for finishing and, again, one that has proved to be very popular.

To produce the croquant, place 1 lb (450 g) cube sugar into a suitable pan with a squeeze of lemon juice and heat, stirring constantly, until a pale straw colour is reached. Remove from the gas, add 12 oz (340 g) medium coconut,

Coconut croquants

roasted, and stir until thoroughly amalgamated, transferring to an oiled slab to cool. Break up for use, sieving to remove the dust, which may be used for flavouring the buttercream.

The method of mixing the biscuits is sugar-batter, though, with the rather lean fat content, very little creaming takes place in the first stage.

Cream together:

1¼ lb (570 g) castor sugar	¼-oz (7 g) salt
10 oz (280 g) shortening	

Add and cream in:

6 oz (170 g) egg

Dissolve, add and break in:

1¼ lb or 1 pt (570 g or 0·57 litres) milk	1 oz (28 g) bicarbonate of soda

Sieve together, add and clear:

2 lb (910 g) weak flour	½-oz (14 g) cinnamon
12 oz (340 g) fine coconut	

Pipe out in fingers and circles on to greased and floured sheet tins and bake at 380°F (195°C).

To finish, join together in pairs with lemon cheese, mask the outsides with lemon-coloured and -flavoured buttercream, to which the croquant dust has been added. Roll in the crushed croquant and dredge lightly with icing sugar, placing a stick along the centre of the fingers.

Fruit Bars

2 lb (910 g) castor sugar	½-oz (14 g) ginger
10½ oz (300 g) glucose	1 lb 5 oz (600 g) shortening
1 oz (28 g) salt	1 oz (28 g) milk powder
1 oz (28 g) cinnamon	1 oz (28 g) bicarbonate of soda

Cream the above to maximum volume, then slowly add:

10 oz or ½-pt (280 g or 0·28 litres) egg

To this add, mix in and clear:

1 lb (450 g) honey

Then add and partially clear:

4 lb (1820 g) weak flour

Finally add and clear:

2 lb (910 g) sultanas	8 oz (230 g) chopped glace pineapple
8 oz (230 g) chopped cherries	

When thoroughly mixed, transfer to a well greased 30 × 18 in (76 × 46 cm) sheet tin and spread level, placing a stick at the end to prevent flowing. Bake at 360°F (180°C).

When cold, cut into 2½ in (6·4 cm) widths, spreading the tops with praline buttercream. Place in the refrigerator for a short period to harden, then re-mask and comb with a suitable comb scraper. Place a sprinkle of green almond nibs along the centre of each, scribble with chocolate and cut into 1 in (2·6 cm) slices.

Malties

This is a line with a unique malted 'nutty' flavour and is certainly unusual. Coupled with this is the added attraction that it provides an outlet for cake crumbs.

1¼ lb (680 g) castor sugar	1½ lb (680 g) cake crumbs
8 oz (230 g) honey	1¼ oz (36 g) bicarbonate of soda
8 oz (230 g) malt extract	½-oz (14 g) salt
1 lb (450 g) golden shortening	¼-oz (7 g) cinnamon
10 oz or ½-pt (280 g or 0·28 litres) egg	¼-oz (7 g) nutmeg
2 lb (910 g) weak flour	¼-oz (7 g) mixed spice
1 lb (450 g) wholemeal or wheatmeal	1¼ lb or 1 pt (570 g or 0·57 litres) milk

Produce by the sugar-batter method, piping out with savoy bag and ½-in (1·3 cm) plain tube, into fingers and rounds (or drops), on to well greased and lightly floured sheet tins. Sprinkle with nib almonds and bake on biscuit wires or upturned sheet tins at 380°F (195°C).

Finish quite simply by joining together with buttercream lightly flavoured with malt extract.

Malties—attractive and unusual

Butterscotch Crunch

Fancy—or weekend special? This line, as can be seen from the illustration, is readily adaptable as either and equally popular. The facts of easy production and good shelf-life make it well worth a trial.

Ingredients needed are:

2 lb 6 oz (1080 g) melted butter, margarine or shortening
6¼ lb (3060 g) Barbados sugar
1 oz (28 g) salt

2 lb 6 oz (1080 g) egg
4¼ lb (2260 g) weak flour
2½ oz (70 g) baking powder
2 lb 6 oz (1080 g) roasted chopped nuts

Place the melted fat and sugar in a machine bowl fitted with beater and start the machine on first speed, gradually increasing the speed and adding the egg.

Butterscotch crunch

When all is incorporated, stop the machine, remove the beater, scrape well down, add the sieved flour, baking powder and salt, partially clear, add the roasted nuts and well clear. These latter, of course, may be of any type to the reader's choice.

Scale the mixing at 4½ lb (2040 g) on to a well-greased and lightly-floured sheet tin, the area measuring 18 × 17 in (46 × 43 cm). Spread level and bake at 350°F (175°C) until firm to the touch, which will take approximately 30 min.

When cold, and to finish, mask the top of one portion with pineapple jam, placing a similar-sized portion on top, upside down. Using a sharp knife, cut into 2½ in (6·4 cm) slices and enrobe with bakers chocolate. When set, re-enrobe and comb.

If for fancies, cut into 1 in (2·6 cm) slices, but, if to be displayed and sold as a large unit, decorate with walnut halves and cut into lengths of the desired size.

Honey Fingers

A line of American origin, it is one with probably much greater palate appeal than eye appeal; it is certainly quickly produced, and very tasty.

Honey fingers

Cream to maximum lightness:

1½ lb (680 g) castor sugar	1 oz (28 g) cinnamon
1¼ lb (570 g) shortening	½-oz (14 g) ginger
1 oz (28 g) salt	½-oz (14 g) mixed spice
3 oz (85 g) bicarbonate of soda	¼-oz (7 g) nutmeg

Add and beat well in:

2½ lb (1140 g) honey

Soak together and add to the above:

3½ lb (1530 g) cake crumbs   2 lb (910 g) water

Add and clear well:

5 lb (2270 g) weak flour

The water content can be slightly variable, depending upon the type of crumb used.

When mixed, place on a well cleaned and greased sheet tin, 30 × 18 in (76 × 46 cm) spreading level, placing a stick at the end to prevent flowing. Scatter quite heavily with sugar nibs, roll in gently to adhere, and bake until firm at 350–360°F (175–180°C). When cold and set, cut into 2½ × 1 in (6·5 × 2·6 cm) fingers.

Honey Almonds

With a slight variation, this is a base that can be totally transformed. Place a portion of the honey finger paste into the refrigerator overnight to set, then rub well down and pin to approximately ⅛-in (3 mm) thick. Cut with a 2 in (5·1 cm) fluted cutter, place carefully on to a papered sheet tin and bake at 370°F (190°C). When cold, sandwich in pairs with praline buttercream, masking the tops also, rolling into roasted fine flaked almonds. Complete by dredging with icing sugar, lightly.

Truffle Fingers

The crumb situation is one that can very quickly get out of hand, and the surprising thing is that many in our industry labour under the delusion that stale or broken cakes do not cost anything! Should any reader doubt this, let him take into his bakery some broken, stale or cake ends and just casually ask at random, 'How much do these cost?' The answers will be interesting.

As is usual with a line of this type, no set recipe exists, the actual mixing depending upon what is to hand. Suffice to say that the mixing comprises: crumbs, walnuts, cherries, sultanas, boiled apricot purée and flavour.

The whole is put into the machine bowl fitted with beater, the machine started on first speed, mixing to the consistency of a slightly soft almond paste. Stop the machine and transfer the paste to a sheet tin lined with silicone paper. Press level, finally rolling level with rolling pin, the finished thickness being in the region of 1 in (2·6 cm). Allow a short time for it to set, then brush over the surface with baker's chocolate. Reverse off the sheet tin when the chocolate has hardened, strip off the silicone paper, brushing over this second surface with chocolate, roughing it to give an interesting appearance. When set, cut into fingers—not too large—and display with the variety of fancies.

This is a line that can be really popular, much depending upon the flavour. In this respect sherry, or a spot of liqueur—room for experiment here—but do not kill it with essence and then wonder why they are not selling!

Truffle fingers

Walnut Slices

Another quick-selling and popular line, which has the advantage of using up quite a large quantity of crumbs.

Line a sheet tin 30 × 18 in (76 × 46 cm) with sweetpaste, spread with apricot jam and produce the following, topping by the sugar-batter method.

1½ lb (680 g) castor sugar	3 lb 6 oz (1530 g) sieved cake crumbs
1½ lb (680 g) margarine	1 lb 14 oz or 1½ pt (850 g or 0·85 litres) milk
8 oz (230 g) chopped walnuts	

Spread level and bake on wires or upturned sheet tins at 380–400°F (195–205°C). When baked and cold, mask with boiling apricot purée, water ice and flash in a hot oven. When cold, slice into 2½ × 1 in (6·5 × 2·6 cm) fingers, or, alternatively, triangular shape.

Coconut Cheese Cakes

Whilst the purist is arguing whether these are cakes or fancies, the realistic, practical confectioner will produce a batch and find that here is another winner both from the customer's and his own angle.

Line the required number of patty tins with well-rested puff-paste cuttings, allow a recovery period and pipe a spot of lemon curd into the bottom of each. Then produce the following recipe by the sugar-batter method:

1 lb (450 g) margarine	5 oz (140 g) cornflour
1 lb (450 g) castor sugar	1 lb (450 g) egg
8 oz (230 g) crumbs	5 oz or $\frac{1}{4}$-pt (140 g or 0·14 litres) milk
8 oz (230 g) coconut flour	spot of oil of sweet orange

Pipe into the tins two-thirds full and bake at 400°F (205°C). When cold, quickly complete with a small button of white fondant, piece of cherry and, if desired, angelica diamonds.

Winter Slices

This is another line which will assist in keeping the crumb problem within reasonable limits and yet also produce a tasty slice in which several varieties of finish may be employed.

Winter slices

Line a sheet tin 30 × 18 in (76 × 46 cm) with sweet-paste and spread with pineapple or other jam to choice. The following recipe is sufficient for one sheet, and should be made by the sugar-batter method.

Ingredients needed are:

1 lb 2 oz (510 g) Barbados sugar	2¼ lb (1020 g) sultanas
14 oz (400 g) butter or margarine	2 oz (57 g) lemon paste
4 oz (110 g) shortening	½-oz (14 g) mixed spice
14 oz (400 g) egg	rum essence
2¼ lb (1020 g) crumbs	chocolate and egg colour
2¼ lb (1020 g) currants	

Spread on to the prepared sheet, fitted with a stick to prevent flowing, and bake at 370–380°F (185–195°C).

One finish, as shown in the illustration, is to soften macaroon paste to thin, spreading consistency and apply carefully just before baking is completed, returning to the oven to finish.

Alternatively, the slice may be sold as it is with a variety of simple fondant finishes, or with marzipan, coloured suitably and marked with a fancy marzipan roller.

Truffle Christmas Puddings

During the Christmas season, extra production means more crumb coming from breakages, genoese ends and wastage generally, which, unless very carefully watched can assume gargantuan proportions. Undoubtedly many bakery staffs conveniently fail to notice the pile-up occurring. It is no one's business in particular to keep this scrap moving so, within quite a short space of time, the pieces are musty and rancid, fit only for the swill bin. This is undoubtedly the quickest method of disposal, but it should be impressed upon all concerned that these ends cost money. Net profit is money that hasn't been wasted, and here is one place where loss can be turned to useful profit and vice versa.

Sieve all the crumbs carefully and, if producing by hand, make a bay. Into this pour boiling apricot jam and a small quantity of melted baker's chocolate, making the whole into a workable paste, capable of being moulded by hand. Flavour with liqueur rum, not essence, and add sufficient plump, washed and picked sultanas. Scale off at 1¼ oz (36 g) or, better still, cut on the divider using castor sugar as dust, though, if correctly made, very little should be necessary. Mould round, roll in baker's chocolate or couverture between the hands and allow to set. Now, pipe on the top a small amount of white or pale yellow fondant to represent sauce, finishing with a very small holly piquet on the top.

This is a line in which many odds and ends of good, usable material may be disposed of. For instance, that chocolate into which water was accidentally

Truffle Christmas puddings, a popular outlet for scrap

spilled, rendering it useless for normal purposes, the odd small amounts of buttercream, that extra pan of chocolate fondant and so on all combine to produce these. If expenses permit, then a good proportion of well-beaten ganache gives a very acceptable flavour. It is remarkable how popular these are with the public, and invariably command both a ready sale and a good price.

Chocolate Rum Truffles

These are an all-the-year-round version of the above.

Using the same mixing as for the puddings, minus the sultanas, roll to a rope, then cut into $2\frac{1}{2}$ in (6·4 cm) lengths. Roll into chocolate between the hands and then into chocolate vermicelli. Allow to lie on the bench until set before being placed in paper cases, otherwise the shape will become distorted.

Hazelnut Snacks

Here is another line to reduce the crumb problem, and one that is extremely popular where introduced.

You need:

3 lb (1360 g) fondant   12 oz (340 g) roasted, ground hazelnuts
1½ lb (680 g) cake crumbs

Soften the fondant slightly, then mix with the remaining ingredients to form a smooth paste, which should be capable of being rolled out in a similar manner to sweet-paste.

Pin to ¼-in (6 mm) thick, using castor sugar for dusting and cutting out with square or oblong cutter, setting on one side for a short time to set.

Enrobe in coffee-flavoured baker's chocolate and, if hand dipped, mark with the dipping fork before completing with a whole, de-husked, roasted hazelnut.

Whilst the illustration was from the recipe above, variations are obviously possible. For instance, flavours or essences may be added, with variation in the type of nut used. Undue softening of the fondant will produce a paste soft in character, whilst the type of crumb has also to be considered and adjusted as necessary.

The use of a different ancillary material for finishing will always arouse customer interest, and the use of candy crunch is no exception. Whilst only one or two uses can, for reasons of space, be indicated here, no doubt several others will readily occur to readers.

Hazelnut snacks

Calypso

Although in appearance this line may rather resemble chocolate almond clusters, both base and flavour are entirely different.

12 oz (340 g) brown sugar
12 oz (340 g) butter or margarine
½-oz (14 g) salt
½-oz (14 g) bicarbonate of soda

8 oz (230 g) egg
1½ lb (680 g) weak flour
4 oz (110 g) milk
1½ lb (680 g) clean, lightly-chopped raisins

Produce by the sugar-batter method, dissolving the bicarbonate of soda in the milk and adding after the eggs have been incorporated and well beaten in. Add the flour, partially clear, then add the raisins and clear.

Calypso

Using a large plain tube and savoy bag or, if preferred, the hands, pipe or shape into balls weighing approximately 1–1¼ oz (28–36 g) on to a heap of strip almonds and coconut well mixed together. Roll into the nuts so that the dough or batter is well covered and, preserving the shape as well as possible, place on to lightly-greased sheet tins and bake at 370–380°F (185–195°C) until able to be lifted off the tin.

When cold, enrobe in chocolate.

Pineapple Cups

Not by any means new, these are, nevertheless, well worthy of a place on any production list for their ease and speed of production, their good, unfinished, shelf-life and, by far the most important virtue of all, their unfailing popularity with the public. Very rich in character, the confectioner should not make the mistake of making these goods too large. The following recipe should produce six dozen, baked in well-greased small custard cups.

1¼ lb (680 g) castor sugar
3 lb (1360 g) butter or margarine
8 oz (230 g) praline paste

8 oz (230 g) roasted ground hazelnuts
2¼ lb (1140 g) weak flour

Cream together all the ingredients with the exception of the flour, finally adding this and clearing after a reasonably light batter has been achieved. Using a savoy bag and ½-in (1·3 cm) plain tube, pipe out into the prepared custard tins. Bake at 370–380°F (190–195°C) and, making use of the 'M' fault in cake-making, the cups are baked when the centre has collapsed. Allow to cool slightly before emptying from the tins, and to go thoroughly cold before finishing.

Pineapple cups

To do this, dip the 'shoulders' into baker's chocolate and allow to set. Into the hollow pipe a liberal amount of pineapple conserve, and on top of this pipe a good whirl of pineapple-coloured buttercream, and nicely flavour by the addition of some of the syrup from crystallising the pineapple. Place a segment of drained crystallised pineapple on the top and a small pinch of green almond nibs to complete.

Florio Slices

Quickly produced and finished, slices are suitable for all classes of trade. The finish can be quick and simple, or more elaborate, whilst thickness and size can, in conjunction with costings, be varied to suit the type and class of trade.

The florio slice is unusual, good to eat and capable of a wide variety of finishes.

Using a 30 × 18 in (76 × 46 cm) sheet tin, with other sizes in proportion, line reasonably thinly with sweetpaste, place a stick at the end to prevent flowing, and sprinkle with a mixture of fruit comprising:

14 oz (400 g) currants   8 oz (230 g) chopped cherries
9 oz (255 g) sultanas

Using the sugar-batter method, prepare the topping from:

1¼ lb (680 g) butter   1 lb (450 g) ground rice
1½ lb (680 g) castor sugar   12 oz (340 g) ground almonds
1¼ lb or 1 pt (570 g or 0·57 litres) egg

Spread level on to the prepared sheet, and bake on wires or upturned sheet tins at 390–400°F (200–205°C). Allow to cool before finishing.

Varieties of Finish

1. Mask the slice with apricot purée, followed by white fondant. Cut into fingers of the desired size, completing with a half cherry and two pieces of angelica.

Florio slices No. 3

2. Mask the slice thinly with white fondant, followed immediately by white desiccated coconut. When set, cut fingers of the desired size.
3. Mask the slice with boiled apricot purée, followed by golden marzipan, previously marked with the basket roller. Cut into $2\frac{1}{2}$ in (6·4 cm) slices,

Neopolitan 'Tutti frutti'

afterwards masking sides with lemon buttercream and roasted, flaked almonds. Cut the slices into fingers of the desired size.

4. Neopolitan 'Tutti Frutti'. Cut the sheet into $2\frac{1}{2}$ in (6·4 cm) slices, masking the tops of these quite thinly with apricot purée. Now roll out coloured marzipan to ropes of approximately $\frac{1}{4}$-in (6 mm) diameter and place lengthwise on the strips. Place on wires, enrobe with white fondant and, when set, cut to the desired shape and size.

Orange Tarts

Mask the base of the pastry with orange curd or, if none is available, with apricot jam to which a little orange paste has been added and well mixed in.

Orange tarts

The filling is produced by the sugar-batter method from:

1¼ lb (680 g) castor sugar	12 oz scone flour
1 lb (450 g) butter	1¼ lb (570 g) weak flour
4 oz (110 g) shortening	4 oz (110 g) orange paste
1 lb 9 oz or 1¼ pt (710 g or 0·71 litres) egg	orange colour

Fill the lined sandwich tins approximately two-thirds full, so that, after baking, the cake will be just level with the top of the tin. Bake at 380°F (195°C) and invert on to a clean cloth as soon as withdrawn from the oven until cold.

This will ensure a level surface on which to mask apricot purée, followed by orange-coloured and -flavoured fondant, after which a simple design comprising orange jelly slices, angelica, cherries and neatly piped chocolate-fondant lines will suffice.

Dexmond Tarts

Here is another line, finished when baked, yet something different, making it a ready seller.

Block the required number of fluted frangipane tins with sweet-paste, sprinkling the bottom of each with strip almonds or, indeed, any type of nut desired, though this could necessitate a change of name.

Produce the filling by the sugar-batter method finally adding the glucose and beating well in:

5 oz (140 g) castor sugar	6 oz (170 g) cornflour
8 oz (230 g) butter	¼-oz (7 g) salt
12 oz (340 g) egg	4 lb (1820 g) glucose

The unusual dexmond tarts

As the reader will recognise from the recipe, the filling is quite soft and should be transferred to a savoy bag fitted with a $\frac{1}{2}$-in (1·3 cm) plain tube, filling the prepared tins two-thirds full. Bake at 380°F (195°C) when, during baking, the nuts will rise to the top, giving a very attractive appearance.

The slight sinking is, of course, a characteristic of this line, caused by the large amount of glucose. An increase of flour would, of course, obviate this, but that would also alter the line altogether.

Punch Tarts

Produce sweetpaste and block round frangipane tins, and baking empty, or 'blind' as it is often termed. After allowing to go cold, empty from the tins—use a baking temperature of 410°F (210°C).

Make a fairly soft mixing of cake crumbs, boiled apricot purée, sultanas and rum to flavour—liqueur, not essence. If the filling appears to be too stiff, a small quantity of boiling water could be added, but do *not* get the filling sloppy.

Punch tarts

Fill the pastry cases level to the rim, followed by a thin masking of raspberry flavoured pink buttercream, placing in the refrigerator to set.

Mask with pink, raspberry flavoured fondant, edging with finely chopped green decor, and completing with a small piece of glacé cherry.

Whilst making sweetpaste for this line, extra could be made for:

Victory Tarts

This time, block patty tins with the sweetpaste, and pipe into the bottom of each a fair amount of pineapple jam. Produce the filling by the sugar-batter method from:

1 lb (450 g) butter	4 oz (110 g) scone flour
1 lb (450 g) castor sugar	3 oz (85 g) coconut flour
1 lb (450 g) egg	3 oz (85 g) ground almonds
1 oz (28 g) glycerine	noyeau flavour
12 oz (340 g) weak flour	

Using a savoy bag and plain tube, fill the pastry cases about two-thirds full, baking at 370°F (185°C) taking care not to overbake.

When cool mask the tops with boiled apricot purée, followed by very pale green fondant. The obvious Christmas finish is a small holly piquet.

Victory tarts

This line is very reminiscent of frangipane fancy, and a few cherries added to frangipane ring the changes on a line that is always popular. For the reader desiring to try this, then about 8 oz (230 g) chopped cherries to 4 lb (1820 g) mixing is about right.

Chapter 10

HIGH SPEED MIXING

It has always been the author's contention that machinery as such is not given great significance in a book such as this. This is not in any way to denigrate bakery engineers, who do a magnificent job for all classes in our industry, and who produce a most varied range of all types at very reasonable prices, but modern advances can so easily outdate the written word, that this aspect is better left for the individual to make his own enquiries. The proof of this is to listen at any gathering of bakers, where the merits of equipment are always a source of discussion. However, since the first edition of this book was published, high speed mixing has, along with the deep freeze, revolutionised the industry to an extent that was not forseeable a short time ago, and therefore deserves special mention. As the writer was involved in the production of recipes for high speed mixing in the early days, it will be of advantage to the reader for some of the more popular recipes to be included.

Obviously, before any machinery purchase is made, the reader will have seen and weighed the pros and cons of all competitive makes, finally arriving at the decision as to what will suit his situation best. Most were originally evolved for the production of bread only, but research and development led to the production of attachments to permit confectionery to be produced.

The first thing to learn, on using high speed machines, is that they do *not* aerate, but only mix. Once that fact is accepted, then adaptation is not difficult. This, of course, means that these machines are unable to cope with some lines. Meringues, at the time of writing, are not possible, nor are sponges by the classical method, the mixes, by and large, are 'all-in'.

All ingredients are placed in the machine together, generally, the exceptions being any fruit in fruit cakes or doughs, but the liquids should *always* be poured in first, otherwise there is a danger that dry ingredients will 'cake' round and under the impellers.

After 30 seconds of any mixing time (less in the case of a short time mix), the machine should be stopped and well scraped down, after which the indicated mixing time can be completed. These mixing times should be strictly adhered to, otherwise quality will suffer. Obviously, all tin preparation should be completed before the mix is commenced, for it has always been my experience that serious deterioration sets in if any cake mix is neglected after mixing is complete,—this holding good whether mixing by high speed or conventional methods.

For the sake of clarity and brevity, the recipes and mixing times only will be given, scaling weights, tin preparation and all relevant details being as for conventional mixes in the preceding chapters to which that particular line refers.

Chou Paste

6 lb (2730 g) medium flour $7\frac{1}{2}$ lb (3380 g) water
3 lb (1360 g) margarine $8\frac{1}{2}$ lb (3830 g) egg

Make a roux in the normal manner, pour the eggs into the machine, add the roux, mix for a total of $2\frac{1}{4}$ min.

Sweet Paste

14 lb (6360 g) weak flour $3\frac{1}{2}$ lb (1530 g) castor sugar
7 lb (3150 g) margarine $1\frac{3}{4}$ lb (800 g) egg

Place egg in the machine, followed by the remaining ingredients. Mix for 20–25 s.

Frangipane Filling

1 lb (450 g) weak flour   5 lb (2270 g) castor sugar
3 lb (1360 g) margarine   2 lb (910 g) ground almonds
1 lb (450 g) shortening   1 lb (450 g) ground rice
5 lb (2270 g) egg   2 lb (910 g) cake crumbs

Place eggs in the machine, add remaining ingredients, mix for 30 s.

High Ratio Genoese

6¼ lb (2840 g) high-ratio flour
5 lb (2270 g) egg
4 lb 6 oz (1990 g) water
7¾ lb (3490 g) castor sugar
4 lb (1820 g) high-ratio shortening

12 oz (340 g) milk powder
4 oz (110 g) baking powder
1 oz (28 g) salt
colour and flavour

Add the colour and flavour to the milk, pour this and the eggs into the machine, add remaining ingredients, mix for 30 s.

Madeira Cakes

7¾ lb (3490 g) high-ratio flour
5 lb 2 oz (2330 g) butter
5½ lb (2500 g) egg
3 lb (1360 g) water
7¾ lb (3490 g) castor sugar
3 oz (85 g) milk powder

5 oz (140 g) baking powder
¾-oz (21 g) salt
10 oz (280 g) glycerine
2 lb (910 g) glycerol monostearate
½-oz (14 g) lemon yellow colour

Place the liquids into the machine, add remaining ingredients and mix for 1½ min.

Genoa Cakes

7½ lb (3480 g) weak flour
1 lb 6 oz (620 g) butter
1¼ lb (570 g) shortening
3 lb (1360 g) egg
3 lb 2 oz (1420 g) water
2 lb 10 oz (1190 g) castor sugar
1 lb (450 g) rice flour
7 oz (200 g) milk powder
3 oz (85 g) baking powder
1 oz (28 g) salt

1 lb 14 oz (850 g) glycerol monostearate
¾-oz (21 g) lemon yellow
2 lb 10 oz (1190 g) glucose
12 lb (5450 g) sultanas
7 lb (3150 g) currants
5 lb (2270 g) cherries
3 lb (1360 g) mixed peel
1 oz (28 g) lemon paste
1 oz (28 g) orange paste

All the liquids should be placed into the machine, followed by the dry ingredients, but *not* the fruit. A total mixing time of 2¼ min is required, clearing the fruit in the last 15 s.

All-in Sponges

7½ lb (3380 g) high-ratio flour
7½ lb (3380 g) egg
7½ lb (3380 g) castor sugar

3 lb 2 oz (1420 g) emulsifier
4½ oz (130 g) baking powder

Place eggs and emulsifier into the machine, sieve together the flour and sugar, adding to the liquids in the machine. Give a total mixing time of 2 min, adding the baking powder in the last 15 s.

Note

If butter sponges are required, add up to 2 lb (910 g) melted butter to the recipe given above. Add this during the last 30 s of mixing time, still adding baking powder in the last 15 s.

Scones

6 lb (2730 g) medium flour	12 oz (340 g) castor sugar
4 oz (110 g) baking powder	4 oz (110 g) milk powder
12 oz (340 g) shortening	3 oz (85 g) yeast
1¼ lb (570 g) egg	8 oz (220 g) currants
2¼ lb (1020 g) water	

The above is for afternoon tea scones, but any of the well known variations are permissable.

Break down the yeast in the liquids, place in the machine, add remaining ingredients, except the fruit, and mix for 30s, adding the fruit over the last 7 s.

Chapter 11

SOME CONCLUSIONS

Whilst numerous recipes and methods for various types of goods have appeared in the preceding chapters, all commercial and capable of being put into daily production, it has been the author's aim to present to the reader a representative selection under each heading.

The ability to run a business successfully, however, depends upon many other factors, so it is not sufficient merely to be able to produce these articles. They have to be produced economically in the correct quantities, and be at the point of sale at the right time, and it is this aspect with which I would like to deal now.

We are all familiar, even if only theoretically, with the factory system, where everything is controlled from the checking in of raw materials to the cash check for the finished product. Small though we may be, I feel that it would be advantageous if we moved in that direction.

First, costings—these are all important, and no longer should rule-of-thumb methods prevail. A gross profit margin should be set, and all lines should earn that profit. Any uneconomical lines should have prices adjusted, and should the public decide that these are too expensive, then they should be rested.

As a musician, with eight notes to the scale of music, can produce tunes in infinite variety, so can the baker and confectioner, with his raw materials, produce many varied productions, and it is an easy matter to turn those raw materials into an entirely different line.

The practice of reducing prices of certain lines because the nearest competitor sells his at a lower price is to be deprecated. The time to worry, I feel, is when a competitor sells a similar article at a higher price.

In many of the smaller- and medium-sized bakeries one finds that the raw materials are open to anyone, delivery notes signed by anyone available, with the occasional consequence that short deliveries, improperly checked, have been signed for as correct. To give the allied traders full credit, shortages are usually made good, if only for the sake of goodwill, but such things should not be allowed to happen.

Whilst the smaller bakeries could not afford the luxury of a full-time storeman, it should be possible for one of the reliable hands to weigh up all the mixings for the following day from a list supplied by foreman, manager or proprietor.

The ingredients used should be entered daily in a daily stock book, and this amount be deducted weekly from the main stock book.

Raw materials, as they arrive, should be entered into both main and daily stock books. Thus, when a traveller calls, it is a simple matter to order from the stock book, rather than hunt the premises from attic to cellar to find out what is required.

Again, any pilfering may be easily spotted, and quite often the knowledge that such a system is being operated is sufficient to deter the pilferer.

With one reliable person weighing all mixings, the odds are considerably reduced that wastage will occur through mistakes in weighing.

Wasteful Practices

So far as is possible, it will be advantageous to have one person only doing the mixings and, when completed, handing over to others to work off, leaving him free to continue with the second mixing and so on. Consideration should also be given that a highly paid and skilled worker does only skilled work; it is a wasteful practice to have workers in this class preparing their own tins, washing up and doing jobs that can well be performed by employees in lower-paid categories.

The oven, as master of any bakery, merits long and earnest consideration. Here, I feel, are many smaller bakeries guilty of wastefulness, for often one finds the staff struggling along with an old-type solid fuel oven, low in temperature through indifferent qualities of fuel and half-hearted firing, and quite often only half filled with goods.

In many instances an oven half the size, gas, oil, or electrically heated, would provide sufficient oven space, provided that the work was so arranged that the oven was always used filled to capacity.

Indeed, I know of one bakery where this was adopted, an electric oven replaced a larger coke-fired oven, and each oven full of goods timed with a clockwork 'timer'. Since this was introduced a remarkable amount of money previously spent on fuel has been saved, goods are always perfectly baked and work generally made easier, with no ashes and attendant dust to be cleared. Left overnight with the oven sole switch on 'low', the oven temperature can be raised first thing in the morning to baking temperature within 20 min.

Despatch

The goods, now baked, await packing, and where two or three shops or vans are supplied from one bakery, it will usually be found convenient to entrust this to a reliable person; quite often an active old-age pensioner will be found suitable. This could take the form of a part-time job, or, should circumstances warrant, full time, with part of the time used in tin preparation, etc.

It is a remarkable thing that few bakers would send out a van on wholesale or retail rounds without a strict check of goods outward and cash returned, yet it is equally remarkable that bakers with two or three shops quite happily see their goods going to the branches with no check whatsoever.

Whilst it can be clearly understood that the shop staffs are quite honest and reliable, I would, nevertheless, urge readers to check all outgoing items in a duplicate book. The original copy should be made up, complete with prices, and delivered along with the goods to enable each manageress to check incoming goods. Similarly, any stales and breakages should be checked in and credit allowed in full. On one set day each week, the branch manageress should render a full stock return, and this will usually be found most convenient on Mondays, when stocks are at their lowest and trade generally quiet.

For checking, the commencing stock should be added to the daily outgoings, these figures being supplied from the duplicate entries. From this should be deducted the present stock and wastage (stales and breakages) and this figure should represent the cash taken. While, theoretically, this system should work to the halfpenny, in practice it seldom does, but provided the weekly leakage represents only a small percentage, there remains very little to worry about. When, however, the discrepancy rises to pounds then, obviously, action is called for. Once again, the mere fact of having such a system in operation is often sufficient to act as a deterrent.

Stopping Leaks

Along with the weekly stock check of shops should go a weekly stock check of the bakery raw materials. These should be balanced against the mixing's list supplied to the acting storeman daily, and thus any discrepancies can only go, at the most, for one week before being brought to light. Leaks, therefore, can be sealed before more serious troubles beset the business.

Figures are, I know, an anathema to the average baker and confectioner, far too many of whom are only concerned with sticking to the bench and producing. I submit, and have proved to my own satisfaction, that half a day spent in the office working out a system similar to that outlined can do a business far more goods than many hours working on production. It is, indeed, remarkable what facts emerge with such a system in operation. Should the reader decide to institute such a system, I have no doubt that the staff will immediately point out the snags, shortage of time for booking out, etc., etc. Insistence on strict adherence to the system, however, will produce within a very short time the necessary co-operation.

Management

Since the first edition of this book was published, great strides have been made in training, the Industrial Training Boards having provided much stimulation, making firms conscious of both the advantages and responsibilities in this direction.

Whilst this is commendable and all to the good, a tendency has arisen, and is being directed to what could be called 'Professional Management', leading one to wonder how much this aspect is responsible for much of the industrial unrest apparent today. Formerly, management, by perseverence, effort, ability and merit rose from the shop floor and, because of the experience thus gained, was able to spot difficulties and correct them before any great harm was done. Today, the professional manager, having moved sideways to such a position, often without depth of knowledge of the industry concerned, is unable to recognise many of these occurrences which are allowed to escalate, often disastrously. Use of correct, modern jargon, often eight words where one would do, is no substitute for proper decision making and firm control. Management unable to give these firm and quick decisions, where necessary, lead to a staff eventually becoming frustrated and disgruntled.

It should always be remembered that a wrong decision can soon be reversed, but no decision means no policy, and no policy means that impetus is lost, to the detriment—if not worse—of the business.

We appear generally to be in the hands of 'experts', change for the sake of change having run riot over many facets of our National life. In many instances this has resulted in serious deterioration and a much more expensive service, quite often with that so important human touch absent. Let one hasten to add, that our industry is one of the few remaining that can generally be absolved from the above criticism!

Management, work study, budgetry control etc., etc., are all important tools, but should *only* be regarded as tools, to greater, speedier and more economic service, with one person in mind, the one at the end of the line, so often forgotten, the customer. When all the 'experts' have done their work, it should be remembered that someone, somewhere, must produce something to sell. This is a fact all too often forgotten, and the article to be sold must be sold profitably, to the customer's satisfaction, otherwise all effort will be wasted. It has to be realised that the strength of the business lies with the artisans, and the quality of goods produced will be no better than the worst of these, setting at nought the best of management theory.

Human Relations

Finally, and most important of all, is the aspect of human relations for upon this depends the ultimate success or failure of the business.

The enthusiasm and drive must come from the top. The manager or foreman will echo this, and so it will go through the staff down to the youngest apprentice. Good humour is essential for good relations and certainly instils confidence all the way round. That, coupled with a fair deal in regard to wages, conditions, and hours, is usually sufficient to ensure a happy staff.

Many of us have memories of greedy employers, whose attitude was one of 'drive' and 'never be satisfied'. Although staff may be constantly changing, they never seem to be able to grasp why. The answer, of course, is to 'lead', not 'drive'.

Similarly, we have experience of employees whose craftmanship and general attitude to any job is to be deplored. However, despite on the one hand, the lack of good employees, and on the other of appreciative employers, it is still possible to run a successful business with a happy team.

Teamwork, with everyone pulling together, is the essential, and the attitude of the staff will be a reflection of the attitude of the management towards the staff.

INDEX

Afternoon tea fancies,
  No. 1, 298
  Nos. 2, 3, 4, 5, 299
  No. 6, 300
  uniform slices, 300
Albumen, powdered, 3
Almond,
  buns, 77
  cakes, 236
  gateaux, 320
Angel flan, 255
Apple,
  crumble, 161
  crunch, 125
  frangipane, 187

Bakewell type tart, 231
Baking powder, 4
Banana,
  gateau, 331
  layer cake, 330
  loaf, 261
  sponge, 329
Banbury cakes, 179
Battenberg, 313
  chocolate, 314
  many varieties of, 315

Batter method,
  flour, 219
  sugar, 218
Biscuits,
  ginger, 201
  linzer, 109
  Shrewsbury, 98
  sweetpaste, 97
Border,
  frosting, 340
  gateau, 340
Brandy snaps, 209
Brazil,
  delights, 149
  nut cake, 341
  pound cake, 247
Buns, small, 228, 229
Bury simnels, 271
Butter, 2
Butter sponges, 26
  gateau bases,
    chocolate, 27
    vanilla, 27
  Melba gateau, 26
Buttercream, 295
  American, 298
  boiled, 296
  boiled meringue, 297
  chocolate, 298

Buttercream (*Contd.*)
Continental fillings, 296
custard cream, 297
fondant, with, 296
gateau, 324
icing sugar, with, 296
lemon, 297
marshmallow, with, 296
sponge, 297
Butterscotch,
crunch, 359
gateau, 342
caramel icing for, 343
filling for, 343

Cakemaking,
flour batter method, 219
general purpose mixing, 227
high ratio cakes, 220
preparing tins for, 226
recipe balancing, 222
'rub-in' or 'all-in' method, 220
sugar batter method, 218
two major faults, 223
Cakes,
almond, 236
almond and raisin, 260
Brazil pound, 247
caramel, 345
caraway seed, 239
cherry, 246
cherry and walnut, 235, 258
Christmas and birthday, 273
coconut No. 1, 244
coconut No. 2, 245
country, 263
date and walnut, 256
Dundee, 247
fig and ginger, 349
fruit, first and second quality, 234
Genoa, 268
Genoese (*see* 'Genoese')
Hallowe'en, 263
honey, 246
hoop, 246
lemon, 238, 240

Cakes (*Contd.*)
Louisa, 248
Madeira, second quality, 235
Madeira, third quality, 236
Maraschino banana, 258
miniature, 279
picnic, 237
pineapple, 252
Simnel, 268
slab (*see* 'Slab')
sultana and walnut, 243
wedding (*see* under 'Wedding')
Calypso, 367
Charlotte royale, 39
Charlotte russe,
method 1, 37
method 2, 38
Cheese straws, 169
Cherry,
banana loaves, 254
biscuits, 130
buns, 78
marshmallows, 123
rings, 260
whirls, 234
Chocmalt milk gateau, 343
Chocolate,
coconut, 345
gateau, 345
slices, 48
fingers, 110
gateau Nos. 1 and 2, 323
rum truffles, 365
Chorley cakes, 94
Chou paste,
cheese eclairs, 193
chocolate eclairs, 194
coffee creams, 198
cream buns, 192
further varieties of eclairs, 195
petits chou, 197
recipe for, 191
rognons, 196
swans, 197
Christmas puddings,
cause of mould of, 268
cooking of, 267
fruit preparation for, 265

Christmas puddings (*Contd.*)
  mixing of, 266
  recipe for, 265
  scaling of, 266
  types of basins for, 264
Cinnamon cookies, 146
Coconut,
  buns, 78
  cheese cakes, 362
  cookies, 355
  crisp fingers, 125
  croquants, 356
  drops Nos. 1 and 2, 353
  honey balls, 53
  honeys, 160
  log, 21
  munchettes, 138
  shapes, 117
Coffee,
  buns, 78
  chocolate bars, 140
  chocolate-nut drops, 150
  fingers, 80
  gateau, 318
Colours, 6
Cream,
  curls, 22
  sandwiches, 33
  shells, 229
  slices, 176
Crispnuts, 114
Croquants, 350
Crystallised ginger cakes, 208
Currant loaves, 244
Currant lunch buns, 229
Currant walnut tarts, 141
Currants, 5
Custards, 91

Date loaf, 242
Despatch, 382
Dexmond tarts, 372
Dobos,
  fudge gateau, 36
  slice, 111
Drescan, 59

Dresden, 20
Dundee cake, 247

Easter gateau Nos. 1 and 2, 333
Eccles cakes, 177
  filling for, 178
Eggs,
  accelerated freeze dried, 3
  pasteurised, 3
  whites, 3
Engadiner torten, 142
Essences, 6

Fig and ginger cakes, 349
Florentine cookies, 142
Floria slices, 369
Flour,
  batter method, 219
  scone, 4
  strong, 3
  weak, 4
Fluted fingers, 55
Fondant dipped fancies, 307
  cocktail parties, for, 312
  enrobe with ladle, 307
  Nos. 1, 2 and 3, 308
  Nos. 4, 5, 6, 7 and 8, 309
  Nos. 9, 10, 11, 12, 13, 14 and 15, 310
  Nos. 16, 311
  Nos. 17, 18 and 19, 312
  preparing for sale, 312
  problems easily overcome, 307
Fruit,
  bars, 357
  cakes, 234
  charlottes, 90
  ginger, 206, 216
  honey, 242
  pie fillings, 89
  squares, 93
  tarts, 89
  walnut, 251
Fruited nut slices, 139
Fudge icing, 37

Ganache, 298
  tarts, 135
Gateau bases, 27, 231
  chocolate, 27
  vanilla, 27
Gateaux,
  almond, 320
  border, 340
    frosting, 340
  buttercream, 324
  butterscotch, 342
    caramel icing for, 343
    filling for, 343
  chocmalt milk, 343
  chocolate Nos. 1 and 2, 323
  chocolate coconut, 345
  coffee, 318
  dobos fudge, 36
  Easter Nos. 1 and 2, 333
  Hawaiian, 325
  hazelnut, 49
    chocolate, 334
    Nos. 1, 2 and 3, 335
    No. 4, 337
  honey, 348
  honey raisin, 342
  lemon, 322, 324
  lemon coconut, 318
  mocha chocolate, 349
  mushroom, 320
  orange, 322, 324
  peppermint, 346
  pineapple Nos. 1 and 2, 327
  plain, 321
  rose, 321
  spice, 338
  St. Honoré, 199
  torte type, 318
General purpose mixing, 227
Genoa cakes, 268, 378
Genoese, 287
  afternoon tea fancies, 295, 304
  cauliflowers, 304
  cherry layer, 317
  chocolate boxes, 294
  chocolate logs, 317
  chocolate walnut layer, 316
  coffee chocolate layer, 317

Genoese (*Contd.*)
  coffee vanilla layer, 317
  cross bow cutter, the, 288
  fondant chocolate coffee layer, 319
  fondant dipped fancies (*see* Fondant)
  fruit slice, 293
  fruits,
    apples, 301
    peaches, 303
  high ratio, 378
  lemon or orange layer cake, 315
  lemon slices, 303
  Nos. 1 and 2, 287
  No. 3, 287, 288
  petits fours glacés (*see* Petit Fours)
  pineapple, 304
  pyramid layer, 316
  rainbow cake, 289
  raspberry layer, 316
  sacher slices, 303
German cheese cake, 155
Ginger,
  biscuits, 201
  bread squares, 204
  buns, 203
  fruit cakes, 206, 216
  fruits, 215
  goods, 200
  honey slice, 214
  linzer torte, 107
  nuts, 201
  parkin biscuits, 202
    methods 1 and 2, 202, 203
  parkin slab,
    No. 1, 205
    No. 2, 206
  rings, 145, 211
  slices, 212
  walnut cake, 209
  walnut slice, 108
Glacé cherries, 5
Glycerine, 5
Golden moulds, 253

Hallowe'en cake, 263
Ham crescents, 171

Harlequin cream sandwich, 233
Hawaiian gateau, 325
Hazelmalt fingers, 54
Hazlenut,
  chocolate gateau, 334
    Nos, 1, 2 and 3, 335
    No. 4, 337
  dainties, 46
  fruit triangles, 111
  gateau and fancies, 49
  rings, 144
  snacks, 365
High ratio cakes, 220
High speed mixing, 376
  all-in sponges, 378
    with butter, 379
  chou paste, 377
  frangipane filling, 377
  Genoa cakes, 378
  high ratio genoese, 378
  Madeira cakes, 378
  scones, 379
  sweet-paste, 377
Hollywood tarts, 138
Honey,
  almonds, 151, 361
  cakes, 246
  fingers, 360
  fruit cake, 242
  fudge slice, 351
  gateau, 348
  gingerbread, 204
  pineapple topping, 249
  raisin gateau, 342
Hoop cakes, 246
Human relations, 384

Iced ginger,
  cakes, 207
  slab cake, 208

Jam tarts,
  small, 87
  using foil plates, 88

Lemon,
  buns, 80
  butters, 113
  cakes, 238, 240
  coconut gateau, 318
  cups, 135
  gateau, 322, 324
  nuts, 158
  split, 241
Lime tarts, 249
Linzer,
  biscuits, 109
  paste, 107
  squares, 108
Louisa cakes, 248

Madeira cakes, 223
  high speed, 378
  second quality, 235
  third quality, 236
Madeleines, 18
Malted lemon walnuts, 143
Malted milk, 344
Malties, 358
Management, 383
Maraschino banana cake, 258
Maraschino cookies, 115
Margarine-cake, 2
Marshmallow ladies, 12
Marzings, 136
Methods of mixing,
  all-in method, 62
  batter, 62
  creaming, 62
  rub-in, 62
Mince pies, 84
Mincemeat, 84
Miniature cakes, 279
Mixed nut cake, 337
Mocha chocolate gateau, 349
Mocha slice, 47
Mochas, 153
Moulds,
  golden, 253
  rum, 252
Mushroom gateau, 320

Navettes, 148
Nut tarts, 157
Nutmeal diamonds, 137

Orange,
    butters, 104
    crunch squares, 185
        topping for, 186
    gateau, 322, 324
    tarts, 371

Othellos, 40
    apples, 43
    chocolate, 42
    coffee, 42
    kirsch, 42
    peaches, 43
    petits fours glacés, 40
    pineapple, 42
    potatoes, 43
    vanilla cream, 42

Paris buns, 79
Paste,
    German, 96
    short, first and second quality, 82
    sweet, 1 and 2, 97
Peach flans, 160
Peanut fancies, 128
Peel,
    citron, 6
    lemon, 5
    orange, 5
Peppermint gateau, 346
Petits Fours glacés, 305
    colours for, 306
    dipping the fancies, 306
    preparing the fondant for, 306
    topping for, 305
Picnic cakes, 237
Pikfeen, 134

Pineapple,
    centres, 159
    cups, 367
    gateau, 327
    orange slices, 354
    tarts, 149
Pitcaithly or Pitkeathly bannocks, 105
Plain fingers, 50
Plain gateau, 321
Powdered aerated goods, 61
Praline cups, 121
Praline fingers, 105, 137
Prune tarts, 129
Puff paste, 163
    apfel strudel, 189
    apple frangipane, 187
    Banbury cakes, 179
    baton glacé, 183
    cheese straws, 169
    coconut cream batons, 182
    continental varieties, 188
    Coventry cakes, 181
    cream,
        coronets, 183
        crescents, 180
        crisps, 184
        horns, 182
        slices, 176
    Eccles cakes, 177
        filling for, 178
    English method, 165
    French or continental method, 166
    fruit or other squares, 180
    fruit slices, 190
    further points, 166
    ham crescents, 171
    jam puffs, 180
    large savoury vol-au-vent, 170
    large sweet vol-au-vent, 172
    lemon cream ovals, 182
    lemon gateau, 189
    mandel gipfel, 188
    Marianas, 186
    mince pies, 180
    orange crunch squares, 185
    puff tarts, 177
    sausage rolls, 169
    Scotch method, 166

Puff paste (*Contd.*)
　small vol-au-vent finishing off, 168
　small vol-au-vent or patty cases, 166
　small vol-au-vent producing the filling
　　for, 168
　stars, 188
　storing the paste, 165
　sugar squares, 176
　sweet varieties, 172
　unit method, 164
　vanilla slices,
　　continental method, 172
　　English method, 174
　　individual, 175
Punch tarts, 373

Queen drops, 233

Raisin,
　fingers, 133
　icing, 339
　slice, 55
Raspberry,
　buns, 77
　slice, 119
　strips, 126
Recipe balancing, 222
Rice,
　buns, 76
　cakes, 245
　cookies, 131
Rich fruit slab, 275
Rock buns, 74
Rose gateau, 321
Rum moulds, 252
Russe slice, 44
Russe tarts, 147
Russian slice, 58

Sandwich,
　cream, 231
　Harlequin, 233
　second quality, 232
　Victoria, 232

Sausage rolls, 169
Savoury cheese filling, 169
Scones,
　American doughnuts, 71
　cherry, 67
　chocolate, 68
　coconut, 69
　commercial rings, 63
　currant tea, 64
　　using yeast and powder aeration, 66
　enriched ring, 63
　fried scone dough rings, 74
　ginger, 68
　treacle, 70
　wheatmeal, 70
　wholemeal, 70
Short paste, 82
Shortbreads, 99
　almond slice, 106
　clover, 119
　coconut, 115
　machine blocking, 100
　rock, 101
　wooden block, 100
Shortening, 2
Simnel,
　Bury, 271
　cakes, 268
　slices, 272
Slab cakes, 280
　buttercream, 283
　caraway seed, 282
　cherry, 283
　coconut flavoured, 283
　combining two slabs, 286
　currant, 286
　Dundee, 285
　Genoa, 284
　high ratio, 286
　iced ginger, 208
　Madeira, 282
　pineapple, 286
　sultana, 285
　tins and frames for, 281
　varieties of Dundee, 287
Small buns, 228, 229
Some conclusions, 380
Spice gateau, 338

Sponge, goods—general hints, 7
  bricks or cakes, 11
  chocolate,
    drops, 10
    fingers, 11
    halves, 9
    sandwiches, 35
  coconut log, 21
  cream,
    basket, 15
    curls, 22
    sandwiches, 15
  drops, 7
  flans, 16
  Madeleines, 18
  moulds, 16
  raspberry,
    drops, 10
    fingers, 11
  sandwiches, 14
    'all-in' method, 33
    high speed, 378
  savoy,
    delights, 11
    fingers, 10
  stopping leaks, 382
Strawberry,
  bars, 126
  fool, 15
  krunch tarts, 161
  mallows, 147
Streusel topping, 126
Suet, 262
Sugar,
  batter method, 218
  brown, 1
  castor, 1
  granulated, 1
  icing, 2
  squares, 176
Sultana loaf, 234
Sultana and walnut cake, 243
Sultanas, 4
Swiss rolls, 18
  cherry almond, 23
  chocolate, 24
  coffee, 24
  ginger, 25

Swiss rolls (*Contd.*)
  hazelnut, 25
  marzipan, 20
  orange fruit, 23
  pineapple, 23
    chocolate, 45
  plain, 19
  raspberry, 23

Tins, preparation of, 226
Torte type gateau, 318
Torten, 27–35
Trifles, 60
Truffle Christmas puddings, 364
Truffle fingers, 361
Tutti-frutti, 44

Vanilla,
  custard, 190
  fingers, 79
  slices, 172–176
Victoria sandwiches, 232
Victory tarts, 374
Vienna jam slice, 120
Viennese,
  orange discs, 103
  shells, 102
  tarts, 101
Vol-au-vent, 166–172

Walfruit slices, 57
Walnut,
  butters, 152
  coconut wafers, and, 351
  fruit cakes, 251
  loaf, 250
  raisin fingers, and, 122
  slices, 362
Wasteful practices, 381
Wedding cakes, 273
  icing and almond paste, 278
  sizes/constituents weights table for, 277
Winter slices, 363

Yuletide kups, 145

INDEX TO ILLUSTRATIONS

Sponge Goods

Marshmallow ladies, 13
Swiss roll as a 'Week-end' special, 19
Dresden, 21
Coconut log, 21
Chocolate roll, 24
Christmas chocolate log, 25
Motifs suitable for piping in chocolate for torte décor, 29
Praline flavoured torte, 29
Chocolate flavoured torte, 30
Coffee flavoured torte, 30
Hazelnut torte, finish No. 2, 32
Hazelnut torte, finish No. 3, 33
Butter sponge bases using the 'all-in' method, 34
Fresh cream torte, 34
Chocolate butter sponge using stabiliser, 35
Chocolate sponge sandwiches—fresh cream/fondant finish, 35
Dobos fudge gateau, 36
Othellos and Petits-Fours glacé, 40
Russe slice, 45
Pineapple chocolate roll, 46
Hazelnut dainties No. 1, 46
Hazelnut dainties No. 2, 47
Hazelnut gateau, 49
Hazelnut gateau fancies from the same base, 50

Plain fingers with alternative finishes, 51, 52, 53
Hazelmalt fingers, 55
Raisin slice, using sheets, 56
Raisin slice, 'trough' variety, 57
Walfruit slices, 58
Drescan, 59

Powder-aerated Goods

Sultana and ginger scone rings, 63
Afternoon tea scones, 65
Cherry tea scones, 67
Coconut scone rings, 69
American doughnuts, 72, 73, 74
Rock, rice and raspberry buns, 75

Short-paste Goods

Small jam tarts, 87
Large jam and lemon cheese tarts, 88
Fruit charlottes, 90
Large fruit tarts, 91
Custards, small, 92
Chorley cakes, 95

Sweetpaste and Shortbread

Fruit flans, 97
Fruit flans, small, 98
Shortbreads, strips, 99
Shortbreads, blocked, 100
Viennese tarts, 102
Viennese fingers, orange discs and shells, 103
Stencil mat as quick production aid, use of, 103
Orange butters, 104
Orange butters, piped, 105
Plain or fancy praline fingers, 106
Ginger Linzer torte, 107
Ginger walnut slice, 108
Linzer squares, two varieties of, 109
Linzer biscuits, 110
Hazelnut fruit triangles, 111
Dobos slices with traditional finish, 112
Dobos slices with more elaborate finish, 113
Lemon butters, 114
Maraschino cookies No. 1, 115
Maraschino cookies Nos. 2 and 3, 116
Coconut shapes, hearts, 117
Coconut shapes, triangles, diamonds and ovals, 118
Raspberry slices, 120
Vienna jam slice, 121
Praline cups, 122
Walnut and raisin fingers, 123
Cherry marshmallows No. 3, 124
Coconut crisp fingers, 125
Two different finishes for Strawberry Bars, 127
Peanut fancies No. 1, 128
Peanut fancies No. 2, 129
Prune tarts, 130
Cherry biscuits, 131
Rice cookie whirls, 132
Rice cookie fingers and drops, 132
Raisin fingers, 133
Pikfeen—a continental favourite, 134
Marzings, 136
Nutmeal diamonds, 137
Hollywood tarts, 139
Fruited nut slices, 140

Currant walnut tarts, 142
Florentine cookies, alternative finishes for, 143
Hazelnut rings, 144
Ginger rings, 145
Strawberry mallows, 147
Russe tarts, 148
Brazil delights, 150
Coffeenut drops, 151
Honey almonds, 152
Walnut butters No. 1, 152
Walnut butters No. 2, 153
Mochas Nos. 1 and 2, 154
Mochas No. 3, 155
German cheese cake, 156
Nut tarts, 157
Lemon nuts, delicious and unusual, 158

Puff Paste

Vol-au-vent cases, 167
Vanilla slices, continental method, 173
Vanilla slices, English method, 174
Vanilla slices, individually produced, 175
Sugar squares, 177
Eccles and Banbury cakes, 179
Jam puffs, 181
Cream horns, 183
Cream crisps, 184
Orange crunch squares, 185
Marianas, 186

Chou Paste

Chou paste cream buns, 193
Piping chocolate fondant, 194
Piping chocolate fondant on to chocolate eclairs, 195
Rognons, 196
Petits chou, 197
Chou paste swans, 198

Ginger Goods

Ginger biscuits with simple pre-packing, 202

Parkin biscuits with characteristic 'crack', 203
Iced ginger slab cake, 208
Brandy snaps with fresh cream and chocolate finish, 210
Ginger rings, 212
Ginger gateau, 213
Ginger slices, 213
Ginger honey slices, 214
Ginger fruits, 216

Cakes and Cakemaking

High ratio cakes, 221
High ratio cherry slab cakes, 222
Recipe balance, the 'M' fault, 224
Recipe balance, the 'X' fault, 225
Buns finished by top decoration before baking, 228
Buns, simple finishes to give variety, 230
Madeira cakes, cheaper quality, 236
Almond cakes, 237
Picnic cakes, 238
Lemon cakes, 239
Caraway seed cake, 240
Sultana and walnut cake, 243
Currant loaves, 244
Brazil pound cake, 248
Walnut loaf, 250
Walnut fruit cake, 251
Rum moulds, 253
Cherry banana loaves, 254
Angel flans, 256
Date and walnut cakes, 257
Cherry and walnut cakes, 258
Maraschino banana cakes, shapes and texture, 259
Almond and raisin cake, 261
Banana loaf, 262
Bury simnels, 271
Simnel slices, 272
Heavily fruited wedding cake, 274
Almond and walnut slab, using wedding cake base, 276
Miniature cakes, 279
Madeira slab cake, attractive, 282
Cherry slab, 284

Genoa slab cake, 284
Dundee slab cake, 285
'Cross bow' in use to level a sheet of genoese, 289
Genoese, a simple gadget for cutting a number of sheets quickly and accurately, 290
Genoese placed in the box ready for cutting, 291
Genoese, cutting the, 292
Genoese, now cut, the pieces are placed on wires ready for enrobing, 293
Fruit slice, ideally presented on a log card, 294
Cutting trough, a simple gadget to ensure accurate cutting, 300, 301
Cake or real fruit? Peaches and apples, which may be produced from genoese or crumb paste, 302
Lemon slices, 303
Genoese fondant dipped fancies; vanilla, shamrock and coffee, 308
Fondant dipped fancies; diagrams for finishing, 311
Battenberg, with the Christmas motif of holly piquet, 313
Chocolate Battenberg, suitable for a festive season if given a seasonal motif, 315
Coffee, mushroom, almond and praline gateaux, 319
Lemon, chocolate and orange gateaux, 320
Gateau, a simple lemon coloured and flavoured, 321
Buttercream finish, a simple, 322
Chocolate gateaux, with autumnal seasonal motif, 323
Buttercream gateau, 324
Multiple ring Hawaiian gateau, 325
Hawaiian gateau, single ring for reduced costs, 326
Hawaiian gateau base, 327
Pineapple gateaux 1 and 2, 328
Banana layer cake produced from banana sponge, 329, 330
Banana gateau bases, 331
Banana gateaux, 332
Almond gateaux with a 'something different' finish, 334

Hazelnut chocolate gateau base, 335
Hazelnut chocolate gateaux Nos. 1, 2, 3 and 4, 336
Mixed nut cake, 338
Spice gateaux, 339
Border gateau, 341
Peppermint gateau texture, 347
Peppermint gateau finished, 348
Coconut wafers, walnut wafers, 352
Coconut drops, using two finishes, 354
Coconut cookies (round), 355
Coconut cookies (fingers), 356
Coconut croquants, 356
Malties, 358
Butterscotch crunch, 359

Honey fingers, 360
Truffle fingers, 362
Winter slices, 363
Truffle Christmas puddings, 365
Hazelnut snacks, 366
Calypso, 367
Pineapple cups, 368
Floria slices, two simple finishes for, 369
Florio slices No. 3, 370
Neopolitan Tutti Frutti, 370
Orange tarts, 371
Dexmond tarts, 372
Punch tarts, 373
Victory tarts, 374